Beyond the Color of Skin

Library of Congress Control Number: 2006909174

To order additional copies, please contact us.
BookSurge, LLC
www.booksurge.com
1-866-308-6235
orders@booksurge.com

CAJETAN NGOZIKA
IHEWULEZI

Beyond the Color of Skin

Encounters with Religions and Racial Injustice in America

Published in South Carolina
by Booksurge Publishing
2006

Beyond the Color of Skin

TABLE OF CONTENTS

ACKNOWLEDGMENTS

My parents always told me as a child, "Seek the truth, say the truth, clear your conscience, and be happy you did." This has been my guiding principle in life and my first inspiration in the writing of this book. Initially, I experienced some fears in writing this book, but when I remembered the above words of my parents, I mustered enough courage to finish it. My people used to say that "the gun with which a child shoots and kills a lion, it is his or her parents that made it for him or her." My parents taught me to be strong in taking decisions. They taught me how to be serious with my education and work hard in whatever career I chose to pursue. I couldn't but be what they trained me to be. For bringing me up in such an environment that enabled me to relate to them and say my mind freely, I am so grateful.

The training given to me by my teachers at Aquinas Institute of Theology to keep daily journals has been very helpful in my ability to pull my materials and sources together. So I am thankful to Rev. Charles Bouschard, Rev. Gregory Heille, Rev. Dan Harris, Rev. Albert Glade, Sister Mary Margaret Pazdan, Rev. Martha Brunell, and Ms Juliet Mousseau. I am thankful for the exposure and support I received from Rev. Dr. Wayne Hellmann, O.F.M., and other members of staff of the Historical Theology Department of St Louis University. I can't forget the encouragement that came from my pastoral care supervisor, Rev. Charles Hart O.F.M., who challenged me in class to put down on paper my experiences in the hospitals while anointing the sick. My pastoral director, Rev. Ellen Hiatt, was so wonderful and supportive by providing me with some of the valuable materials I needed to support my points.

At a point, I needed to interview bishops, pastors, rabbis, and lay members of the different American religions covered in this book. I also needed people to help me make contacts with the people ready to grant me interviews. I am so grateful to Debra Moll, Betty Switzer, Rev. Jay Kanzler, Stephnie Edwards, Harry Charles Rosso, and Akebi Fisher for helping me make the contacts. I appreciate so much the support I received from Members of St. Vincent De Paul society of St Clement Parish, Marge and Ed Meiners, Osy and Chinwe Kokelu, Jim and Dorothy Ganser, John and Ruth Hertel, Dr. Emanuel Uwalaka, Theresa and Bshara Kswani, Chris and Terry Oliver, Benny and Bonnie Dehahn, Donna and Larry Marlers, Theresa and Robert Siefker, Mike and Georgia Millers, Dr. Paula T. Trzepacz, Dr. Robert W. Baker, Dr.Patrick J. MC Cann, Rev. Micheal and Mary Elaine Suden, Frank and Susan Gumerlock, Lisa and Ndu Ezeamii, Mr. J.P. Cummings, Alys L. kehr, Kuehle Janice, Ginger Shives, Sister Concha, Sister Marie Louise Ruggeri, Anthony Dolce, Heather Sieve, Juliet Escobar, Marcy Farrell. I am thankful to Sylvester Brown of St. Louis Post Dispatch for his encouragement.

It was not easy to get people to accept interviews and to publish the information I gathered from them. For granting me the opportunity to interview them and to make use of the information I got from them, I am so grateful to the following pastors and Rabbis: Monsignor Frank Blood, Rev. Eugene Morris, Rev. Grenham J.P., The Rev. John Kenneth Blair, Rev. Cannon Renee L. Fenner, Rev. William G. Gillespie, Rev. Mamie A. Williams, Rev. B. Kevin Smalls, Rev. Gregory Howard, Rev. Damon J. Powells, Rev. Dr. Richard C. Dickinson, Rev. Charles Ebelebe, Rev. Peter Osuagwu, Rabbi Carpers Funnye, and Rabbi Randy Fleisher. The content of this book would not have been as comprehensive as it is without the interviews granted me by the following lay women ministers: Deaconess Addie Wilkins, Jessie Thomas, Leodia Gooch, and Juanita Dick. I am also thankful to all my interviewees whose names, for some personal reasons, I am not able to include.

Finding a suitable editor for this work was also not easy. Editing this book was as painstaking as writing it. The person who made the sacrifice of bearing the demanding task of going through this work and making the necessary corrections was Sister Pat Chaffee. I am so grateful to her. I also received some proof reading and library assistance from Mira Tanna, Nini Harris, Louise Harris, and David Chance. Last but not least are my former hosts and pastors of St. Cecilia parish, Fr. Chuck P. Tichacek and Fr. Richard Hadel. They were wonderful in helping me with some theological arguments and reflections. My new host Father Gary M. Meier of St. Teresa and Bridget parish, has been wonderful in encouraging me in the last efforts I made in the final production of this work. For all these supports, I am so grateful.

To
His And Her Royal Highnesses
Daniel And Cecilia

INTRODUCTION

My first encounter with Christianity was during the Biafran war in Nigeria. This was a civil war between the Eastern region of Nigeria, the home of my ethnic group, the Igbo, and the Federal government. When the British colonizers left after independence in 1960, the political process that followed led the country into a bloody civil war. At this time, my people were being slaughtered everywhere in the country. At times, we had to hide inside the bushes and beneath dead bodies to protect ourselves from the shootings, air raids, and artillery bombardments.

Over one million Igbo people were murdered or died of starvation because of our ethnic background. I lost many of my peers through starvation and through air raids by senseless mercenary pilots bombing civilian targets. As a little child, I was so scared and terrified. At the same time, the war made me strong, tough, and determined. It also made me conscious of people's rights to live their lives in freedom and justice. It was at this time that I encountered Father Buckley, CSSP, and the other Irish Holy Ghost priests who came to us with the message of Christ, as well as food and supplies. Their kindness and mercy captivated me. I knew then that it was my calling to be a Catholic priest and to love and protect others.

At the same time, during the 1960s, the less bloody, but just as important, Civil Rights Movement was going on in America. Through peaceful protest, great things were accomplished for freedom and equality. Throughout my education and my years in the Church, I came to know much about America. I was, therefore, happy and excited, in 2001, to be asked by the Holy Ghost Fathers of Nigerian Province to come to America, *the home of the Free and Equals*, to do my doctoral studies. I was surprised, as soon as I arrived, to hear so many complaints of racial prejudice, inequality and marginalization of some Americans because of the color of their skin, especially African Americans and Hispanic Americans.

I was, and remain, shocked and disturbed to learn that, although laws no longer support racism, it is experienced not only in American society and the justice system, but also in our houses of God! I was brought up in a society where no person is made to feel superior or inferior, where the color of one's skin makes no difference in one's treatment by others. I had never encountered this type of discrimination before, and never did I expect to find it in America. Although, I experienced a kind of discrimination based on tribe in my country, it was not based on who is black and who is white, or who is superior and who is inferior, or who is middle class and who is lower class. However, evil is evil no matter where it is done, the form it takes, and who is involved. It was beyond me and what I expected, to notice that people could feel that they still lack basic human rights such as the right to praise God equally with believers of another color.

In this book, I contribute to the search for true racial justice and peace in America by reporting what I have heard and experienced personally in regard to racial prejudice in the churches and synagogues, which are called to be prophetic in speaking out for the defenseless and the poor. I have interviewed bishops, pastors, evangelists, rabbis, and other popular figures in American society, men and women willing to be honest and talk about this problem with the intention of finding solutions to it. I give the victims of this racial crisis a platform to tell their stories, stories that will touch our hearts, and make us think about our own lives and how racism is affecting each of us here.

Though a foreigner, I still see myself as part of the American society. Whatever affects this society also affects me, as no one is immune to racial prejudice. This book is not an attack on any person, any church leader, any church, or the state, but an honest effort to know the truth, and to appeal to every heart and mind to tolerate, accept, and love every human being created in the image and likeness of God without regard to color and any other condition.

I know how sensitive it is to talk about racism. We may not, however, run away from talking about it, as it continues to be a problem and affects people's lives. Paul Kivel is right in saying that it is good to talk about racism.[1] He also asserts, "Racism is a gross injustice which kills people of color, damages democracy, and is linked to many of our social problems. Talking about it helps make our society safer for people of color and safer for us as well. Talking about racism keeps us from passing it on to our children. Talking about racism allows us to do something about it."[2]

As a matter of fact, I have spent just as much time worrying about upsetting people with this book, as writing it. I have worded and reworded things so as to say what needs to be said without causing ripples. However, it is like telling someone that he has cancer. There is no way to say it without causing stress, even though there could be some solutions. I do not want to sound like the ranting angry people who scream about racism on the radio, television, and internet, without suggesting solutions to the problem. By so doing, they are spreading hate and tension among the races.

I have also been warned by my peers that merely by writing this book; I could possibly lose my career, my home, my visa, my ability to be allowed to graduate from my university studies, and even suffer physical attack. But my soul will not let me rest, as I have become a slave of my conscience. What I have found in my research and interviews and my experiences in this country has deeper meaning than my own comfort. So I take this chance and turn the results over to God.

CHAPTER ONE
ENCOUNTER WITH A TAXI CAB DRIVER

I came to the United States of America to study at St. Louis University in 2001. Through the generosity of the Archdiocese of St. Louis, I lived in a beautiful parish, St. Cecilia. I received the warm welcome of my Caucasian host and former pastor of the church, Monsignor Frank Blood. He lived with me as a real brother. Although I am black, I never received any indication of racism from him. For some time, I was unconscious of this evil!

The neighborhood where I lived was mixed; whites, blacks, Hispanics and Asians live comfortably together. It took me two Sundays to discover that there was a problem with Mass attendance. I saw a huge number of blacks in the neighborhood and at the shopping malls, but I did not see them attending Catholic Church on Sundays. I noticed only two to three black families that occasionally came to church, in a neighborhood that also has a huge black population. I was a pastor of a church in Nigeria where people gathered and worshiped together in the same church, irrespective of color. I saw something different here and I began to ask questions about why the blacks in my neighborhood did not attend Catholic Church. I was told by a few friends that African Americans do not like the Catholic Church because it is a racist church or a white man's church.

The next question I asked was why is it that the blacks see the Catholic Church as racist or as a white man's church? I could not get a satisfactory answer. When I asked the pastor I was living with, he told me that many African Americans feel that way because of this country's history of slavery and segregation laws. He also told me that efforts are being made to correct the mistakes of the past, but that a lot is yet to be done in the Christian churches (not only Catholic) to change such feelings. He then challenged me to reach out to African Americans in our neighborhood. He said how happy he would be to see many African Americans look at the Church differently, and begin coming for Mass.

This encouraged me to start visiting black families in my neighborhood and to stop along the streets to talk to some of them.

I was lucky to have made some friends among my neighbors. Many of the black families welcomed me, but a few made me feel that I was not very welcome in their homes. Because of my Nigerian accent, many did not understand my English; therefore, I could not develop enough rapport to continue talking with them. A few looked at me with some suspicion; they were not sure what I really wanted in their homes. When I noticed that they were not comfortable with such visits, I did not continue going to them. Although I was a bit discouraged, still I did not give up my efforts to know why they had such feelings about the Church, and to see if I could help bring about a change.

Emotional and Revelatory Meeting

A chance occurrence made me decide to carry my findings further. I needed a Social Security number to get my driver's license, open a student bank account, register at school, and shop easily. Since I had no car, I called the taxi cab to take me to the Social Security office. Within a few minutes, a taxi cab pulled up to the front door of the rectory. When I entered, I noticed that the driver was an African American man in his early sixties. I greeted him and introduced myself to him as a Catholic priest. He also introduced himself and told me that he was both a retired teacher and a retired pianist of a Baptist Church. He asked me if I came from Africa. I told him yes, and that I came to do my studies at St. Louis University. He said, "Your accent made me suspect that you are either from Haiti or from Africa."

"Oh yes, many people tell me that," I replied.

"Do you like it here?" he asked.

"Yes, America is really big, beautiful, and blessed."

"What type of study are you going to do at St. Louis University?"

"I have just started my orientation, to do a master's program in Historical Theology, but I do not know if I will do my doctoral program in it or change to something else." I saw this as an opportunity to engage in a discussion with him, to be able to get more information on why black Americans see the Catholic Church as racist.

"May I discuss something with you, sir?" I asked.

"Oh yeah, go ahead."

"I discovered that most African Americans here do not like attending the Catholic Church."

"That's true," he said. "Though there're some black Americans who are Catholics, a greater majority have this impression that the Catholic Church is racist or a white man's Church because of what happened in the past."

"Okay, I now understand why you are a Baptist. So the Baptist Church is not a racist Church?"

"No, that's not what I mean. I am a black Baptist. You see, the Baptist Church was so racist that it split into white and black Baptist Churches. So we're more welcome in the black Baptist Church and that is why many of us are Baptists. The black Baptist Church, which I belong to, is a church of liberation."

"Thanks for telling me that. I can see that there may be some reasons why African Americans feel more welcome in the Baptist Church than in the Catholic Church. Within the Baptist Church itself, you feel more welcome in the black Baptist Church than in the white Baptist Church and see it as your church of liberation. I will be very happy if you tell me more about why things are this way."

"Sir, the problem is not only in the Catholic Church or Baptist Church; it is the same problem in all the Christian Churches as far as whites and blacks are members."

I nodded my head; I could notice a change in his mood as he spoke. He was looking sad now. I was filled with pity.

"We have really been beaten down and marginalized economically, socially, politically, and even religiously, from the foundation of this country because of the color of our skin. It used to be worse before the 1960s because of the segregation laws. Even now when the segregation laws have been removed, we are not yet fully integrated in all aspects of the life of this country. In most cases, we are not given equal opportunities as our white counterparts."

"That's sad." I replied.

"The impression created in the hearts and minds of many people in this country because of those racist laws, which lasted for almost a hundred years, and how things are still going on in this country after the removal of the laws, are still affecting the lives of the people of color in very negative ways."

I was surprised to hear what he said because that was not the impression I had about America before I came. The impression I had was that of the land of equality and freedom or a country where every citizen is given equal opportunity irrespective of color, class, race, sex, and age. Is he telling me the truth? So I asked him, "What have the churches been doing about this?"

"The churches have been struggling, but have never been very effective in stopping racism and all the evils connected to it. Like I told you, it's a problem of color. The color of the skin is so emphasized in the American society! The white folks in both church and society look at us as inferior human beings because our skins are black and see themselves as superior because their skins are white."

I turned and looked at him in amazement. I know that the color of the skin is accidental and God's own making. It should be neither a credit nor a discredit to any human person.

"There are hate crimes every where. Our black churches are burnt in many parts of the country by hate groups that also claim to be Christians. Sometimes we experience racism even in churches and this makes us ask where the love of God is."

"I thought that such things are no longer happening in churches since the removal of the laws."

"There are so many ways racism is still going on in our churches. Their reactions to racist behaviors and comments by their members in and outside the churches are still very cold. Sometimes church leaders prefer being silent and feel unconcerned about what is happening to the people of color. The churches are not listening enough to our concerns."

I asked him, "What of myself, am I not black? I am a Catholic priest; I live with a white Catholic priest who treats me like an equal and as a brother. I have neither had any problems with him nor the white parishioners since I came to this place."

As soon as I said that, he became very angry. I noticed that I had made a mistake by talking in a way that he saw as doubting him. I did not really mean to make him feel doubted.

"Come on man! Do you doubt me?"

"Not really, sir."

"You said you are from Africa?"

"Yes, sir," I replied.

"Right," he said. "As soon as you entered my cab, and I heard your accent, I didn't see you as different from one of those Africans who collaborated with the white man. You people sold our ancestors into slavery over four hundred years ago and subjected us to this type of treatment we are receiving from the white majority in this country."

I turned and looked at him again in amazement and shook my head. I became very uncomfortable. It looks like the old animosity still exists. I felt so sorry.

"We were cut off against our will from our loved ones in Africa, our culture, and our God. We answer to names that do not depict our culture, and worship the God, who, though we are convinced is a loving God, still looks foreign to us because of the unequal and unjust treatment we are receiving in this country."

When he said that, I sighed. I wish we could re-write history.

He continued, "Do you support racism yourself?"

"No, sir! I am very sorry if I offended you by saying that. I was only trying to let you know that I have not experienced racism since I came here."

"How long have you been in the United States?"

"I have been here for three months, sir."

"Is that enough time for you to doubt a man who was born and brought up here? I was in my twenties during the Civil Rights Movement. I need to tell you more and, by the way, do you think that three months in America is enough time for you to feel immune to racism?"

I decided at this moment I'd better do more listening than talking since he was still angry and I needed more information from him. Shouting at the top of his voice he said,

"Do you know that being a pastor doesn't stop you from being a racist? Do you know that there were pastors and bishops who had slaves and were openly racist? Okay, let me tell you this story. You may believe it or not. A bishop was so racist that every one noticed it. He had a black slave, a young man, even after the abolition of slavery. When the black slave died, the bishop during his funeral service openly said to the public: *'This boy, son of Ham, was a good boy and I believe that he is in heaven.'* Then he said, *'When I get to heaven, this son of Ham will still be cleaning my shoes.'* This angered many of the blacks who were there for the funeral, and many of them stopped going to church."

I found it difficult to believe his story. I felt that it was one of those jokes which non-Christians use to mock Christians. I could not argue with him because that would upset him the more. I closed my eyes in disbelief and opened them only to notice that the man had become emotional with tears running down his face. I looked straight at him as he drove the cab and became sad myself. It was then that I noticed that the man meant every bit of his story.

We had reached the Social Security office a long time ago. We were both carried away by the discussion and did not know that we had spent a very long time talking. He apologized for taking my time telling me all the stories. I accepted his apology, but thanked him for sharing his stories with me.

I said to him, "I can now understand how you and most people of color feel in this country and why it is so. I apologize to you and to the other African Americans on behalf of the Africans whom I represent, for what our ancestors did with their white business friends. Ignorance of the dignity of the human person was the problem of the people of their age. Slavery and racism are evil and against the will of God for all of us. They are not in keeping with the life and teachings of Christ who loves every human being without condition, and whom all the Christians--white, black, and other races--claim to profess. We regret what our ancestors did. If there was any way we could turn the clock backwards, we would have undone what they did!"

He nodded his head in acceptance of all I said.

"I apologize to you and to other people of color; if there is any way the Christian denominations did not do enough to help you, I am so sorry for that."

He nodded, as tears rolled down his cheeks. Looking at him I could not hold my own tears.

"It is unfortunate that the bishop in your story called his black slave *the son of Ham*. I know that such a title hurts you so much. It was a very wrong interpretation of the Bible to find reasons to dominate others."

"Thank you, sir. I am happy to hear this," he replied.

"Let me tell you, my brother, you are not inferior and your color does not make you inferior. No human being has any right to make you feel inferior, because you are created in the image and likeness of God. That is the truth and any other theory or ideology is not only baseless but also unscriptural. God's own ideology supersedes human ideology. Since all of us are created in the image and likeness of God as the Christian and Jewish Bibles tell us, what is really inferior or superior in different peoples? Can the Spirit and the image of God be inferior in some people because their skins are black and superior in some people because their skins are white? Is the superiority based on the skin that will die and turn to dust? Which is greater, the Spirit of God or the color of human skin? So you can see that those ideologies have no theological backings. Racism is human fantasy and not of God because it is good moral life that makes a person pure and good, while it is wrong doing that makes a person impure and bad. That is what should be emphasized and not skin color."

"Yeah, man, you got it. You see, I was not thinking about it that way. That's true man!"

"The whole issue of being superior or being inferior, as you complained, depends on one's belief system. Personally, I do not believe that God created me superior or inferior to any one. I believe that God has blessed each one of us with talents. I believe in education, I believe in discipline, I believe in prayer, and I believe in hard work to develop the talents God has given to me. Above all, I believe in justice and fairness to allow others to develop their own self esteem without suppression of any kind. Living and letting others live is love and love is religion, without love religion is void. Are you with me, sir?"

"That's true, man!" he shouted. "Yeah, man, you got it!" he shouted again.

I noticed another change in his mood. He didn't look angry any more. He had really met a friend.

"I won't keep you any longer. I don't blame you for how you felt when you were telling me your story because I felt the same way. One thing I am convinced about discrimination of any kind is that directly or indirectly, it affects both the oppressed and the oppressor. *A prison guard is also a prisoner. Any one who holds his brother or sister on the floor is also on the floor. True freedom comes only when everyone is free. Sometimes, the most armed and most protected could be the most afraid. We can have peace in this world only when we learn how to give unreserved justice.*"

"Yeah, man! Yeah! You are right brother!"

"I have taken note of all you told me and I am going to study about racism in the churches. After finding out the truth, I hope to make some meaningful suggestions to the church authorities of the different denominations for the eradication of this problem which has really burdened you. We all must join hands, whites, blacks, Hispanics, Indians, Jews, and Asians to fight against this social evil in words and in actions, to be able to bring true healing to all. May God help us!"

"Amen. Oh Jesus!" he replied with eyes closed.

He opened his eyes, looked at me, and smiled, I returned his smile and he hugged me and said, "You are not only a friend but also a brother for listening to me, crying with me, and for talking to me the way you have done. I believe that my meeting you today is providential. This conversation with you has made my day."

"Thank you, sir, for listening to me," I replied.

Freedom of Speech and Story Telling

I love the freedom of speech in this country. The taxi driver had no problem pouring out his heart before me. Not many citizens of many countries in the world enjoy that much freedom of expression. Freedom of speech, which I see as a credit to this country, not only helped the taxi driver to tell me his stories without fear, but also helped me to listen to him without fear. In listening to his stories, I came to understand his identity, his community, his feelings, and the feelings of his community. David A. Hogue in his book *Remembering The Future Imagining The Past* observes, "African American experiences are best understood in the telling of personal and communal stories and in the relating of stories to the biblical narratives."[3]

I listened to my taxi driver's pain and observed him begin to heal. This reminded me of the double effects of story telling as described by Hogue. The first effect is pain. "Some stories are painful and intrusive. Their persistence and unwelcome presence do not bring healing or wholeness; instead, they continuously re-wound us."[4] Hogue gives examples with victims of sexual abuse, combat veterans, and victims of domestic violence, who often find memories painful and troubling. The same thing happens to victims of racial discrimination. Telling stories of how your fellow human, because of difference in color, deprived you of equal opportunities with others and made you feel less important and less human is troubling, as it happened to the taxi driver.

Personal stories are most painful when one gets to the point of telling his or her hearer that a loved one or a loved institution who or which should have rescued or protected the person, turns to be either the oppressor or one of the sources of oppression. For example, in my discussions with many victims of sexual abuse, I discovered that a victim feels the pain most and finds it more difficult to overcome her painful experiences when she remembers that it was her own friend or even her own father, who should have protected her, who turned to be the one who abused her. She finds it very difficult to say that her father was the one who abused her, and when she eventually says who did it, she releases a bitter cry from her heart.

I discovered the same feeling from the taxi driver. In telling his stories, the taxi driver cried out when he got to the point of telling the story of a religious leader who had a black slave whom he referred to as *the son of Ham*, whom he imagined cleaning his shoes in heaven. The taxi driver must have imagined that if there is any place where a person should find refuge or defense when discriminated against or marginalized, it is the religious institution. When religion is a source of discrimination, instead of defending the marginalized person, and when religion defends the unjust system with the word of God, it is most painful.

The taxi driver, like a girl sexually abused by her own friend or father who should have protected her, had every reason to cry out from his heart. I cried with him and I could not but give him a good listening ear, feel with him, and make him know that he was not alone in his feelings. "The ability to walk in another's shoes or see the world through another's eyes is central to being human."[5] This is also central to being Christian if we are serious about being our brother's or our sister's keepers regardless of the color of skin. To have no feeling of empathy for victims of racial discrimination, as if that is the way God made it to be, is very improper and against love.

Another effect of story telling, which Hogue talks about, and which I also observed in the taxi driver, is that story telling can also bring healing, especially when the victim sees someone who could listen to him or her and share in his or her feelings. "By telling those stories, victims can weaken the stories' power over them. Untold stories and secrets can harm and destroy more quickly than stories that have been shared."[6] Hogue goes on to explain, "When we tell our story to someone who has never heard it, in a sense we are telling that story to someone for the first time. It is reassuring: our own lives make sense all over again."[7] My listening to the story of the taxi driver and feeling with him was a source of healing. I could see him smile after crying. He felt much more fulfilled and happier after talking with me, because I cared to listen. For him, the churches are not listening enough.

How do I find out the Truth?

Because the taxi driver raised the issue for me, I started to ask the following questions:

1. How involved were the mainline Churches in slavery and racism before the removal of the segregation laws in 1964?

2. How involved were the Churches in the abolition of slavery?

3. When the segregation laws were imposed on blacks by the government, how effective and prophetic were the Christian Churches in speaking out for the liberation of the African Americans and other people of color before the prophetic voices of Martin Luther King, and the Civil Rights Movement of the 1950s and 1960s?

4. Was there any practical resistance against the laws from any member of the Churches for almost a hundred years before the historic action of Rosa Park?

5. If the Churches did not effectively speak for African Americans, against segregation laws, what could have been the possible reasons?

6. Since the removal of the laws in 1964, is there still evidence of racial discrimination in these Churches as the taxi driver claimed?

7. If there is still evidence of racism in them, what forms is racism taking now?

8. Are there ways in which racism in the Christian churches has affected American Judaism and the way the European American white Jews treat other Jews of color in and outside the American Synagogues?

9. How has racism affected the pastoral ministries of these Churches among the people of color and how have the Churches

been able to respond to the greatest effect of racism (poverty) among people of color?

10. What are the possible measures that could be applied in the American mainline Protestant Churches, the American Catholic Church, and the American Synagogues to fight against racism?

The problem remains, how do I find out the truth? There is no better way of knowing the truth than historical research of these three early American religions, Protestant, Roman Catholic, and Judaism.[8] We refer to the past in order to understand the present, and to create a better future.

CHAPTER TWO
THE PROTESTANT ROOTS OF SLAVERY AND RACISM IN AMERICA 1600-1964

In this chapter, I investigate the role of Episcopal, Presbyterian, Methodist, Baptist, and Lutheran Churches in the institution of slavery and racism from the period when these Churches were brought to America, to the Civil Right Movements of the 1960s, when the segregation laws were removed. I will first give an overview of how Protestantism generally helped to shape racist ideologies and theories before looking into how each of the above Churches played its role in the development of "racism as a factor in American history. . ."[9]

Over View of Protestant Involvement

After the exploration of the Americas by Christopher Columbus and his companions, the Native Americans, and later the black Africans were subjected to forced slave labor in the south by the Spanish and Portuguese colonizers and business men. At the same time, The British colonizers and business men were doing the same in the British colonies in Northern parts of America, now known as United States. Joseph T. Leonard, S.J., describing the origin of racism argues, "It was unknown to the ancients, who, if they possessed others, did so because of cultural, political, or religious differences, not because of race. Racism did not appear until the discovery and colonization of America."[10] The need to supply cheap labor from Africa to work on the plantations made slavery a very lucrative business starting from the fifteenth century and extending to its abolition in the nineteenth century. The first shipment of Negro slaves was taken to a Virginia colony, Jamestown to be specific, aboard a Dutch ship, in 1619.[11]

Meanwhile, as the shipment of thousands of blacks from Africa was going on, many Northern Europeans, mostly from the British Isles, were migrating to North America in great numbers. Most of these early immigrants were Puritans running away from religious persecutions in Europe. According to Virgil Elizondo, "The United States began after the Protestant split in Europe and the majority of the early settlers were escaping various forms of religious tyranny in Europe."[12] Being people who had suffered from persecution, they came to America in search of freedom. They saw themselves as the new people of God marching to the Promised Land. "From the very beginning, the first Northern European immigrants to North America saw themselves as the New Israel. They believed they were elected by God for a special destiny and a special role in the formation of the kingdom of God on earth."[13] With this impression about themselves, these early European immigrants and the colonial Englishmen convincingly saw themselves as a chosen people. Thomas Powell argues that this conviction became American, lasting far beyond independence and shaping American national relations with the rest of the world.[14]

These immigrants with such feelings of divine election were mostly Protestants. According to Frank G. Kirkpatrick, they believed that it was the will of God that America should be made Protestant.[15] The Catholic immigrants from Ireland, Italy, France, Portugal, Germany, Poland, and other parts of Europe joined them later. Initially, the Protestant immigrants who came first were anti-Catholic because they saw Rome as the oppressor. The presence of Catholics who were loyal to the Pope was seen as a symbol of the presence of Rome, which never allowed them religious freedom. This feeling made the early Protestants oppose the presence of Catholics. "The Protestant population was easily stirred into anti-Catholicism, given its sense that American liberties and institutions depended upon Protestant teaching and practice . . ."[16] They feared that as Catholics grew in number and power, the United States would come under papist domination. So Catholics had to prove that they could be loyal to Rome and also prove their patriotism as Americans by being loyal to the American governments, which were Protestant dominated. Moreover, for the American Puritans, the primary ecclesial reality was not the universal holy church but a local congregation of those elected to salvation.[17] It is not surprising that they were hostile to Catholics, who had a different view about the church, salvation, and divine election, as the Catholic Church, consistently, rejects all forms of heretical predestinationism.[18]

The feeling of divine election by these Protestant immigrants was then translated into nation building (United States), and into racist ideas of being superior over the other groups of Americans (blacks, Indians, Latin Americans, Jews, and Asians) and other religions (Catholicism and Judaism). In the words of Robert P. Lockwood, "Catholicism was identified as the religion of people deemed inferior by the white Anglo-Saxon Protestant establishment."[19] James H. Smylie in his article *Racism, Religion, and the Continuing American Dilemma,* placed much emphasis on how white Anglo-Saxons, mainly protestant, have asserted superiority and the right to subjugate, govern, and exploit those whom they have considered inferior—especially Indians, Africans, and Asians, among others, according to the racial color formation.[20] Virgil Elizondo also observes that "this sense of divine election has become one of the deepest collective traits of the white Anglo-Saxon-Protestant-English-speaking people of the United States of America."[21]

At this early period, the color of the skin was introduced by the colonial Englishmen as the clearest difference between them and the other races. In the words of Winthrop Jordan, ". . . taking the colonies as a whole, a new term appeared—white."[22] This indicates that there was no sense of feeling whiteness, until the Anglo-Saxon Americans encountered the other races that make up the United States of America. This is why Powell asserts, "Their fairness—a typically ambiguous term referring to either skin or disposition, or somehow to both—meant that Englishmen were favored, by God, through Nature; favored with membership in a category or great class of men: membership which was literally conducive to salvation, and to progress."[23]

The American Anglo Saxon language and culture were then taken to be superior to other cultures and languages and also taken to be the product of a favored nature.[24] Those who were regarded as real Americans were whites and it was only those who migrated from north-west Europe that qualified to be whites.[25] It was in the late nineteenth century and in the early twentieth century that the Irish, Spanish, Italians, and other immigrants from east Europe, including Jews, were assimilated into the white fold.[26]

American Protestantism, the Anglo-Saxon Myth, and Racist Ideologies

In the nineteenth century, this Anglo-Saxon racial ideology captivated American racial thinkers and theologians. The Anglo-Saxon myth was postulated by Robert Knox, an English man. He loved democracy and so did not like the undemocratic system of the British government under the queen. He wanted to prove that such a government could be fit for the Celtic people but unfit for the English or the Saxon race, which he saw as the superior race. He asserts, "Everywhere, Saxons were smashing the shackles of tyranny and someday, he predicted, on American soil would arise a mighty republican empire as the apotheosis of nature's democrat—Saxon man."[27]

Robert Knox's racial postulation had no Biblical or scientific foundations. It was simply the imagination or the dream of one man, who was politically motivated. His ideas were later used by American Protestant theologians and racial theorists to push forward their racial ideas to find reasons to dominate the other races. The racial ideologies formulated on Knox's premise permeated deep into the American intellectual and religious minds, to the extent that philosophical theories and the religious sermons of that time supported them.

> In 1844 Robert Baird, considered the first major American Church historian, wrote: 'In a word, our national character is that of the Anglo-Saxon race...and men must study Saxon institutions, and Saxon laws and usages...for Germanic or Teutonic are the chief supports of the ideas and institutions of evangelical Christianity and hold in their hands the theoretical and practical mission of Protestantism for the world.'[28]

Biblical Arguments to Support Racism and Slavery

In addition to the Anglo-Saxon myth, the early European Protestant immigrants also tried to apply skewed biblical interpretations of the King James Bible to support their racist ideas of the time.

> From the Bible they learned about God's creation of Adam and Eve, the parents of the human family, and the teachings of Jesus

and Paul about how God made of "one blood all nations of men to dwell on all the face of the earth" (Acts 17:26 KJV), and loved and saved them, calling them to love one another (John 3:16). They also brought stories about Noah, who cursed his son Ham because of his disrespect and blessed his other sons, Shem and Japheth. According to tradition, these sons became the sources, respectively, of African, Asian, and European stock, although no reference to racial coloring appears in the texts (Gen. 5-10) (Ex. 3ff).[29]

In American society in the 19th century, Darwin's theory of evolution was also wrongly interpreted by the social Darwinists to mean that "the races had evolved slowly over time and that the white race was naturally selected for racial superiority."[30] Darwin himself (1809-1882) believed that "the human races were of the same species and that racial distinctions were only minor variations."[31] Given the above racial theories--the Anglo-Saxon myth and the feeling of divine election by white Protestant immigrants--the white Americans saw their feeling of being superior over other immigrants--the blacks, Jews, Asians, and over Native Americans as *divinely established*. American theologians and racial theorists from different Christian denominations in the nineteenth century were teaching that "Because of their race, nonwhites were intellectually incapable of rising to the level of Anglo Saxon Americans and could never be successfully assimilated into white America."[32]

Like the Anglo Saxon myth, white supremacy has no reliable Biblical and scientific foundation. According to Joseph T. Leonard SJ, "Scientists may disagree over various points regarding race, but there is practical agreement that no scientific basis exists for considering any race superior. They do not deny existing differences between races—social, physical, educational, or cultural—but most of these differences can be explained by environment, and do not demonstrate innate inferiority or superiority."[33]

Inderjit Bhogal observes that "slave masters, makers of apartheid, biblically—heretically justified the enslavement of people by preaching 'God cursed Canaan. The lowest of slaves shall he be to his brothers.'"[34] Bhogal also describes this interpretation of the curse on Ham the father of Canaan (Gen:18-27), which racists saw as a curse on blacks to serve whites as "a lie, a massive misinterpretation."[35] He argues that it was Noah who cursed his son Ham and not God, as the racists preached. When these racial themes went unchecked by the church authorities, "these themes were particularly attractive to slaveholding American southerners who were intent on preserving the institutions of slavery."[36]

Most British Protestant slave owners in North America did not want to baptize their black slaves as the Spanish and Portuguese Catholics were doing in Latin America. They feared that "to Christianize enslaved Africans could result in economic loss and social disorder..."[37] They tried to justify Christians enslaving people by arguing whether blacks were human beings with souls and could be deemed for salvation. Though the slave-owners came from Europe to exercise religious and social freedom, "Slavery on the other hand was a form of persecution, which in the eyes of colonial America had to be justified. Therefore, the black slaves became an easily identifiable group targeted as being inferior, subhuman, and destined for servitude."[38]

Declaration of Independence and the Contradiction of Freedom

The Declaration of Independence in 1776 meant freedom and liberty for white men only. The founding fathers who were mostly Christians and also slave owners contradicted freedom and liberty by continuing the enslavement of blacks and Indians after independence. "In the Constitution of the United States, the nation's founders, Christians of various types, treated American Indians as foreigners in their own land, and postponed the end of slavery. . ."[39] Freedom in the era was denied to non-white races, since they were not considered as human beings. Even during the period of Revivalism or the Second Great Awakening of faith (1797-1820), the Bible was used by some preachers to support slavery, despite the fact that the period of slavery was a period of humiliation, abuse, oppression, and manipulation of the black slaves by their Christian masters.

Abolitionism and Civil War

When at last slavery became unpopular and had to be abolished, Quakers and Mennonites and other Protestants from the North, led an attack on slavery.[40] Southern religious leaders, lay members, and religious institutions opposed the abolitionists. Many of the Christian slave owners fought against the Union that advocated for the emancipation of the slaves during the Civil War (1861-1864). The Protestant Churches were much divided during this period, mostly over the issue of slavery. Their divisions due to slavery occurred within as well as between the various denominations.[41] The major reason why the Churches could not oppose slavery with one voice was materialism. The churches in the South and their leaders were gaining a lot from the lucrative business of buying and selling human beings. They needed slaves also to keep the cotton fields and the cotton business in the South flourishing. This materialistic quest was so strong that the Southern Christians fought a deadly war with the North, which threatened the Union.

The war was led by Abraham Lincoln, a Presbyterian church-goer from Illinois, who is also described as another Moses.[42] He is described as a Moses of the black slaves because on January 1st 1863 he issued the Emancipation Proclamation.[43] Was the war primarily fought with the intention of freeing the slaves or to keep the union together? There are arguments among historians whether the war was fought to keep the Union or to free the slaves. According to Kivel, "The Civil War and the end of slavery occurred because of economic tension between North and South, and political differences about state's rights, more than it did because of an outcry against slavery."[44] Some people do not agree with Kivel because for them, without slavery, there wouldn't have been a Civil War. However, despite the outcry against slavery at that time, the war seems to have been fought primarily to keep the union together, as Lincoln gave no voting rights to the blacks after the emancipation. Lincoln made his intention for fighting the Civil War clear in the letter he wrote to Horace Greeley:

> Dear Sir: I have not meant to keep any one in doubt . . . My paramount object in this struggle is to save the Union, and is not either to save or destroy slavery. If I could save the Union without freeing any slave, I would do it; and if I could save it by freeing all the slaves, I would do it; and if I could do it by freeing some and leaving others alone, I would also do that. What I do about slavery and the colored race, I do because it helps to save the Union.[45]

The American Civil War ended with the emancipation of black

slaves; still their problems were not over. "The early post-slavery period offered little hope of change."[46]

Protestant Churches Complied with Segregation Laws

After the declaration of emancipation of most slaves by Lincoln in 1863, "Reconstruction Congresses finally emancipated all slaves, even those in the North, but did not rescue African Americans from second-classdom."[47] The African Americans were still to be subjected to another form of slavery with the passing of the Jim Crow laws based on the racial theories, which the Christian abolitionists were not ready to speak against. The post slavery African American was declared free but with nothing to begin a new life. He or she was faced with lots of problems, such as lack of money, food, clothing, medical treatment, unemployment, and the attacks of white supremacy groups most especially in the south. "Because of these needs, he became an easy subject to denial, rejection, exploitation, and the consequences of unjust laws."[48]

Reconstruction came to an end as early as 1876 because of the racist activities of the Ku Klux Klan white supremacy groups in the south and due to national politics.[49] The hope of a better future for the African American was finally shattered in 1896 with the formal imposition of the segregation laws by the US Supreme Court.

> After the emancipation of slaves at the end of the Civil War, southern politicians used the new racial theories to justify their disenfranchisement of blacks. As a whole, the United States after the war became a culture that adhered to a legal policy of racial segregation. In 1896 the U.S. Supreme Court issued its decision in *Plessy v. Ferguson* which provided that the separate public facilities for the white and black races were constitutional as long as they were equal in quality.[50]

Though many of the Christian groups helped to oppose slavery, Protestant denominations from both North and South failed to oppose segregation laws. "By the 1890s segregation was not only a fact of the church life; it was the law as well."[51] It is not surprising that most religious leaders from both Catholic and Protestant denominations did not oppose the above racist policies and the governments that promulgated them. Segregation laws favored white European Americans, and the Churches were mainly white Churches. So it was like white churches could not oppose white government policies even when the policies went against the Christian teaching of love and justice. So this could answer the question why the churches did not speak in defense of the African American against the segregation laws.

There seemed to have been a racial solidarity between the churches whose leaders were white and the governments whose leaders were also mostly Christian and white to propagate the interest of the white race at the expense of the other races. Materialism was also one of the reasons why the churches could not opposed segregation laws because the laws were simply applied so as to dominate the other races economically, politically, socially and religiously. William Sinclair argues that the South opposed reconstruction and gave an out cry of "negro domination,"[52] when they saw that despite the suppression, which blacks received from over four hundred years of slavery, they were measuring up to participate in the different aspects of the nation's life. These points will be made clearer when we start looking at the roles the different churches played, one after the other.

As blacks and other minorities were segregated in society, they were also segregated in American Christian Churches. As blacks were not allowed to sit with whites in the front seats of the buses and trains, blacks were not allowed to sit together with whites in the Christian churches and cathedrals. "Some whites wished to keep relationships as they had been before the war, with former slaves sitting in the galleries. Freedmen thought differently and left their former masters' churches in large numbers."[53] Slavery brought about disagreement and division between most Christians in the North and most Christians in the South, but both sides did not disagree and divide over segregation laws. "Segregation in public conveyances, schools, and the churches, for example, was the rule. Even those whites who held up the abolitionist flag, often at the risk of social ostracism in their own families and communities, rarely conceived of a reconstruction of the North along lines of perfect racial and social equality."[54]

However, the mass exodus of blacks from the white churches due to the hypocrisy of segregation was more pronounced in the South. "Virtually all black Baptists and Methodists left churches controlled by southern whites. Presbyterians, Episcopalians, and Lutherans retained a remnant of black communicants but did not allow them to hold significant leadership positions."[55] This led to the formation of black churches in most denominations with little or no contact with white churches. The activities of the Ku Klux Klan members also worsened race relations in the churches as most of their members were Protestants. According to Smylie, "Most Klansmen, largely of Scots ancestors who traced their lineage to the lost tribes of Israel, belonged to Baptist, Methodist, and Presbyterian churches. To warn of danger, they practiced witchcraft, donned hoods, held rallies, and burned crosses, as they did in Scotland."[56]

Lynching of Blacks and the Protestant Churches

Lynching was one of the most regrettable aspects of American history, which worsened race relations and demonstrated the failure of the Protestant Churches to speak out against evil and government unjust practices in the early and middle twentieth century. Thousands of black men were murdered by angry white mobs mostly in the south to protect the racial purity of white women from what they called Uppity, Niggers or Negro Coon or Brute.[57] Most of the black men who were either burnt alive or hanged due to this aspect of the Jim Crow law were not tried before execution. Many were innocent of the crimes for which they were executed.

Ralph E. Luker in his book, *The Social Gospel in Black and White* told the graphic story of the hanging and the burning of two black men on Holy Saturday, 14th April 1906 in Springfield, Missouri. The two black men were accused of assaulting a white woman. The white employer of these two men vowed that they were working somewhere else at the time of the alleged assault and the victim could not identify the offenders. Despite the testimony of their white employer, an angry white mob broke into the county jail, released fourteen prisoners, dragged out the two black men, hanged them, and burned their bodies.[58]

They also, without trial, hanged and burned a third black man accused of murder. The following day, being Easter Sunday, as they were walking to church on Easter, the white Christians of Springfield, Missouri stepped around the burned bodies of the three black men.[59] After proper investigation when the three men had already been killed without trial, according to Luker, "A grand jury concluded that the white woman had not been assaulted and that the mob had released from jail the man who was probably guilty of the murder. But all charges against the mob were finally dropped."[60] The southern Protestant religious leaders were not effective in speaking out against the lynching laws and were blamed by L.B. Brooks for the continuation of the inhumane practices, in these words:

> The white preachers of America can break up the lynching, clean up the debauching evils of destructive prejudice, injustice and civil robbery in all parts of our land; if the true dispensation of the Gospel is preached and practiced! . . . But we find thousands of white preachers who hold the pulpits of the churches where lynchers are members, there men and women sit in the pews each Lord's Day who are members of State Legislature, where corrupt laws have been enacted, lawyers, judges of the courts, and jurors who are vile and unjust to men because of their color or race; and are too cowardly to raise their voices against these criminals in high places. God cannot use these preachers because they are slaves of wicked man.[61]

The Protestant Churches initially did not see any thing wrong in hanging and burning blacks without trial, at least to be found guilty before execution; if at all the crime justified the death penalty. The irony of burning and hanging Negro Male Coons or Bruts is observed by Fitts in these words, "Southern whites, at the same time, used as common-law wives, the daughters, sisters, and cousins of the same so called Negro brutes."[62]

Blacks were not the only people subjected to racial discrimination during this period. The other minorities such as the Indians, Asians, and Jews also suffered from discrimination. There were restrictions on where they lived and the kinds of jobs they had, and so they found themselves in the lowest income status in the country. According to Stanley I. Kutler, "The great majority of whites, including major educators and scientists, justified this condition on the grounds that non whites were biologically inferior to whites."[63]

Most religious leaders and theologians from different denominations during this period shared this idea. This could be another reason why the Churches were not effective in speaking for the minorities against segregation laws. "In the United States, religious education, economic, political and communications institutions have all worked together to confirm and reinforce the conviction that white, Anglo-America was indeed God's chosen vessel--a superior people destined by Divine Providence to rule over all the lesser people of the world."[64] This was what motivated William MacDougal in his racist ideas of the early twentieth century.

> In 1921, William McDougal, a well known English psychologist at Harvard, published *Is America Safe for Democracy?* He fed Anglo-Saxon phobia for racial and ethnic mixing. As a partial remedy for this fear, Congress passed restrictive immigration acts in 1921 and 1924. Congregationist President Calvin Coolidge approved: 'America must be kept America.' And in 1925 thousands of KKKers marched on Washington to demonstrate for racial purity and against Roman Catholics and Jews.[65]

Some Christians from different denominations did, however, attempt to improve interracial relationship and good will. The Federal Council of Churches of Christ in America and some other Christian organizations such as Young Men's Christian Association were advocating for better racial relationship, though they were not very effective instruments in bringing about the removal of the segregation laws. When they were calling for desegregation of America, their church denominations were still segregating against blacks. The churches were still complying with the racist laws for almost a century until the Civil Rights Movement of the 1950s and 1960s. All the mainline Protestant Churches were already observing segregated seating arrangements in church worship from the antebellum period, long before the Jim Crow laws became effective.[66] In this case, one may be right to argue that Jim Crow must have been inspired or encouraged by the discrimination already taking place in the churches. Most government officials are members of the denominations or religions, who expect the church or religion to lead the way to justice and peace. When religion sets a wrong example, the state could make wrong laws.

Protestant Churches and the Civil Right Movement

Rosa Park, a 42 year old Christian woman, resisted the evil laws on December 1, 1955, and sparked off the Civil Rights Movement.[67] Martin Luther King Junior, a Baptist black pastor, and his followers started the bus boycott without violence, which led to the removal of the segregation laws in 1964. The bus boycott was effective and led to the granting of numerous demands by the city authorities.[68]

Some white members of some Protestant denominations really supported the Civil Rights Movement, while some did not feel concerned. "While African Americans took leadership in this contemporary struggle, they were joined by Anglo-Saxon Americans, American Indians, Asian Americans, and others who had grown more active politically in dealing with racism."[69] A new era of the American history was created when "President Lyndon Johnson signed into law the Civil Rights Act of (1964) and the Voting Rights Act (1965), thus ushering in a *Second Reconstruction*."[70] Though the Civil Rights Movement made a lot of achievements and gave blacks new hope, there were also tremendous negative consequences against blacks especially in the south. According to John L. Kater, there were "murders and maiming of civil rights leaders and those whose only fault was attempting to vote; scores of burned homes and churches across the South (thirty-eight churches in Mississippi alone by the end of 1964)."[71]

"In 1968 Martin Luther King Jr. an African-American Moses and Nobel Prize Winner was assassinated. Even as he took a stride toward freedom, it cost to be black and different."[72] His assassination came at a time when he was leading his people toward a total dismantling of racism. Since his assassination, no religious leader or prophet of his caliber has risen from any of the white or black churches. King's murderer did not want racism dismantled; he wanted to create fear in any one who would resume the leadership of the Civil Rights Movement.

The *Third Reconstruction* which should bring racism to its final defeat and bring about equal treatment and equal opportunities to every one, at all levels, regardless of color, as wished by the taxi driver, is yet to be achieved. People of color need another Moses who will take them to the real Promised Land, or they may not need just an individual to do it this time. They really need the Christian Churches and other religions to play their prophetic roles well. They also need the different governments to be sincere with their plans and what they wish the people of color to be in this country.

Poverty among the people of color, which is the greatest effect of racism, due to a long period of economic exclusion, as revealed by hurricane Katrina, is yet to be effectively addressed. Unequal treatment based on color is experienced on daily bases in different aspects of the post modern American life. The removal of the laws is simply another stage of the evolution of racism from human enslavement, to segregation laws, and from segregation laws to the present inequality, which is experienced either in subtle ways or in overt ways, individually or institutionally. In the following sections, I will describe how each Protestant denomination contributed to this racial divide.

The Anglican Church (Episcopal)

The English immigrants who settled in Jamestown, Virginia colony in 1607 "marked the permanent beginnings of the Church of England in America."[73] The Anglican Church changed its name to Episcopal Church after the American Revolutionary War. In 1789, American Episcopalians met in Philadelphia and decided to reorganize their denomination and also change its name to Protestant Episcopal Church because of the activities of the Church of England in the war. "This marked the beginning of the fully structured Protestant Episcopal Church in the United States. . . "[74]

Pastoral Ministry Among slaves

As the Church of the colonial oppressors and slave masters, its missionaries did not do well in ministering among blacks. "For many African Americans, memories of Episcopalians as slaveholders were vivid and off-putting."[75] The Episcopalian Church, for its own part, found it difficult to persuade its slave owners to allow their slaves to receive religious instructions and be baptized. There was a widely held perception that the slaves were incapable of instruction and so could not be incorporated into the fellowship of Christ's religion, not only because of cultural differences but because of racial distinctions.[76] The Episcopalians also felt that making slaves Christians would be an economic detriment, as Christianity could open their eyes to know their rights and what Christian love should be. "Christianity made blacks too much like whites and raised troubling questions of conscience."[77] To protect their interest, the Episcopalian slave owners demanded that missionaries instruct slaves to obey their masters.

The missionaries of the Society for the Propagation of the Gospel in Foreign parts (SPG), during the period of the Second Great Awakening (1797-1820), when Episcopalians started to admit blacks, had to convince the slave owners that "far from being an economic detriment, converted slaves do better for their Master's profit than formerly, for they are taught to serve out of Christian Love and Duty."[78] To satisfy the slave masters, the epistles of Paul were particularly used by Episcopalian missionaries to instruct slaves, for example, Ephesians 6:5: Servants be obedient to them that are your masters.[79] The admission of African Americans into the Episcopal faith was, therefore, conditional. Missionaries preached a Christianity that justified slavery and racism.

Episcopalians and Slavery

Like those in other denominations, many members of the Episcopalian Church, both clergy and lay, had slaves. "In Louisiana, the bishop was himself a slave-owner who sought to provide a role model for the rest of the Episcopalian plantation owners. Bishop Leonidas Polk (1841-1864) had some four hundred slaves and several plantations. He built several chapels for them and encouraged the other slave masters to follow his example."[80] This reminded me of what the taxi driver told me about bishops and pastors having slaves. There were Episcopalians involved in arguments in support of the institution of slavery. Episcopalian slave holders, especially in the south, argued that black slaves were inferior human beings and should not be exposed to education because education would make them unruly and dissatisfied with their status. The best thing to do to make them remain in their condition as slaves and work hard to serve their white masters was to keep them out of education.[81]

There were also some Episcopalian missionaries who argued against the treatment given to slaves and condemned the institution of slavery as not justified. "In 1711, William Fleetwood, Bishop of Asaph, preached a remarkable sermon before the SPG at its annual meeting in which he declared that Negroes had potentially the same intellectual power as whites, that they were in no way inferior, and that they would work for wages. He conceded that baptism did not free a slave but quickly added that slavery was not justified."[82]

Episcopalians and Abolitionism

Before the Civil War, many white Episcopalians resisted the abolitionists and the emancipation of the African slaves, especially those in the South. The Episcopal Church did not experience division over the issue of slavery like many other Protestant denominations.[83] However, "the official silence of the Church over the slavery issue and the split in the Union, coupled with its continued hands-off policy with regard to freedman Black Episcopalians during Reconstruction led to mass defection among these churchmen."[84] Robert A. Bennett estimates that, "in some southern states 90% of the Black Episcopalians left to become African Methodist Episcopalian or Colored—now Methodist Episcopalians."[85]

The Episcopal Church Complied with Segregation Laws

After the Civil War, the Episcopal Church respected and complied with all the racist laws of the American governments, by denying their African American members equal opportunities to worship and hold leadership positions like their white counterparts. Bennett reports that, "They were forced into slave galleries and had services held for them at special hours in separate buildings."[86] Bennett goes on to assert, ". . . the remnant Black Episcopalian, though totally segregated in his diocese already by 1870 was given neither voice nor vote. Both north and south, the Church resisted efforts of churchmen to develop their own leadership; many parishes were excluded from diocesan conventions."[87] Negro missionaries were not allowed to go overseas and their delegates were not allowed to take part in General Conventions.[88] It was this type of racist attitude of the Episcopal Church towards the black Episcopalians that caused W. E.B. DuBois in his book *The Negro Church*, to remark that "the Episcopal Church has probably done less for the black people than any other aggregation of Christians."[89] Due to their depressed condition in the national Church scene, the remaining black Episcopalians struggled to defend their rights to speak up for themselves and to be able to vote in the General Convention of the Church. An example of this effort to have a voice in the national Church level was the action of Alexander Crummell who called "the Conference of Church Workers into being in 1883 to thwart the southern effort to segregate Black Episcopalians into a disenfranchised appendage of the Church."[90]

Harold T. Lewis summarized the historic encounter between African Americans and the Episcopal faith in these words:

> The Anglicanization—the Christianization—of slaves, therefore, during this period can only be seen as conditional, since evangelistic efforts were undertaken in order to help ensure the continuance of the institution of slavery, itself predicated on racism. Since emancipation, when it came, could change laws not necessarily hearts, the descendants of slaves had to contend against the legacy of this institution. The struggle of subsequent generations of black Episcopalians for recognition in the life of the Church must be understood in the light of this historical framework.[91]

From the above statement, one could rightly say that African Americans have never been fully integrated into the American Episcopal Church as they continue to struggle for recognition. There is no doubt; the African Americans in the Episcopal Church have also been patronized, some times marginalized, and even ostracized. The presence of an African in the Episcopal Church, if seen as an anomaly, reflects the general condition of blacks in American society from the beginning.[92] The Church is described as heavily white because of its 94 percent white membership in the country.[93]

The Episcopal Church and the Civil Rights Movement

The Church started to support the Civil Rights demand for equality, and there were efforts to start integrating the African American members of the Church, especially after the US Supreme Court's historic *Brown v. Board of Education* decision of 1954.[94] The activities of the

Civil Right Movement challenged the Episcopal Church to realize that discrimination within the body of Christ was an intolerable scandal. This, however, did not stop some Episcopal bishops from adopting the chameleon-like attitude of advocating for gradual change. Bishop Burrill of Chicago commented that "change must come slowly, as the Episcopal Church is congregational in nature and the Bishops have no power to do more than invoke change."[95] The struggle by black Episcopalians for recognition and against inequality continued even after the removal of the segregation laws in 1964. In the next chapter, we shall see the extent white Episcopalians have tried to improve their relationship with colored Episcopalians since the 1960s.

Presbyterian Church

Presbyterians are described as one of the earliest groups of immigrants that came from Europe to America. "The Reverend Francis Makemie (d. 1708), an Ulster Scot immigrant to the American wilderness, often has been referred to as the father of American Presbyterians. He settled on the eastern shore of Virginia in 1683, planting churches in Maryland as well as Virginia."[96] The first Presbytery was formed in Philadelphia in 1706 through the able leadership of Makemie.[97] As more immigrants continued to make their way into the new world, the number of Presbyterians continued to grow. In 1716, the first synod was organized in Philadelphia and three other Presbyteries, namely New Castle, Long Island, and Snow Hill—were carved out of the original Philadelphia Presbytery.[98]

Pastoral Ministry among Slaves

The fast growing Presbyterian Church in America, like other denominations, had its own challenges with conversion and acceptance of slaves as members of the Presbyterian Church. During the period of the Second Great Awakening, some Negroes were accepted as members of the Church, but equality of black and white members remained a problem as in other Churches. "Black slaves were introduced to and frequently adopted Christianity in the antebellum period. Although the races were segregated in worship services, they attended the same churches and listened to the same ministers."[99] The problem of equality of black and white members brought about conflicts among Presbyterians in Philadelphia and this led to a schism and the formation of a black Presbyterian congregation (1807).[100]

Presbyterians and the Institution of Slavery

Northern Presbyterians and Southern Presbyterians were divided over the institution of slavery. "New school Presbyterians especially supported the voluntary mission and reform societies, and many in the North called for the immediate, uncompensated emancipation of slaves in the 1830s."[101] On the other hand, the Old School Presbyterians insisted that slave holding should not prevent any one from communion.[102] The unresolved issue of the institution of slavery was so strong that the Southern Presbyterians seceded from the national assembly. The seceded Southern Presbyterians, in 1861 in Augusta, Georgia, organized their own assembly as the General Assembly of the Presbyterian Church in the Confederate States of America.[103]

Presbyterians, Abolitionism, and Civil War

At this period, many notable Presbyterians in the North, such as Harriet Beecher Stowe, James Birney, and Henry Highland Garnet, wrote and spoke against slavery, and called for its abolition. In the South, some Presbyterians such as Charles C. Jones and Thornwell, defended slavery using both biblical and philosophical arguments.[104] Also, as recorded by Joel L. Alvis, "Southern Presbyterian ministers led in the defense of slavery."[105] During the war, most members in the South fought against the abolitionists and against the Union. "Old and New School Presbyterians, South as well as North, supported their own governments. They sent soldiers and chaplains into the fields of combat, and they helped organize the Christian Commission to minister to all those who bore the brunt of the war."[106]

The Presbyterian Church Complied with Segregation Laws

After the Civil War, the Presbyterian Church faced the issue of relationship between the white members and the freed black members. Although Northern Presbyterians and Southern Presbyterians disagreed on the acceptance of blacks and on the freedom of the slaves, the racist laws introduced by the government to affirm inequality and segregation between whites and blacks in 1896 were complied with by both Northern and Southern Presbyterians until the 1960s. "American Churches cooperated with the segregated system—indeed they contributed to its rationalization."[107]

In the Presbyterian churches, blacks were forced to either sit at the back or in the galleries for almost a hundred years. "Southern whites, who composed 98 percent of the PCUS membership, were ambivalent about the plight of black Presbyterians, and this attitude arose in large part from simple indifference. Some tried to establish a separate black Presbyterian Church, but those efforts failed. Black Presbyterians were eventually included in a segregated system of church government."[108]

However, there were some groups and organizations formed in the mid 1900s which some Presbyterians helped to organize, to foster better race relations. The Black Presbyterian Leadership Caucus was formed by the PCUS "to help deal with racial and ethnic issues among Presbyterians and in Society."[109] However, this organization and some others were not as effective as the Civil Rights Movement of Martin Luther King Jr., in prophetically speaking out boldly for the removal of the oppressive laws.

The Presbyterian Church and the Civil Rights Movement

Many Presbyterians supported the Civil Rights Movement calling for a change and the removal of the evil laws in the American society. "In the civil rights movement of the 1950s and 1960s, Presbyterians faced the racism left over from the Civil War."[110] They supported the peaceful protests advocated by Martin Luther King, Jr., and his followers.[111] Though many Presbyterians supported the Civil Rights Movement, does that mean the end of racism in the Presbyterian Church in the United States? We shall see in the next chapter, how much effort has been made by white Presbyterians to improve their relationship with colored Presbyterians since the 1960s.

Methodist Church

The Methodists were among the early immigrants that came to America from Europe in the middle of the 18th century. "In 1760, the Irish Robert Strawbridge from Ulster organized a group of Methodist preachers in Maryland; the following year another group of Irish immigrants from County Limerick founded the first Methodist meeting in New York."[112] As immigrants with Methodist connections continued to flock into America from England, Scotland, and Ireland, the Church started to grow in strength and in number. As soon as Wesley observed how progressive Methodist work was in America, he sent lay-preacher missionaries to facilitate its progress. Francis Asbury (1745-1816), was the most popular leader in early American Methodism.[113] John Wesley, an Anglican clergyman, was able to send lay missionaries to America because he was the founder or the organizer of the societies under lay leadership within the Anglican Communion, which later developed into a separate denomination after the American Revolution.[114]

Pastoral Ministry among the Slaves

Methodist missionaries converted and accepted black slaves into their fold as members during the period of the Second Great Awakening. They were admired like the Baptists for their belief in the equality of all believers under God's rule and also "preached against those in power who oppressed the weak and the poor."[115]

Black Methodists later discovered, however, that the white Methodists were not serious about equality of all believers. The white members were forcing the black members to sit in the gallery, while the white members were asked to sit in the front pews inside the churches. The missionaries were also infected with the *Anglo-Saxon virus,* which made all Northern European immigrants to feel inherently superior to all other races. The black Methodists could no longer take the hypocrisy of those who preached the word of God to them, professed equality of all believers, and at the same time made them feel inferior. This issue led to division between the black members and the white members.

In 1787 Richard Allen (1760-1831), an African American Methodist preacher, led a group of African Americans that walked out of St. George's Methodist Episcopal Church in

Philadelphia when they were mistreated by white members of the Congregation. Allen and his companions in 1816 formed a new denomination, the African Methodist Episcopal Church, devoted to Wesleyan theology and a Methodist form of organization. Allen was its first bishop. The second schism caused by racial division occurred in 1796 in New York City under the leadership of James Varick (c.1750-1827), Christopher Rush (1777- 1827), and Peter Williams (c. 1750-1823). African American members of the John Street Methodist Episcopal Church, reacting to the discrimination by the white congregants, left the church and in 1821 formed the African Methodist Episcopal Zion Church with Varick as their first bishop.[116]

Methodism, Slavery, and the Division

The issue of slavery was another problem the Methodist Church had, as argument went on for many years on whether the institution of slavery was justified or not. "In the early days of small and simple beginnings, Methodists were able to take a strong stand against the evil institution."[117] According to Chester Jones, "The early Methodist preachers called for the abolition of slavery and demanded that all Methodist slave-holders free their slaves immediately."[118] Despite this call, the issue of slavery brought about a major division between the Northern members and the Southern members as many Methodist pastors continued to defend slavery and own slaves.

A well known Methodist preacher, George Whitefield, advocated and supported slavery for the economic development of the colony. He had slaves and was more concerned with the economy of the colony than the freedom of the slaves.[119] According to William Warren Sweet, "In 1844, there were at least 200 traveling Methodist preachers owning 1,600 slaves; while there were at least a thousand local preachers who owned 10,000; while there were at least 25,000 Methodist laymen holding more than two hundred thousand."[120] When the General Conferences of 1840-1844 could not get the problem of slavery resolved, "Numerous individual Methodists withdrew and joined other denominations, while in May 1941, a small group in Michigan formed themselves into a congregation and took the name Wesleyan Methodists and in two years reported more than a thousand members and seventeen preachers."[121] Some other antislavery groups broke away from the General Conference.

The Free Methodist Church formed in 1860 was also organized by one of the antislavery groups to dissociate itself from the main group, so as to propagate freedom for the slaves and freedom of worship. "At the 1844 General Conference, antislavery forces were able to require that James O. Andrew, bishop of Georgia, either discontinue functioning as a bishop or free the slaves he owned."[122] The slaveholding states in support of Bishop James O. Andrew "created a new church in which ownership of slaves was acceptable."[123] The name of the new Church formed in the South, in which slaveholders were welcome was Methodist Episcopal Church. The African American members who used to be members of the newly formed Methodist Episcopal Church got fed up with their second class position and formed the Colored Methodist Episcopal Church in 1870.

The Methodists Complied with Segregation Laws

Though the Northern and Southern Methodist churches split over the issue of slavery, both groups complied with the segregation laws that were enforced by the government a few years after the Civil War. Blacks were still forced to sit at the back of the churches and in the galleries. In 1939, some of the breakaway Methodist denominations such as the Methodist Episcopal Church, The Methodist Protestant Church, and The Methodist Episcopal Church, South, were reunited to form the Methodist Church, which also gave rise to the central jurisdiction.[124] As if racism were not enough at this stage, "the central jurisdiction relegated African American churches and annual conferences wherever they were located in the United States into a separate and unequal jurisdiction. Not until 1968, with the formation of United Methodist Church, was the central jurisdiction abolished."[125]

Methodism and Civil Rights Movement

During the Civil Rights Movement of the 1950s and 1960s there is evidence that some Methodists supported the movement, while some others opposed it. Many took part in some of the protest marches organized by Martin Luther King Jr. and his followers to dismantle the segregation laws. When the laws were removed in 1964, the American Methodists also started to adopt some integration policies. Though some Methodists supported the Civil Rights Movement, the question remains, what is presently happening in the United Methodist Church between the black members and the white members since the removal of the segregation laws? In the next chapter, we shall see the extent white Methodists have tried to improve their relationship with colored Methodists since 1960s.

Baptist Church

The Baptists were among the Puritans that migrated to the United States in search of religious freedom and to escape the religious persecutions in Europe. "Under the leadership of Roger Williams, founder of Rhode Island, the first Baptist Church in the colonies was established at Providence in 1639 and two years later the first Baptist Church of Newport was started by John Clarke."[126]

Baptist Pastoral Ministry among Slaves

The Baptist Church did not find it as difficult as the Anglicans to convert and to accept black slaves into their fold, because the conditions they placed on their missionaries for the conversion and the acceptance of black slaves were lighter than those of the Anglicans.[127] The Baptist Church really made a lot of progress, especially in the North, in the conversion of the black slaves and the freed slaves. Due to the Baptist teaching of equality of all believers and its open preaching against those in power who oppressed the weak and poor, many black slaves became more disposed to follow them. A large number of black slaves were converted and accepted as Baptists, especially during the Second Great Awakening of the eighteenth and nineteenth centuries. [128] Helpful was the fact that, "evangelization was tolerated by the slave owners, who hoped that it would make slaves more obedient and less prone to rebel against their circumstances."[129] Indeed, "many clergy were compelled to assure slave holders that conversion to Christianity changed only the eternal status of the African, with no effect on their earthly situations."[130]

Because of the Baptist belief in equality of all believers, blacks and whites were closer to each other in the Baptist Church. However, division set in between blacks and whites when blacks found out that there was a contradiction and insincerity among the white Baptists with regard to the teaching of the equality of all believers. Black members of the Church, as in the Methodist Church, were subjected to staying in the galleries and to sitting in the back benches during worship with their white counterparts.[131] The first African American Baptist Church came into existence because of the racism in a white Baptist congregation.[132] Nancy Good Sider and Cheryl Talley also commented on this:

> The Baptist Church of Richmond, Virginia was founded in 1780 during the Revolutionary war and masters and slaves worshiped there together. By 1841 the number of slaves outnumbered the number of masters in the congregation. That year the slaves were given the building, which was called the First African Baptist Church of Richmond, and a new church was erected for the white parishioners. For the last 159 years the two churches have been primarily racially segregated.[133]

The two Baptist Churches side by side came into existence simply because the white Baptists did not want to sit on the church pews with blacks as equals. Secondly, as the number of blacks was getting far bigger than that of the whites, the whites feared that blacks might become leaders of the Church. The whites, therefore, left the church for blacks and erected another one for themselves. They would rather worship in small numbers elsewhere than be under the leadership of the black Baptists, who were seen as second class members.

The Baptist Church and Slavery

The Baptist involvement in the institution of slavery was very surprising and raised a lot of questions, when considering their origin and the reason why they migrated to the new world. "How could a group so exposed to persecution in Europe support the oppression of black men and women from Africa? How could a people who supported the freedom of conscience issues fail to recognize the evils of an institution styled to enslave both body and conscience?"[134]

These questions, whether answered or not, point to the common trait of those who seem to have suffered persecution either through religious intolerance or through racism. Immediately they get their freedom, they treat others exactly the same way the oppressor treated them and sometimes worse. We shall see this common trait occurring as we discuss the type of discrimination which the other religious bodies and groups of people in America suffered and how they turned to be the oppressors of the people who used to suffer oppression with them, after they were assimilated or accommodated by the original oppressor. When they reached the Promised Land, they forgot when they were in the wilderness and those who are still in the wilderness.

According to Robert G. Torbet, "An estimated two fifths of all Baptist clergymen in South Carolina owned slaves."[135] However, the issue of slavery later became a controversial issue in the Baptist Church.

Baptist Controversy over slavery and the Division

Before the Civil War, "the issue of slavery became so controversial that unity of Baptists was hopelessly impaired."[136] The Northern Baptists supported the emancipation of slaves, while the Southern Baptists wanted to continue the institution of slavery. "In the 1840s, the Southern Convention was formed because they wanted the right to own slaves."[137] The Southern Baptists used biblical arguments to support the institution of slavery, as found in Ephesians 6. However, African Americans, conscious of this hypocrisy, held fast to the liberating elements of the Christian gospel as evidenced in the songs of slavery.[138] This was the reason why, "after the Civil War, African Americans, sensitive to their second-class status, left white Baptist churches to found their own congregations and denominations."[139] There was a mass exodus of black slaves after the Civil War. About one million black Baptists in the south left the white dominated churches and formed their own congregations.[140]

Baptists Complied with Segregation Laws

In both North and South, the segregation laws against the people of color were complied with and applied in the church worship to reflect what was happening in the wider society. Historically, the Southern Baptist convention has been described as one of the most racist denominations in the country. "In the 1950s, they stood in opposition to equal rights."[141] Garner Taylor also observes:

> Baptists have a large stake in the whole cause of human rights in America, upon which the fate of the nation may well hang. For better or for worse, Baptist people are in the majority in the religions where human rights heretofore have been most rigidly proscribed and where the ugliest forms of racism have until recently had their greatest expression.[142]

The mass exodus of black Baptists caused by the racist attitudes of white Baptists brought about little or no contacts between black congregations and white congregations. I remember the statement of the black taxi driver. "The black Baptist Church, which I belong to, is a church of liberation." In the next chapter, we shall see if there is improvement in the relationship between black Baptist congregations and white Baptist congregations from the period of the Civil Rights Movement to the present twenty-first century.

Baptists and Civil Rights Movement

Many white Baptists really supported the Civil Rights Movement while some who were racist minded, especially in the South, even protested against it. However, officially, "the American Baptist Convention passed resolutions giving moral support to the aspirations of the Negroes. These resolutions were backed up by many churches and individuals as they supported legislation or participated in demonstrations to gain recognition of the Negroes' basic civil rights."[143]

Martin Luther King Jr., a Negro Baptist pastor played a leading role in the Civil Rights Movement which led to the removal of the segregation laws in the 1960s.[144] The gift of Martin Luther King is a credit to the Baptist Church as a denomination, as no other religious denomination was able to produce such a fearless challenger of the Jim Crow laws. However, it took the Baptist Church almost a hundred years to produce a black minister who boldly and without minding the cost, prophetically spoke out for justice and for the liberation of people of color. He needed to be a black man to brave it, as no white pastor or bishop from the

Baptist Church itself and from any other Christian denomination was inspired to lead the Movement. Is prophecy determined by color?

However, this achievement was not without a cost; Martin Luther King was assassinated in 1968. Also the violence that arose as a white reaction to the Movement resulted in "the murder of civil rights workers in Neshoba County, Mississippi, as they participated in the Freedom Summer Project of 1964."[145] At present, many black Baptist Churches are being burned down in the south by hate groups. The Baptist Church, like the Methodist Church, started as a more liberal group, but ended up before the 1960s as a Church with a complicated racial past.

Lutheran Denomination

Lutherans came to America in the eighteenth century. Among the early Lutherans that came to North America were German speaking Lutherans and Lutherans from other parts of Europe. "By the year 1700 there were about 1,000 Swedish and Finnish Lutherans on the Delaware and perhaps 300 Dutch Lutherans on the Hudson."[146] However, it was in 1742 that Henry Muhlenberg, who is regarded as the father of American Lutheranism, formally and systematically organized Lutheran churches in the colonies.[147] The Church continued to grow as more immigrants continued to pour into the new world. "From the 1830s through the end of the century and beyond, Lutheran immigrants from the German territories, as well as Norway, Sweden, Denmark, and Finland, organized new congregations and synods throughout the United States, but principally in the Midwest."[148]

Lutherans and Slavery

The Lutheran Church, like other Christian denominations at that time, did not find the issue of slavery very easy to handle. Initially, slavery was forbidden among the Lutherans. When Muhlenberg, the father of American Lutheranism, visited Charleston, South Carolina, he for the first time noticed that Lutherans were enslaving human beings. He was not happy that those who pretended to be Christians were using fellow human beings who have been redeemed along with themselves as mere body slaves. He wondered if that was not going to produce severe judgment.[149]

Despite his observation and condemnation of slavery, the use of slaves started formally due to the shortage of labor in most German colonies and colonies of other nationalities that had Lutheran ties. They also found reasons and arguments to justify slavery "on the ground that Negroes were spiritually and physically better off as slaves in America than as freemen in Africa."[150] It is on record that Muhlenberg refused the gift of a slave while his son Peter had many of them, as many other Lutheran members had.[151] According to Douglas C. Stange, many Lutheran pastors owned slaves as did many other Protestant pastors of different denominations.[152]

Lutheran Pastoral Ministry among Slaves

Like other Protestant Churches, there were efforts to convert slaves to Lutheranism during the antebellum period, but the success was not so encouraging initially.[153] However, there was an official arrangement to receive slaves into the Lutheran fold, "in 1809 when the North Carolina synod authorized its pastors to baptize slaves—provided the owners did not object."[154] A similar decision was taken in 1814, and a formal catechetical program was designed for the evangelization of slaves, but different from that of the white members. In the words of George Anderson,

> The program suggested that elders in each congregation see that some place be set aside for the instruction of slaves. After adequate instruction and demonstration of good conduct, the slaves could be baptized. Then, in contrast to white members, blacks would undergo an additional probationary period during which they were to receive more instruction. Then, after an unspecified time, the slaves could be admitted to Communion, but only at their master's church. Slaves could have their children baptized and could stand as sponsors at baptism. The most awkward rule concerned marriage. Slaves were to remain faithful to their spouses as long as they are not separated by their master, in being removed to a distance. In that case, they were not to marry again until given permission by the minister or by their owners.[155]

It was the right of the master to determine how long marriage lasted between a black man and a black woman and whether any slave had the right to remarry.

In most Lutheran Churches during the antebellum period, masters and slaves worshiped together in the same church but were not allowed to sit together. There was a common seating arrangement practice, in many Lutheran churches, especially in the churches of the Northern states. They marked "a certain section of pews, with letters 'B.M.' meaning Black members. Here is where the Black members are supposed to sit."[156] In most Lutheran Churches in the South, slaves were also forced to stay in long galleries or at the back of the churches during worship. In some cases, different churches were built for slaves where white pastors or approved colored pastors ministered to them, according to the type of pastoral care approved for them.[157]

Lutheranism, Abolitionism, and Civil War

Like other Protestant denominations, the issue of slavery and racism brought about division. "Then the Spirit of sectionalism expressed itself in terms of anti-slavery and pro-slavery, and this momentous issue absorbed all other political questions until after the Civil War."[158] Most members in the South supported slavery and fought against abolition and against the Union, while members in the North supported total abolition of slavery and fought in support of the Union. "The South Carolina synod passed resolutions expressing their strongest disapproval of the conduct of Northern Abolitionists."[159] General synods like that of Hartwick could not resolve the issue of slavery, as members "voted instead to postpone the subject indefinitely."[160] In 1842, the Franckean synod, formed in 1837 to advance the call for the total abolition of slavery, "sent an appeal to every other synod in the United States, calling for them to express themselves on the abolition issue."[161]

Many Lutherans spoke out against slavery as the confusion continued between the North and the South. "One of the most outspoken Lutheran opponents of slavery was William A. Passavant. The Pittsburgh Synod, which he had been instrumental in organizing, labeled slavery as a moral and national evil."[162] Despite the efforts of the Franckean Synod, the

Pittsburgh Synod, and some other Synods, such as the Ohio Synod of 1852, the issue of slavery remained dormant and unresolved. "The position of the Missouri Synod, not unlike the attitude of southern churches, held that according to Scripture slavery in itself was not sinful. It was considered a judgment of God as a punishment for sin."[163] Through this statement, the Missouri Synod justified and approved the continuation of slavery. The Civil War broke up the General Synod along the line between North and South.[164]

Lutherans Applied Segregation Laws

Like other Protestant denominations, the Lutheran Church both North and South, complied with the racist laws established after Reconstruction. As already indicated, blacks were forced to sit at the back of the church or in the galleries during church worship. "The Lutheran Church – Missouri Synod had tacitly assumed the position of racial segregation in missionary and educational programs."[165] The Lutheran leaders could not do much about the segregation laws because the prevailing attitude was that segregation was a social rather than a theological or spiritual problem and that the Church's sole concern was to preach the Gospel.[166] There was less emphasis on the fact that preaching the Gospel of Jesus Christ also involves being prophetic to whatever keeps people under bondage. However, segregated seating arrangements and segregated pastoral ministry for the blacks had been the formal practice in the Lutheran church during the antebellum period, even before the government imposed segregation laws against the people of color.

Lutherans and the Civil Rights Movement

Many Lutherans supported the Civil Rights Movement of the 1950s and 1960s, while many, mostly in the South, did not give a damn about it. Before this period, the Lutheran leaders were being criticized for being guilty of social ethical quietism.[167] Lutheran theologians and boards of social action had to define well the role of the Lutheran Church in the face of social tension. They made it clear that the doctrine of righteousness by grace through faith does not forbid a Christian from seeking righteousness on earth and from responding to the call for social justice and peace.

At the same time, the theologians reaffirmed that what a person needs to become a Christian is not social action or works but grace which an individual gets through faith in the Word of God.[168] This really encouraged some Lutherans to support the Civil Rights cause while some were not happy and charged that "the 'spiritual' character of the Church was being eroded by a new 'liberalism.'"[169] What type of 'spiritual character' is more important to such Lutherans than love, justice, and peace that should come through fairness and equal opportunity with others?

CHAPTER THREE
RACISM AND THE PROTESTANT CHURCHES
FROM THE 1960S TO THE PRESENT

The mid 1960s ushered in a different and a new American society without the formally institutionalized segregation laws which had kept people of color as second class citizens in their beloved country for almost a hundred years after slavery. Though the laws are gone, we still need to know whether their effects are gone along with them or not. This is why we have to look at the following questions to know what is happening at present.

1. How has the Civil Rights Movement affected the relationship between white Protestants and Protestants of color since 1964? Is there still racism in all these Protestant Churches? If yes, what forms is it taking now?

2. Are Protestant churches presently committed to speaking for equal opportunities for every American citizen socially, economically, politically, and religiously?

3. How have these Protestant Churches, through their pastoral ministries responded to the greatest effect of racism, which is poverty mostly among African Americans and Hispanics, for example, as we saw in the case of Hurricane Katrina?

4. What are the measures that could be applied by the Protestant Churches to fight against racism among their members and outside their congregations?

In this chapter, we shall see the improvements that have been made from the sixties to the present day and what still needs to be done.

About The Interviews

I tried to interview pastors and lay members of these churches from different parts of the country and of different races. I carried out interviews with as many Protestant pastors and lay people as possible, to be able to get enough information about the recent happenings in these churches. Many of the individuals I interviewed did not want me to mention their names or to publish the details of my discussions with them, for fear of what the members of their churches would say. Some individuals even fear retaliation or physical attack from hate groups.

Some of the Protestant clergy and lay persons in charge of institutions such as schools and hospitals were afraid of speaking out to avoid losing the patronage of some of the rich white members of their churches who fund their institutions. Some were afraid of losing their positions as deans of theological colleges. My experiences while interviewing them makes me feel that poverty and fear of physical attack are two major reasons why some people try not to talk about inequality in this country. Poverty is a strong point because some reputable persons of color swallow the truth that could have freed their brothers and sisters from the same poverty.

Violence or physical attack is another major reason why people are not ready to say the truth about injustice. I can understand them because violence has been one of the crudest methods of silencing those who have a different definition of truth in connection with racial oppression in this country. Unfortunately, some religious leaders make bizarre public comments that seem to make one feel that religion supports violence here. I was shocked in August, 2005, to hear Rev. Pat Robertson, a well known American Television evangelist with the CBN, advising the American government to take out the president of another country.[170] I am not interested in whatever politics is going on between countries, but at the same time, I feel that there is no way the president of another country could be taken out by a foreign power without blood shed and hurting innocent people. Christianity is not a bloody religion but a religion of love, justice, peace, and friendship even with enemies. When the Samaritans did not allow Jesus and his disciples passage to Jerusalem through their town, Jesus did not allow his two disciples James and John to call fire down from heaven to destroy them as they requested (Lk. 9: 51-56). By cautioning his disciples, Jesus did not allow an abuse of power. Our religion should guide and model our politics and not our politics controlling our religion. We religious leaders should be instruments of love, peace, justice, and reconciliation nationally and internationally.

I do not have any of the above fears because I am simply a student reporting the truth based on objective research, with the good intention of encouraging this society and the churches not to relent, in their efforts to look for true justice and equality for all. By so doing, I am bearing witness to the truth. So, I do not see the reason why I should be afraid of any sort of victimization from any one or any group. I am not reporting anything new from what people already know; at the same time, it is good that a foreigner, who came with a different view of things, is also making the same observations. However, I will present in this book only the few interviews of those who allowed me to do so. Some of the interviews include a personal confirmation of my research, while others offer new information of current happenings.

Episcopal Denomination

The Civil Rights Movement in both church and state, put pressure on the Episcopal Church to move towards change. The pressure to move faster towards integration and to instill self awareness among its members resulted in the formation of the interracial action group known as the Episcopal Society of Cultural and Racial Unity (ESCRU), and in the establishment of the General Convention Special Program (GCSP) in 1967.[171] Among the developments that helped to create the consciousness of black Episcopalians in the late 1960s to work for self determination and stronger representation in the Church was also "the formation of the Episcopal Church Black caucus, the Union of Black Episcopalians (UBE) in 1968, providing a forum and lobby for Black interests in the Church . . ."[172]

So we can say that the African American struggle for recognition in the racially divided Episcopal Church, which became more serious in the 1800s, yielded some remarkable results in the late 1900s. Robert Bennett also records some areas of strength and gains in the status of African Americans in the Episcopal Church in the 1970s.

> Gains in the status as well as strength of Black Episcopalians can be seen in the greater representation and voice in diocesan conventions and the National General Convention and the wider participation of Black Clergy and laity in Church executive position as well as in its missionary outreach, particularly in urban centers. As a sign of the Church's new readiness to serve and evangelize in the Black community, the already

traditionally urban-oriented Episcopal Church is placing Black priests at the head of its programs of outreach to the new Black city dweller. A dozen have been attached to cathedral staffs as Urban Missioners.[173]

Though some progress has been made by the Episcopal Church to integrate its members of color, Harold T. Lewis argues that the little that has been gained "was done not of the Church's volition, but as a result of pressure exerted on the Church from within and without. It can be argued, then, that the Episcopal Church, in addressing matters concerning its black constituency, has been given more to reaction than action, more to response than initiative, more to acquiescence than advocacy."[174] For example, the beginning of the consecration of black bishops was as a result of pressure from black leaders of the Conference of Church Workers among Colored People (CCWACP), who demanded that blacks be included in the hierarchy of the Church. However, after the consecration of such black bishops, they were limited to ministry in black communities.[175]

Despite the main changes, Lewis feels that the Episcopal denomination's purpose has been "to preserve the status quo, and not to champion the cause of the oppressed."[176] He feels that "it has been the black Episcopalians who, with a steady beat, have faithfully provided a corrective."[177] The following interviews will help us to know how much effort the Episcopal denomination has made to improve the relationship between the white and colored members since the Civil Rights Movement of the 1960s.

Interview with the Reverend John Kenneth Blair, CPC-C, CSAC

The Rev. John Kenneth Blair.

The first Episcopal priest I talked with was the Reverend John Kenneth Blair. Father Blair is the rector of All Saints Episcopal Church, St. Louis, Missouri. Sitting face to face with Father Blair in his well furnished office, I asked these questions.

"As racial discrimination is very much noticed in the wider American society and in most Christian denominations, do you believe that it is also experienced in the Episcopal denomination at present?"

"Yes, I do believe, but at the same time I need to explain myself. I was not ordained in the Episcopal Church, and I attended a non-Episcopal seminary. I was ordained in the African Orthodox Church which was a breakaway Church from the Episcopal Church. It was formed in the twentieth century under Marcus Garvey's United Negro Improvement Association. The blacks were disappointed because they did not have any black clergy and bishops in the Episcopal Church, and so they left to form their own Church as their own empowerment movement of the people of color. So that is my background before coming into the Episcopal Church. In this diocese of Missouri, I am the only active black male

Episcopal priest, and my church is the oldest black Episcopal Church west of the Mississippi. My predecessor is retired, but he was also the only black clergy in the diocese. Recently, there is a black female priest who was just ordained and is serving as an assistant in the Cathedral."

"Yes, the Episcopal Church is one of those churches that have recognized the right of women to become priests. Tell me, Reverend, what you have experienced recently as racist in your denomination."

"Within my short stay here, I have noticed what I may call racism of apathy or lack of interest, because whenever the Episcopal Church is planning to build new churches, they never think of including North St. Louis and North County where the majority of blacks are. I do not think that it has been a priority in the Episcopal Church, especially in this diocese, to reach out to the African Americans."

"It is surprising to hear that, Reverend. Do you think that there is anything the authorities in this denomination are doing to solve this problem of apathy and racial prejudice as you have mentioned?"

"Well, in terms of racism, I think that the Episcopal Church is one of the most liberal, because we have a commission that looks into such matters but at the same time we just have to accept the fact that it has not been a priority of the Episcopal denomination to reach out to the African Americans. It is a question of isolation and they do not know what to do about it for now."

"So what do you recommend that should be done?"

"I recommend that when planning for the expansion of the Church, African Americans should be included and be provided for, because the Episcopal Church in the United States is not a very big denomination. It has a population of about two million members nationwide and the population of the African Americans is just about two percent of the population of the entire Episcopalians in the country. So, there is need to reach out to them, to have more people of color become members."

"Many people in this country who feel with the African Americans and the other people of color are saying that it is time for the federal government to really discuss the racial crisis in this country and to address the poverty of African Americans and Hispanics. People started asking for a dialogue after the horrible revelation of the extent of their poverty by Hurricane Katrina. Are the Episcopal authorities in this country doing any thing to appeal to the government to discuss this problem and see ways to fully integrate some of the minorities who have been complaining of economic marginalization and exclusion?"

"I do not know, but I do not think that anything is being done yet. However, the church helps the poor through social services."

"That's good, but self reliance is the best condition for the poor. I am happy the Episcopal Church is helping the poor through social services. That is what I may call giving the poor the *fish*. What do you think about giving them the *hook* to do the fishing by themselves, by the Episcopal Church with other churches appealing to the government to discuss their poverty especially the type that was inflicted in history through long period of economic exclusion?"

"That's true. I really do not think that the Church has done anything to appeal to the state for the full economic integration of the African American and the Hispanics who are the poorest in this country."

"Thank you, Father Blair; I have enjoyed talking with you."

Interview with Reverend Canon Renee L. Fenner

Rev. Canon Renee L. Fenner

The next Episcopal priest I interviewed was the Reverend Canon Renee L. Fenner. For many years, she was a member of a Catholic religious community, and she felt the call of God to the priesthood, but because the Catholic Church does not ordain women, she left the Catholic Church and joined the Episcopal Church. She was recently ordained to the Episcopal priesthood. She told me that she did not leave the Catholic Church in anger, but to respond to the call of God to the priesthood, which she felt was a greater call than being a member of a particular church. Rev. Fenner is currently assisting in the Christ Church Cathedral of the Missouri diocese. We met in her office, and after her gracious reception of me, I began the interview:

"Do you believe that discrimination or racism exists in the Episcopal denomination?"

"Yes, racism does exist. I have relations, friends, acquaintances, and classmates to whom some questionable things have happened even within the Episcopal denomination that show that racism does exist and that the Church may not even be better than the government in this case. Inequality also happens even in the seminary."

"Could you explain please?"

"I am one of those who recently graduated from the seminary; I had classmates who are African Americans, some from the Caribbean. We can all speak of different things that did happen to us while we were in the seminary about being ignored sometimes. I thought that all of us were pretty intelligent; otherwise, we would have not been able to withstand the rigors of the seminary training. What used to happen was that some one could just paraphrase what we just stated without first clarifying with us. Sometimes it looked so embarrassing as if we did not know anything."

"Do you experience any form of prejudice here?"

"In terms of administration in this Cathedral, I noticed that there are just two persons of color in the chapter, which is equivalent of parish council in the Catholic Church. I am not noticing people of color as members of the other Church committees here at the Cathedral. Well, I could be wrong; I guess what I am saying is that I wish to see more."

"Thanks, Rev. Fenner, for saying your mind. In your brief tenure with this Church community, do you see anything the Episcopal community here is doing to be more inclusive in whatever it is doing to represent the multiracial character of this denomination?"

"Yes, I have noticed that in our Sunday school those who teach the children tend to be very inclusive. There are posters and books with pictures and illustrations from different cultures. I mean I have seen a lot of evidence that they are inclusive. It is not a question of here are some white faces in this book or poster that look in a particular way, as only good. The other ethnic groups are also represented."

"I can see evidence of what you are saying even here in your office. I can see some pictures in this office depicting white, black, Asian, and Indian and so on. I am happy that in this Cathedral community, those who teach the Sunday schools are very inclusive. That is the way it should be. It is good to make people, and, in fact, the younger ones, to know that as Jesus could be painted as a white man, he could also be painted as a black man. God has no color. If God was to have color, He or She would be God of all the colors as every thing is possible for him."

"Exactly."

"So what advice can you give to the Episcopal denomination nationwide to be more inclusive in what ever it is doing?"

"We need to invite more people of color into our faith and to leadership positions in the Episcopal Church. We are not doing that well at all."

"Lastly, do you feel that the Episcopal denomination is doing enough to respond to the cries of the poor for justice? By this I mean not just giving them money to buy cigarettes, but getting to know why America is the richest country in the world, but still the number of poor African Americans and Hispanics is so great. I feel that the church can still do something to help them, or at least speak for them."

"About that, honestly, I do not think that we are doing enough. We really need to do something to show that we are concerned with the extent of poverty in this country."

"Thank you, Reverend Fenner, for talking with me."

Comments

The above research and interviews indicate that there is still racial inequality in the Episcopal Church. Though the interviews do not cover all the dioceses in the United States, at the same time they give a good idea of what could be happening in other dioceses. The Episcopal Church in the United States of America is still challenged to do more to eradicate all forms of inequality in both church and society. This question still remains: what measures can still be applied to fight against racism in both the Episcopal Church and in the entire American society? We will consider these measures when we have heard the story from other Protestant Churches, the Catholic Church, and from the Jewish point of view.

Presbyterian Church

The pressure from and the achievements of the Civil Rights Movement of the 1950s and 1960s also challenged the Presbyterian Church in the United Sates (PCUS) to be more committed to desegregation of the Church and to encourage the white members to reconsider their racist positions against their black brothers and sisters. "Tension over how to relate to black Presbyterians plagued their white brethren, while the General

Assembly adopted a position that aligned the denomination in support of the goal of desegregation and integration."[178] Despite the decision of the General Assembly to address the race issue in the 1970s, the PCUS did not find it easy to address the issue of black identity within the denomination. There was a need to create awareness among the members about racial inequality in the Church.

Despite the effort made by the PCUS to integrate the minorities, the sincerity of this effort was tested. "Leadership opportunities continued to elude many talented black leaders. Rumors persisted of racial prejudice limiting opportunities. And in cases where blacks assumed leadership positions, they found their opportunities limited."[179] Betty J. Durrah wonders why the Presbyterian commitment to diversity and inclusiveness is seen more at the General Assembly level and less at the Synod and Presbytery levels. She feels that "there is still limited contact across racial lines."[180]

According to the response of the Racial Ethnic Ministry Unit in the 203rd General Assembly of the PCUS in 1991, it was accepted that there is "an appalling lack of commitment and action for social justice at every level of the Presbyterian Church."[181] Though the Presbyterian Church had adopted some policies and had made some studies, to purge itself of any racial prejudice, it is still being described as ineffective.[182] It is, therefore, being presently urged to "stop talking and studying and begin to act."[183] I took time to discuss with some Presbyterian ministers and lay members to find out more what is happening at present.

Interview with Reverend William G. Gillespie

Rev. William G. Gillespie.

The first Presbyterian minister I interviewed was Reverend William G. Gillespie of the Cote Brilliante Presbyterian Church in North St. Louis. Pastor Gillespie has been in the ministry for 50 years and had a lot of experiences about what used to happen in the Presbyterian Church and what is happening now between white and black Presbyterians. I addressed him on the main reason why I came to spend some time with him.

"Reverend, having had a lot of experiences as a pastor in the Presbyterian denomination and having had a lot of interactions with your white counterparts in the ministry, do you feel that racism exists in the Presbyterian Church as it exists in the wider American society?"

"Oh yes. The reason why I am saying this is that about forty years ago, I came to St. Louis and this church was in a changing community. There was a law being passed that you can not just segregate against people because of their race. There was a black couple also that had the opportunity to move into this community. There were meetings inside this church to keep black people out of this community. The white pastor who was in this church bought a home near his house and had it occupied by another white family because he did not want any black neighbor.

Since the segregation laws were no longer enforced, blacks gradually started coming to live in this community and also started coming to Cote Brilliante church to participate, but they were not allowed to participate."

"What was the effect of this in the church?"

"The denomination was messed up here by this, as blacks were not allowed to attend Cote Brilliante church. This was a time when Presbyterian leaders declared by word that the Presbyterian Church was to be taken as a non-segregated Church in a non- segregated society and that they were going to work towards that. It was a big contradiction because the few blacks who had come in to live and worship with the white members were not allowed into Cote Brilliante church. I was not surprised myself because I was brought up in the South where we were always segregated as far as church worship was concerned."

"So the removal of the segregation laws by the state meant nothing to them at that time?"

"Yes, I knew at that time that the integration of the churches was going to bring a problem in the church, and it happened. Cote Brilliante church had to be closed for some months because of the crisis. I was invited after some months immediately I came out of the seminary to become the first black pastor of this church. They were hopeful that everybody both white and black will be part of it when it was reopened."

"Did all co-operate?"

"On the first day of starting this church again, there were only two white men that were here to worship with us and there were about eighty-six black men and women present. Now we do not have any white membership as part of this church. So you can see then that when you talk about the Presbyterian denomination, it is still a segregated Church, even now. It is mainly affluent blacks that could be found in a white congregation. So in the actual sense or in practice, the Presbyterian Church is a segregated Church in a segregated society. I have never seen equality."

"What are the effects of the decisions taken in the past?"

"When it comes to problems like racism, the Presbyterian Church is very fast in making statements in condemnation of it. You know, as I know, that most times people make proclamations, but in actuality, they don't keep to their decisions. We are about four black pastors in this community and sometimes the Presbytery brings together all the churches within a particular community, both white and black, for a meeting. There is very little co-operation among the ministers and when you go for such meetings you immediately find out that there is racism. So it is still a segregated Church. We do not have so many blacks in top positions in the Presbyterate, although we have had about four or five blacks in such top positions, but most times you find out that those elected into such top positions are those who speak what we call here *Uncle Toms*"

"What does that mean?"

"It means those who speak the language the white man wants to hear. We have such people even in the government. They dance the music which the white man plays and they are not there to advance the cause of the black people. Their only concern is the self. We have such people in the Presbyterian Church. They will tell you if you have to go further, you have to understand the system. If you do not understand the system, you are not going to hold any top position."

"Please could you explain?"

"We have some committees that are formed to look into the problem of racism. These committees often come out with some proclamations and after reading them to everyone, that is the end of them and nothing happens. However, such committees sometimes are liberal with giving money for projects, scholarships, and so on, but in terms of coming to the black ghettoes to live and feel with the blacks in their living conditions, you do not see them. In our school system, we found out that in most schools that are black schools, no white families enroll their children to such schools because the type of education given to black kids in the United States is still inferior, because the black schools are not as equipped and maintained as white schools. The white families who are Presbyterian are ready to go miles to register their children in white church schools."

"Are these schools Presbyterian schools or public schools?"

"Some are Presbyterian schools, while some are public schools."

"I have heard and read a lot about inequality in school funding by state governments. The black schools or mixed schools are poorly funded in the urban areas while all white schools in the suburban areas get everything they want. If schools are equally funded and children are given equal opportunity to learn, one may find it difficult to notice the type of disparity between the performance of white kids and black kids which some people seem to take interest in making big news over the television."

"Correct."

"Reverend, since it is clear that racism is still a problem in the Presbyterian denomination, what are the authorities doing to overcome this limitation in the Church?"

"Well, as I have already said, there are committees that were formed to look into such problems. Meetings upon meetings are held and in such meetings the blacks complain that they have been discriminated against, decisions are taken, but at the end, nothing happens. Since I have been a minister in this denomination, I have never seen any member or church that is punished for not integrating its black members well. So it is just like a joke. I always say my mind but I have no fellowship because they do not always agree with me. I say things the way I feel and see them."

"Lastly, Hurricane Katrina exposed a lot about the rate of poverty of the people of color in this country. This is now a national concern as many Americans are calling for a national discussion on the major cause of poverty in the country. What is the Presbyterian Church doing to appeal to the government to call for a national discussion on how to eradicate poverty and all forms of inequality still being experienced in different forms across the country?"

"I do not think that any remarkable thing is being done towards that direction yet."

Interview with a White Woman Presbyterian Pastor (Name and Picture withheld)

Having heard from an African American Presbyterian pastor, I needed to discuss Church racism with a white pastor also, so as to hear from another side about what is happening in the Presbyterian Church (USA) today. I was privileged to discuss the issue with a woman Pastor from one of the Northern states. My discussion with her was an interesting one also. I asked her:

"Pastor, racial discrimination is still a problem in the American society of today and many people are of the opinion that it is not only a problem in the American society, but also a problem in the American churches. Do you believe that?"

"Yes."

"As a pastor in the Presbyterian Church, do you believe that there is still racism in the Presbyterian Church?"

"Absolutely."

"Can you tell me the forms it is taking now?"

"Well, I believe that we are still separated or segregated because we have white congregations and black congregations and the level of contact between white and black congregations is limited. For instance, the issue of coming together to worship is not yet as it should be."

"And you people are worshiping the same God?"

"Yes."

"Why are things still that way?

"I do not know why, probably or partly because of difference in style of worship or due to other reasons."

"Is there anything the Presbyterian authorities are doing to encourage more integration or a sort of coming together to appreciate the diversity in the modes of worship among the different races that make up the Presbyterian denomination in the United States? The reason why I am asking this question is because it is by coming together that people come to know more about the problems of one another and how to help one another or speak for one another. If there is separation, the white congregations may not know what the black congregations are passing through and vice versa."

"I do not know much about what is happening in the national level, but I know that in my local congregation, we have three or four African American families in our membership."

"Reverend, in the American society today, the cause of the poverty of the minorities, especially the African Americans and Hispanics as we saw in the Hurricane Katrina experience, is a big concern to a lot of sympathetic people. It should also be a concern to the American churches. Do you feel that the authorities of the Presbyterian Church are doing anything to appeal to the government to discuss the problem of racial inequality in America in order to identify the main reason why a quarter of a whole black race in America is below the poverty line and see how to economically integrate them?

"I do not know. Probably, I do not know very much about the activities of the denomination. I know more about what is happening in my local congregation. I just don't know about the political movements at the denominational level."

"Reverend, discrimination here is not only by color but also by sex and age. As a woman pastor, are you accepted in your congregation on equal bases as male pastors in your denomination?"

"In my local congregation, I am very well accepted just like any male pastor. However, I know that there are some conservative Presbyterian congregations that would not call me or want to receive my pastoral care."

"Thank you so much, Reverend, I have enjoyed talking with you."
"Thanks."

Comments

The above research and interviews indicate that the Presbyterian Church in the United Sates is still struggling with the problem of racism among its members since the removal of the segregation laws. Though the interviews do not cover all the Presbyteries, at the same time, it gives a good idea of what may be happening in other Presbyteries in the United States.

Methodist Church

The success of the Civil Rights Movement also put pressure on the Methodist denomination to move towards change from its racist positions. From the late 1960s, some efforts to correct the disunity and inequality caused by slavery and racism were made. It was when the United Methodist Church was formed in 1968 that the central jurisdiction was abolished and African American congregations became fully part of the Methodist family again. According to Chester Jones, "The uniting action by the church in 1968 was a first step in reaffirming the equality that God has in creation."[184] This uniting conference of 1968 as described by Yolanda Pupo-Ortiz, "took away from the church the shame of a segregated jurisdiction."[185]

Though the elimination of the Central Jurisdiction helped to bring about inclusiveness, "this effort, however, also brought about the diminishing of Black leadership within the church and the debilitation of the Black Church."[186] However, efforts were also made to take care of this problem. "The plan for strengthening the Black Church for the Twenty-First Century, first adopted by the 1996 General Conference, addresses the vacuum created by the merger."[187]

As part of the effort to correct the mistakes of the past, the United Methodist Church a few years ago apologized to the colored members as a sign of repentance for its racist past.

> Delegates and visitors to the 2000 United Methodists General Conference last May in Cleveland participated in an act of Repentance for Reconciliation with representatives of the three historically black Methodist denominations. Apologies were made for acts of racism that prompted the creation of separate black denominations and also for a segregated unit in the predominantly white Methodist Church from 1939 to 1968.[188]

Despite the apologies, there have been suspicions of white Methodists' sincerity: "Pointing to the difficulties of getting white congregations to accept black pastors, the Rev. Daryll Coleman, a CME pastor from Los Angeles, asked if racism identified in the study is "history or today's new?"[189] He asked that question to make sure that the Church was going to be serious with its decisions to eradicate racism among its members. During the Nashville meeting of the United Methodist members of the thirty six member pan-Methodist commission, the Rev. Sylvester Williams, a CME pastor from Birmingham, Alabama asked the white members this question in connection with their apology, "How sincere are you in terms of bringing to fruition what you say?"[190]

Yolanda Pupo-Ortiz says the minds of the Methodists of color, criticized the apologies as not deep and comprehensive enough if it addresses only the historical events that led to the formation of The African Methodist Episcopal Church (AME), The African Methodist Episcopal Zion Church (AMEZ), and The Christian Methodist Episcopal Church (CME): "The Black Methodists who remained in the house, as well as Asian, Hispanic, Pacific Islander, and Native-American Methodists, have also suffered from the internal oppression of racism, and repentance and confession is due to them as well."[191]

It was the above suspicion and the need to find out what is happening in the United Methodist Church today, whether the apologies are being matched with actions that made me enter into some meaningful discussions with some Methodist ministers form different parts of the country.

Interview with Reverend Mamie A. Williams

Rev. Mamie A. Williams.

The first Methodist pastor I interviewed on this issue of racism was Reverend

Mamie A.Williams. She was a pastor for twenty three years, but currently is the executive Director of the Multi-Ethnic center for ministry of the Northeastern Jurisdiction of the United Methodist Church, Columbia, MD. I addressed her as follows:

"Rev. Ms. Williams, there are evidences that racism exists not only in the secular American society, but also in most Christian churches. Do you think that it also exists in the United Methodist Church?"

"Yes, racism exists in the United Methodist Church in the United States because it reflects this culture. However, the denomination recognizes this problem because it has adopted resolutions and programs to address this sin in its midst."

"Is it possible to explain the different forms this is presently going taking?"

"This is a difficult question to answer because each ethnic group, white or black or other groups, experiences the manifestations of racism in different ways. Each group tends to worship and have ministries reflective of its respective cultures. But, more and more, there are multicultural ministries and services emerging and meeting the needs of the membership."

"From what you have just told me now, it means that there is division in the membership. What caused that division, why and how is that division still going on?"

"The division was caused by the fact that blacks were brought to this place from Africa against their will as slaves. The white slave owners used Scriptures, especially Ephesians 6, to subjugate and control slaves. As a result, a more liberating form of worship and understanding of the Scriptures emerged among the slaves and their descendants. Inherently, there was conflict with these styles of worship and theological understanding. So that is why these groups have preferred to stay on their own."

"Reverend, I have read a little about the history of the Methodist Church since it was brought to this land by the European immigrants during the founding days of this country. The information I got was that during the Second Awakening when the slaves were allowed to become Christians, the white Methodists did not want to worship as equals with the blacks, and that brought the division, which also led to the formation of churches according to race. Was that what happened?"

"Yes. The issue of slavery was very strong in the church in its formative years. In the early 19th century when the nation was on the verge of Civil War, the white leadership of the denomination voted to split according to those parts of the Church which condoned slaveholding and those which opposed it. Also, around that time, there were some persons of African descent who got fed up with the segregation, and established their own churches which eventually became separate denominations."

"So it was not a question of preferring to stay on their own because they came as slaves, but because they were rejected by their white counterparts."

"Yes. Methodists of African descent have never excluded persons from participating in worship or membership because they were a different ethnic group."

"It is good to make things clear. Is that division according to race still in existence?"

"Yes. The black denominations from the Methodist heritage,

including the African Methodist Episcopal, African Methodist Episcopal Zion and Christian Methodist Episcopal Churches continue as vibrant manifestations of the Wesleyan heritage. At the same time, within the United Methodist Church there continues to be predominantly white congregations and predominantly black congregations; however, it is a matter of choice of the members, and it is not a legal or denomination-imposed separation."

"Then how united is this denomination now, to be answering this name *United Methodist Church*, since this division is still going on according to color. What makes it really united?"

"The name United Methodist Church is related to a "union" based upon ethnicity; it does not mean that black churches are supposed to be mixed with white churches as one congregation. The United Methodist Church, as a denomination, was created in 1968 when the Methodist Church and the former Evangelical United Brethren Church merged to form the United Methodist Church. The name of the present denomination is a blend of the names of the two predecessor denominations. About the same time that merger was taking place, the segregated organizational structure of the Central Jurisdiction to which most of the black congregations were assigned, was also eliminated. That means that the predominantly black churches are included in the annual conferences; the basic denominational structure exists according to geographical location rather than race."

"Thank you, I now understand. Reverend, now it is clear that racism still exists in both church and state and racism brings about injustice. What efforts are the leaders of the United Methodist Church making to improve the relationship between the races and to create a society free of injustice?"

"The United Methodist Church tries to be intentional at every level about addressing racism, from the local church through all of its various levels of structure to its global manifestation. The General Conference, the highest decision making body, is representational of the ethnic groups in our membership. It has created policies and structures to help address racism within the life of the church as well as in society."

"What of listening to the cries of the minorities against racial prejudice in the entire American society and doing something to help them or at least speak for them?"

"In our denomination, we have agencies that are empowered to listen to the complaints of minorities and also to do something to address their problems. Sometimes these are individual issues that are addressed personally; other times there are systemic issues that require action by the General Conference, the highest legislative body in the church. For me, it is important to know that my denomination, The United Methodist Church, takes seriously the teachings of Jesus Christ that we are all created in the image of God and thus all are equally responsible for living as sisters and brothers in the family of God."

"I am happy that in your denomination, you have agencies that are empowered to address the problems of the racially oppressed. I hope your church agencies are doing well in speaking against injustice in both church and society. As a foreigner, I have seen a lot of things that make me wonder if some of these church human rights agencies or offices of social justice are really doing their jobs well. On several occasions, over the television, I have observed groups of white police men beating up black men or black suspects along the streets without fair trial. This was the picture we used to have about Apartheid South Africa. I was surprised to come here to see public beating of black men by the police without fair hearing, in the twenty-first century. This is a serious violation of human right. It only reminds me of the historic and notorious lynching of blacks without trial during the era of Jim Crow laws.

In most American cities I have visited, government facilities such as roads and parks in black parts of the cities are not as well maintained as the ones you see in white parts of the cities. Integrated and all-black schools in the cities are not as well maintained and funded as the ones you see in the suburban areas where mostly white children go. Some politicians and media men make abusive statements over the televisions and radios against blacks and other minorities as they like. It could be that I am looking at things through the lens of a foreigner; at the same time, do members of such agencies need the eye of a foreigner to see that many things people see as normal here are not really normal? However, Reverend, I know that you are not a member of such agencies to answer these questions. Thanks a lot for speaking with me."

Interview with Reverend B. Kevin Smalls

Rev. B. Kevin Smalls.

The second Methodist pastor I discussed racism in Churches with was Reverend B. Kevin Smalls. He is the Associate Council Director for the Baltimore-Washington Conference. After introducing each other, I began,

"Reverend, there are many complaints by the minority people of this country about racial prejudice in both religion and state. Do you believe that there is racial prejudice in the Methodist denomination?"

"Oh yes."

"Can you explain some of the forms it has taken?"

"Racism has affected Methodism since its inception in America. The first major racial battle the denomination suffered was in 1848 because of slavery. One of the bishops, Bishop James O. Andrew, owned slaves and the church split because it was forbidden for a bishop to own slaves. Another reason was that the South wanted to keep having their slaves which the North objected to and that also brought a split between Methodism in the North and South. They got back together in 1939, but they created a whole separate section for the African American segment of the membership. The separate section was objected to and abolished in 1967, and in 1968 the Church became the United Methodist Church. The last conference to join the merger was in South Carolina in 1972; they had the largest number of African American membership. So today the problem is how does an African American congregation keep its African American distinction in a much larger white congregation?"

"Exactly. Tell me more about what is happening now."

"Unfortunately, racism is still a problem, and we have not yet fully addressed it. It is a question of power within the denomination, and it is always a white person's problem. It comes down to the issue of planning the agenda for the denomination. The African American feels some how excluded. I used to work in one congregation or the other, but now I work in a conference center, which is at the leadership level of the denomination. It gives me a better view of how we relate to each other. I still feel that we are not yet comfortable with the racial identities of each other. We still do not know how to relate to each other, not only the African Americans, but also the Latinos, and the Asians."

"Could you please be more specific?"

"Sometimes, racism may not be very obvious. We also have the problem of classism, and by this I mean those who have and those who have not or the rich and the poor. The greater majority of that class of poor people is African Americans and the Latinos. It is very clear in the society and also in the Church. We have congregations that are very rich and congregations that are very poor. So in this case, it is very difficult to create a homogeneous church or a unified church to accommodate the rich and the poor as one. The church is becoming classified between those who are rich against those who are poor. There are lots of poor black people and Latinos. The question is how does our denomination empower the poor people, which is the same as to ask, how does our denomination empower the African Americans and the Latinos who are members? It is not enough to make a black person a bishop or to send a black person to a white congregation or to give a clergy person an opportunity. These things are very good! But it is a question of how to empower a whole people or give a whole people opportunity. You know that money is power, if you do not have money even in the church, you have no power."

"That is true, my brother."

"There is another form of racism we are experiencing and that is black against black, which of course is perpetrated by white racism against blacks. There are some very successful African Americans who may like to be included as part of the larger white European communities, while the white communities may not even want them. They in turn discriminate against and look down on their poor African American counterparts.

"That is a very sad occurrence."

"I agree with you, my brother. I observe a lot of superiority and inferiority complexes in this country. It looks like many people feel *whiteness* when they are having economic progress and they would like to prove to the others who are poor that they are no longer in the same social and economic condition with them. In a way, economic progress then becomes a justification for discrimination against the poor. It is really sad."

"That's right. The whites feel superior while the blacks are made to feel inferior."

"That's not proper. So reverend, is there any thing the United Methodist Church is doing to address this racial problem or to improve racial relations in the Methodist denomination?"

"Yes, in the last general conference, there was an apology made by the white church to the African Americans church, due to the history of slavery and racial discrimination."

"Reverend, many apologies have been rendered to the people of color by so many dioceses, churches, and communities, but most of these apologies turn out to be empty words, as racial discrimination continues on daily bases both in the church and in the society. So do you feel that this apology will be translated into action?"

"I wish and we are watching."

"Reverend, the apology is a healthy development. Apart from the apology, what do you recommend for the Methodist authorities to do first?"

"I recommend that there should be a dialogue among the different races. I am happy; the authorities know that racism is a big problem in the Church. So it requires discussion or a serious dialogue to know the best way out of it."

"Do you think that this kind of dialogue or discussion of the racial problems in this country is also necessary in the secular society in both federal and local levels?

"Absolutely, it needs to be discussed."

"Reverend you said something about the poverty of African Americans and the Latinos in your denomination. Recently, Hurricane Katrina made Americans and, in fact, the whole world aware of the extent of poverty in this country. What is the United Methodist Church doing to appeal to the government for a dialogue to know how to fully integrate the African Americans and the Latinos to be more self reliant and to improve their social construct."

"Honestly, we are not doing any thing for now to bring about such much needed dialogue."

Comments

The above research and interviews indicate that racism is still a problem in the United Methodist Church. Though the interviews do not cover the whole Jurisdictions, it gives a good idea of what may be happening in other Jurisdictions in the United States of America.

Baptist Church

When one talks about racism in the American Baptist Church, the focus is more on the Baptist Southern Convention. "The color line was not so clearly drawn in the North."[192] However, the period following the Civil Rights Movement of the 1960s brought a new and positive development in the relationship between the white and black Baptists in the South. "During the 1970s, the convention began a massive attempt to bring black Baptist Churches into the American Baptist Churches, USA. A committee of the Southern Caucus at the American Baptist Convention was appointed to organize the work of the American Baptist Churches in the South."[193] The committee really worked hard and laid the foundation for the unification. It achieved its purpose of bringing together for the first time, black Baptists and white Baptists in the South to form a new regional structure within American Baptist Convention. "By 1970, nearly one hundred black Baptist and white Baptist churches entered organic relationships with the convention."[194]

Under the leadership of Rev. E.B. Hicks, the committee also worked hard to prepare the minds of both races to share power. This was a big challenge for the white Baptists who for the first time were urged to share power with their black brothers and sisters. "For some, this was a welcome trend, while others were forced psychologically to adjust to a new order of things in race relations."[195]

One of the most significant achievements of this alliance between white and black Baptists was the election of the Rev. Thomas Kilgore to be the first black man ever to lead the national body of American Baptists. "He brought to the convention one of the most innovative programs ever attempted by black and white Baptists. This was the Fund of Renewal project—a joint effort with the Progressive National Baptist Convention to raise seven million dollars to revive America's financially troubled black colleges."[196] This effort was welcomed by both black and white Baptists.

Although progress has been made in the racial relationship between black and white Baptists, there is still an obstacle to more progress. The biggest challenge to the progress in the union between the two races is the decrease in the personal attendance to the local and regional meetings by Southern white Baptists. "There is a conspicuous absence of white American Baptists."[197] However, it is hoped that the continued cooperation between white and black Baptists, even if not perfect now, will indeed strengthen the "New South," which according to Fitts, "has come to represent a radical departure from the segregation, discrimination, and violence of the "Old South"[198]

Another significant development in the relationship between Southern black and white Baptists in the Post-Civil Rights era was that the Southern Baptist Convention in the year 2000 apologized to African Americans for its long history of racial discrimination. "At its 150th anniversary meeting June 20-22 in Atlanta, the Convention adopted an 18-paragraph resolution repenting past racism."[199] Skepticism, however, lingers among local black Baptists who say that "the public apology is meaningless without significant deeds."[200] The suspicion is based on the feeling of many black Baptists that the apology came as a result of pressure from black critics.

Some black Baptists feel that if let alone, the Southern Baptist Convention wouldn't have taken the initiative to apologize. Whatever is the case, it is a good development that the Convention acknowledged that it had made mistakes because of racial prejudice. The challenge, of course, is for the Convention to match its words with action as a repentant Convention. Summarizing the present state of relationship between black Baptists and white Baptists in the Southern Baptist Convention, Fitts quotes Rev. McCall: "I think we have come a long way. I definitely think we have made progress. We are a long ways from where we were, but we still have quite a ways to go."[201] To have an idea of what is happening in the Baptist Church presently, I also engaged in discussions with some Baptist Pastors across the country.

Interview with Reverend Gregory Howard

Rev. Gregory Howard

The first Baptist pastor whom I interviewed was Rev. Gregory Howard, pastor of Jerusalem Baptist Church in Caroline County, Virginia. After expressing my gratitude to Rev. Howard for allowing me to discuss church racism with him, I addressed him as follows:

"As a Baptist pastor, do you believe that racial discrimination presently exists in the Baptist Church?"

"Yes, definitely, I would say that there is racial tension still residing within the Baptist denomination. For me, it is still obvious as it was to Martin Luther King Jr. that Sunday mornings are the most racial times in American society. You can visit the countless Baptist Churches just like any other denomination and witness with clarity the picture of either all black or all white congregations. The demographic speaks for itself. So, in my opinion, most of the congregations are racial not necessarily discriminatory, but racial in this composition."

"Can you explain in your own understanding how this racial divide started between whites and blacks in the Baptist denomination."

"It started in some instances as early as the late 1700s and into the 1800s when blacks were invited by the whites to fellowship with them in the same church. Blacks were asked to stay at the back of the church or in the balcony just as they were expected to position themselves in society in general. They were not allowed to hold any type of leadership positions; they could not preach, could not be deacons, could not be trustees or financial officers, could not be clerks, and were not served communion until all the whites had received. When blacks wanted some of these issues to be addressed, especially when some of them felt that they were also called to preach and to be ministers, the whites, instead of allowing them on equal grounds, encouraged them to break away and to build their own churches, working closely under white supervision. Baptist Churches were racial, and are still racial today, because racism is part of their heritage.

"I have read something about that in the history. Is that story still affecting the members of both white and black churches?"

"For example, the church in which I serve now, broke away from a predominantly all white church. This happened in 1866. It was because of the aforementioned reason that this Church was established so that we could acknowledge the godly uniqueness of our people and to speak freely about our condition of existence. Today, both churches are almost placed side by side as sister churches, one black and the other white. There is tension still existing between these two churches today. From my understanding, their pastor has made some reconciliatory moves by inviting blacks to come and share with them and we are currently scheduling a joint fellowship. His attempts to reconcile the races have often times met a lot of obstacles due to the criticisms of the people in his church who do not want to see or be a part of a kingdom that is multicultural and multiracial. They are more willing to work and live along side with blacks than to fellowship with blacks."

"I am surprised to hear this Pastor Howard. Is their pastor white?"

"Yes, he is white. He is an advocate of racial harmony. He started recently, just a few months ago to extend a hand of friendship to the

African Americans but he is still facing a lot of opposition from his people."

"What type of Christianity are we practicing here?"

"I wonder, and in no ways am I suggesting that this is the mind of the majority, but many churches are nothing more than ideological clubs."

"Are there other areas in which you notice racism in dealing with other white Baptist Churches?"

"I see racism in the type of attacks which black churches and religious leaders receive from the local media. For instance, when a black minister or member makes a mistake, the news about his or her mistake is spread as rapid as a wild fire and makes front page news, but when a white minister or member makes a similar or even more serious mistake, it is not echoed as loudly or receives little or no attention. But is this fair for the other, which takes a collective hit from the storm of sensationalism?"

"Pastor Howard I feel it is unfair. The reports should not be conditioned by color or race if they must be publicized. The intention for having such reports publicized should be the same for all."

"The reports have racial overtones, just like any other type of crime you see being reported in the news paper. They highlight the race of the perpetrator. Pictures are shown, and he or she is quickly shown as an African American, or Mexican, or a Latin American person. Most times, you do not see pictures of whites who are committing such crimes who are even in the majority. Think of the psychological impact this has on its viewers. Therefore, the black religious leader receives heightened attention. Central Virginia has just experienced two well publicized accounts that were on the local and at one time national news stations on daily bases."

"Reverend, since you have made it clear that racial prejudice still exists in the Baptist Churches more than forty years after the removal of the racial laws, are there some efforts being made by the Baptist leadership in all the conventions to eradicate racism in the Baptist Churches and improve race relations?"

"We are not doing much, as a whole. Individual churches, yes, but I see no collective effort. The Southern Baptist Convention in the summer of 1995 publicly apologized to the African Americans for their support of slavery and racism. Billy Graham who is one of the most well-known Baptist preachers of the Southern Convention declared that it was long over due."

"As racial inequality continues, have the Baptist authorities done any thing to appeal to the government to discuss the racial problems of this country and find ways to fully integrate the people of color especially into the economic mainstream of this country?"

"Honestly my brother, I have not personally observed any move along that line. If there is any, I do not know."

"What advice do you give to your black brothers and sisters?"

"One of the greatest problems we have among blacks is that as people who have for a long time been subjected to second class status; we nevertheless find it difficult to liberate our minds to this reality. I urge us all to use our ancestral religious experiences to come to the godly realization that we are all created equal in the likeness of God and that there is no superior or inferior human being as they were made to believe. We need to work on racial and cultural harmony as we should but nevertheless stop seeking affirmation from the majority. Open our eyes to the realism that race matters, but don't consider heaven to be that of being accepted by the other, but more so accepting the other. "

"Thank you, Reverend. I enjoyed talking with you."

Interview with Reverend Damon J. Powells

Rev. Damon J. Powells

My second interview with a Baptist pastor was with Reverend Damon J. Powells, pastor of King's Way Baptist Church, St. Louis. I addressed him on the subject of our discussion in these words:

"Reverend Powell, racial discrimination has been a problem in the American society right from the foundation of this country. Unfortunately, it is also said to be existing in the various Christian denominations in the United States. Having been a pastor for many years, do you believe that racial prejudice also exists in the Baptist Church?"

"Yes sir. This is because historically or traditionally blacks and whites have their own churches. This started about four hundred years ago during the time of slavery when blacks were not allowed to worship with whites equally and this initiated the separation. Unfortunately, the separation which started four hundred years ago is still being carried out today because blacks tend to stay with blacks while whites tend to stay with whites. This is because of what has been handed down to us. A lot of it is not that there are any more laws now, which say that we should not associate with one another, blacks with whites or whites with blacks. It is mainly because this is the way it has been. I still hope that in our churches, blacks and whites could be better together. I believe that was what Dr. Martin Luther King had in mind during one of his speeches when he said that the most segregated times in America are the Sunday mornings, at church."

"It seems that changing of the laws doesn't change people's hearts."

"The laws have changed, the legal things have changed, but segregation still goes on in the heart, and manifests itself physically in one way or the other. In our churches, often times both blacks and whites feel uncomfortable worshiping with one another. The reason why they feel uncomfortable worshiping with each other seems to be more on how the city is structured. People seem to abide more by what is obtainable in the part of the city where they live or are made to live. For instance, St. Louis, like many American cities, is still a segregated city. Those blacks who live in the North St. Louis who have little or no contact with Caucasians may feel uncomfortable worshiping with whites, unlike those who live in South St. Louis where blacks and whites are more mixed. The same thing happens to whites who live exclusively in the West County and in the South County of St. Louis. They may be surprised to see a black person enter their church to worship with them."

"That's true, but in those areas or churches in the South St. Louis where blacks and whites are mixed, how are the blacks who go to worship with whites treated by their white counterparts?"

"That is the problem. In some cases, you are made to see yourself as different. For instance, on one of the occasions we went to South St. Louis to worship, we were the only blacks there for a singing ministry. During the time they were to introduce us to friends from other churches, they said, "Here are the members of our black family." So instead of referring to us as their Baptist members from North St. Louis, they used the word *black* or referred to the color of our skins to make us feel that we are different from them. We had to correct them and tell them that we understand that we are black and in a white congregation, but using the word *black* to refer to us makes us feel that we are not fully part of you as Baptists or we are a different type of Baptists. The emphasis should have been on the fact that we are all Baptists. The emphasis on *color* is what we did not like mainly because of the long history of presenting a black person as inferior to a white person which we do not want to hear and accept, or else we may be saying that the Bible is wrong for telling us that God created all in his image and likeness. The African Americans are not asking that the government should change their color from black to white, but that what ever is the color of any human person, there should be equal opportunity given to every one. To put some people first in every thing because they are white and some people second or last because they are brown or black is evil and corruption of its own kind."

"Yes, I understand that there is much emphasis on *the color of the skin* and it seems to be what determines most times how people respond to others here. I was shocked when I came to this country and noticed that this is the culture. The most shocking thing is that many people see it as normal and how things should be."

"Absolutely, you are right."

"Reverend, in America, when you talk about racism, the blacks seem to accuse the whites more. In your Baptist denomination, have you observed racism coming also from the side of the blacks against the whites?"

"Oh yes, there was a time we had a problem with our church building and we were looking for contractors who would fix the building for us. The problem was that there were some members who did not want any white contractors to come and fix the building. I told them that it was crazy; all we wanted was who could do the job well. It does not matter if the contractor was white or black. However, it is also the same in white congregations. They may not want a black contractor because to many whites, anything black is inferior. So that is where leadership comes in. It is the duty of the leaders in the Church and even in the state to set an example, but in most cases it does not come that way because many of the leaders in both church and state are racists and may not be better than those whom they are called to lead."

"You are correct Reverend. If the church leader himself or herself is racist, no one corrects the members. Thank you so much for talking with me."

Comments

The above research and interviews show that there is still racial inequality in the Baptist Church in the United States of America. However, the interviews do not cover the whole Baptist Conventions; at the same time, they give good ideas of what could be happening in the others.

Lutheran Church

The Lutheran Church, like other Protestant denominations, supported the Civil Rights Movement due to pressure from the Civil Rights activists, which also became a challenge to a faith that preaches love, to practice the love it preaches. It was also in the 1960s and 1970s that the black Lutherans saw the effect of their long struggle for self determination in the American Lutheran Church and for the structural integration of the Black work of the Synodical Conference into the organic union of the Lutheran Church—Missouri Synod.[202] Dr. Dickinson in his book *Thorn and Roses* observes that, before the integration, "Many white Lutheran congregations located in the North, South, East, or West, flatly refused to accept Negroes in their worship services or at their altars. Many white congregations of the Synod perished on the vine when their communities changed from white to Black rather than accept Blacks into their membership."[203]

There has been some improvement in the relationship between black Lutherans and white Lutherans since the 1970s. Some verbal condemnation of racism in both church and society has been made by the various synods. However, Dr. Dickinson still observes that the full integration of the black Lutherans in the district and congregational levels is yet to be achieved, as the African American and other people of color are not well represented in the administration of the denomination. A look at the interviews I had with some Lutheran ministers could help to clarify what is happening in the Lutheran Church at present with regard to the continued struggle against racism in the denomination.

Interview with Deaconess Addie Wilkins

Deaconess Addie Wilkins

The first Lutheran minister I discussed the racial problem in churches with was Deaconess Addie Wilkins. She has served for many years in Transfiguration Lutheran Church in St. Louis. Deaconess Wilkins also served as a member of the Lutheran district board and also as a member of the Lutheran family and children services. My talk with her went as follows:

"Deaconess, many pastors have told me how racism is still affecting love and unity that should exist among the members of their churches. Do you feel that racism is still a problem in the Lutheran denomination since the removal of the segregation laws?"

"Yes, it is clear that racism is still being experienced in the Lutheran denomination in the United States."

"Is it possible to tell me the forms it is taking now by your own experiences?"

"Yes, let me give you an example with what happened when I went to Valparaiso University, Indiana to take theology courses to complete my basic requirements for the deaconess program. The first Sunday I spent there happened to be the day the whole nation remembers Dr. Martin Luther King Junior. I attended service in a Lutheran chapel called the Resurrection Chapel with some other students. To my greatest surprise, the Lutheran pastor who was presiding over the service did not mention any thing about Dr. Martin Luther King Junior in his sermon and during the entire ceremony. Instead of talking about Martin Luther King whose day was that day, the pastor was talking about one Lutheran theologian that is not even known for any wonderful work he did for the nation."

"How did you feel about it?"

"I got so angry and cried over it. After the service, I went to the pastor and confronted him on the issue and asked him why he did not say any thing about the only black man who was being remembered that day in the whole history of the nation. He did not even use that opportunity to preach against racism which is what Martin Luther King suffered and died for in this country. The pastor said, 'these kids do not know any thing about Martin Luther King.' I was so upset due to the attitude and the response of the pastor and I felt that there is no other reason why the pastor did what he did apart from racism, since he left the man who was supposed to be remembered and was talking about another person who even happens to be a white man like himself. If George Washington was being remembered, would the pastor have left talking about him and talk about a black theologian who did nothing wonderful for this nation? I also told the pastor that my own children knew nothing about George Washington, but they were taught about him and they are expected to respect him on the day he is being remembered."

"Deaconess, you are saying the truth. Some of us who are pastors are also racists. You can find racist pastors in different churches and religions. As you rightly said, such pastors will never preach against racism in their sermons. However, thanks for sharing your experiences with me. Is there any other form wherein you have observed racism in the Lutheran denomination?"

"Yes, there is something I also observed that is not proper and I feel it is also racist. When a young man finishes his seminary formation to become a pastor, the person is normally sent to one of the Lutheran churches to do what they call vicarage. There was this young man I know who was sent to an all-white church made up of old German American Lutherans and they rejected him. He had to look for a black church to do his vicarage. So I feel that racial segregation is still being experienced in one way or the other in the Lutheran Church."

"It is very unfortunate, Deaconess. Our Christianity has a long way go to translate words into practical love. Thank you so much, deaconess. I have enjoyed talking with you and I have learnt a lot from all I have heard from you."

Interview with Rev. Dr. Richard C. Dickinson

Rev. Dr. Richard C. Dickinson

The next Lutheran minister I had the opportunity to interview was Rev. Dr. Richard C. Dickinson. He has been a member of the Lutheran Church for about eighty years. He has also served as pastor in many black Lutheran congregations in the Missouri Synod and was the director of black ministry of Lutheran Church Missouri Synod. He has written many books about the Lutheran Church and about African Americans in the American Lutheran Church. I started the interview as follows:

"Reverend, my discussion with you is going to be more on racism as it is being experienced in the American Lutheran Church today. The aim of this interview is to know what is happening in the Lutheran denomination between the white members and the black members as the church struggles to eliminate racial discrimination among its members. In one of your books, you said a lot about racism as it existed in the 1930s, 40s, 50s and 60s in the Lutheran denomination. Do you feel that there is still racism going on in the Lutheran Church presently?"

"Yes, there is still racism going on. The Lutheran denomination is basically a white denomination and whites are basically in control of everything. The Catholic Church is even better than the Lutheran denomination in many efforts to integrate the blacks. We have black Lutheran congregations and white Lutheran congregations and there is little interaction between these two congregations of the same denomination separated by the color of the skin. There is still tension when these two groups meet, because they have not fully agreed that the conferences should be one."

"You made mention of the Catholic Church doing better in integrating its black members than the Lutheran Church. Is there anything like cross posting of pastors from the white congregations to work in black congregations and black pastors to work in white congregations as it happens in some cases and in some dioceses in the Catholic Church?"

"In most cases, black congregations accept white pastors while in most cases, white congregations do not accept black pastors. Since over eighty years I have been a Lutheran and since over fifty years I have been a pastor, I have never been accepted to minister to any white Lutheran congregation."

"Reverend, I am surprised to hear this. What is the Lutheran denomination doing or what has it done to continue the struggle against racism which is still a problem in the church and in the society, especially to appeal to the government to discuss the greatest effect of racism on the minorities, which is poverty?"

"To be honest, during the Civil Rights Movement, the Lutherans tried to identify with the civil rights activists. Since then, there is little or nothing the Lutheran denomination is doing to respond to the racial problems in the Lutheran church and in the American society. It looks as if every person is feeling that racism is gone with the removal of the laws, but what has been happening proves that racism is far from over both in the church and in the state."

"Yes, Reverend, I can see. Even as a foreigner, I can observe that the poverty of some people here is worse than those in the so called third world countries."

"Poverty due to centuries of economic exclusion is still a problem here. The churches feel that it is not their business to speak about economic injustice. They will try to dodge their responsibilities to humanity by claiming that there is separation of church and state while injustice continues. Separation of church and state does not mean that the church should not speak for the liberation of the poor whose origin of poverty was imposed by their fellow humans in history."

"Dr. Dickinson, I love listening to you talk. Based on your long years of experience in both church and state, as a pastor, what advice can you give to the young black men and women and the youths of other minorities growing up in this country?"

"They need to be more serious with their education. If someone tells you that you are inferior, you need to prove to that person that he or she is not different from you. I remember the type of education we used to receive when we were kids. I was taught as a child in a segregated school to believe that the black person is inferior to the white person and that the white person is the most evolved man, while the black person is the missing link between apes and the white man. Some of us still did not allow such rubbish to affect us psychologically and we still had to struggle to prove such teachings wrong. I do not know if they are still teaching children such nonsense in the Lutheran schools and the public schools now with the evolution theories."

"I do not think that they are still teaching such things now because of the recent findings that the evolution theory may not be a valid theory in the twenty first century. The *St. Louis Post Dispatch of November* 9th 2005 carried an editorial which says that evolution is officially thrown out as a flawed theory in Kansas. I did not know that there was a time when such teachings were given to children in schools. This must have created a psychological defect in them to think that they are really inferior. It is terrible because when children at their tender ages are given such wrong teachings, it will be hard for them to compete with their white class mates. I am happy that people like you were able to prove it wrong, to show the younger African Americans that someone can still have the will power to succeed and achieve his or her self esteem even under such oppression. At the same time, I know that such wrong teaching must have taken its psychological toll on so many other black children by then."

"That was before some of you were born. They may not be teaching such things now, since the Civil Rights Movement, but that does not mean that some parents may not be giving their children such false doctrines about the races in their homes now. What I am trying to say is that things have improved now in the type of education the black children are receiving, though it may not be still perfect with the disparity in the government funding of black schools and white schools. There is still deliberate racial stereotyping to make the public believe that black kids can not compete with white kids. The do not talk of where black kids excelled more than white kids."

"Yes, I have read in some newspapers of such complaints about not funding all-black schools in the cities, as all-white schools are funded, especially those in the counties or in the suburban areas."

"So my advice to the young black children is to leave any thing that will distract them from finishing their education, make use of the opportunities they have now, which we did not have in the past. I believe that with seriousness in their education, they will be able to achieve their self esteem, be experts in various fields and be able to psychologically and physically disabuse people's minds from past racist ideologies and false doctrines preached even in churches to keep non white races down."

"Thank you Dr. Dickinson, I have enjoyed talking with you."

Comments

From the above research and interviews, it is clear that despite the Lutheran support of the Civil Rights Movements in the 1960s, like other denominations, there is still racial discrimination in the Lutheran Church in America. Though the interviews do not cover the whole synods, they give a good idea of what may be the story in other synods.

CHAPTER FOUR
THE CATHOLIC CONNECTIONS TO SLAVERY AND RACISM IN AMERICA 1600-1964

We have already seen how slavery and racist ideologies were rooted in the North American British colonies, now United States of America, with the earliest immigrants who were mainly White European Protestants. In this chapter, I will survey how the Catholic immigrants, who came later than most Protestant immigrants from Europe, were also involved in slavery and in shaping racist ideologies from the foundation decades of this country to the removal of the segregation laws in the 1960s. One of the driving forces behind the writing of this book is to find out why the African Americans view the Catholic Church as a racist church or as a white man's church, as claimed by my taxi driver. What really happened? Despite some efforts already made, is there anything that could still be done to correct this impression which some people of color seem to have today?

As the European explorers and Protestant immigrants were coming to the British colonies with their religions, "Spanish and French explorers brought Roman Catholicism to what is now the United States in the sixteenth and seventeenth centuries."[204] In the seventeenth century also, English Catholics migrated into the new world along with their Protestant counterparts.[205] The English Catholics first settled in Maryland, which was founded in 1634 by an English Catholic noble man called Cecil Calvert, along with a small band of English colonists. "The colony became the center of the Catholic presence in the English Colonies. St. Mary's City in southern Maryland became the capital of the colony, where Jesuit missionaries from England and Europe established farms."[206]

The condition of the English Catholics in the British colonies was different from that of the Spanish and French who settled in the South, specifically, in areas like Florida, Louisiana, and some other Gulf colonies. The Protestant population was larger in number than the English Catholic settlers and clergy who formed a minority.[207] However, their minority status did not prevent them from occupying a high position in the colony. This is why Jay P. Dolan says that "they were always in a position of prestige and power so long as the Calvert family was in control."[208] In Maryland also, a Catholic family known as the Carroll family of Carollton was one of the most prominent families. Some of its members held high positions in both church and society. "Charles Carroll became one of the first great political leaders in the English colonies. His cousin John Carroll, a Jesuit, in 1789 became the first American Bishop. . ."[209]

The Catholic population burgeoned in the first half of the 19th century, due to immigration from different parts of Europe. "Once large scale immigration began in the 1820s and 1830s, America's Catholic population increased dramatically. Many thousands of Irish and German Catholics arrived in the United States prior to the Civil War."[210] As the Catholic population continued to increase, it attracted hostility and discrimination from the Protestant population that earlier felt that they were the only people divinely called to build a Protestant empire in America. The Puritans, Baptists, Deists, and the Quakers did not trust the presence of Roman Catholics, whom they felt were loyal to the pope, whom they saw as anti religious freedom. Their opposition to the Catholic presence resulted in physical attacks against Catholics in the 1800s.[211] Jay P. Dolan records, "In the antebellum period a Protestant crusade against Catholics swept across the nation. Anti Catholic riots took place and convents as well as churches were destroyed. The crusade reached its height in the early 1850s."[212]

Catholics and Slavery

Like most Protestant clergy and laity, the Catholic clergy and laity also took an active part in the slave trade. According to Kenneth J. Zanca, "Catholic bishops, clergy, and religious were among slave owners. This means they were involved in the business of buying and selling slaves. They were supporters of the institution and benefited from it."[213] In trying to indicate who started the inhuman trade, Zanca, first points out the fact that Protestants started it. He also urges that slavery was established on American soil long before the Catholic Church came to America and before any bishop was consecrated.[214] Although Zanca accepts that Catholics were also slaveholders, he maintains that they were always much outnumbered by the Protestant slave owners, who owned 90 percent of all the black slaves in the country.[215]

Cyprian Davis, in *The History of Black Catholics in the United States*, indicates the fact that though the number of Protestant slave owners may have been greater than that of the Catholics, the Catholic clergy and laity were as deeply involved in slavery as the Protestants. Men's religious congregations, such as the Jesuits, the Vincentians, the Sulpicians and the Capuchins took an active part in buying and selling slaves. In Perry County south of St. Louis where the Vincentians settled in 1818, they were major slaveholders.[216] Stafford Poole and Douglas Slawson, also point out:

> The Vincentians had the policy of selling, hiring, and lending their slaves among their various houses and parishes, not only in Missouri but also in Louisiana, where they also owned many slaves. Beginning in 1840, the Vincentians followed a policy of divesting themselves of their slaves through sale to the Catholic slave owners in the neighborhood. They continued, however, to hire the slaves of others. Nonetheless, it seems that the Vincentians in Missouri owned slaves until the beginning of the Civil War.[217]

Some women's congregations, such as the Ursuline nuns, the Carmelites, Daughters of the Cross, the Dominicans, the Religious of the Sacred Heart and the Visitation nuns also had slaves.[218] The Sisters of Charity at Nazareth, Kentucky, had slaves not only at Nazareth itself but also in their various foundations.[219] Camillus Maes, also points out, "In the same year and in same locality, the Belgian priest Charles Nerinckx founded the sisters of Loretto, who also owned slaves. In the beginning of the convent at Loretto, the sale of her personal slave to Father Nerinckx by Mother Ann Rhodes, the first superior, enabled the sisters to purchase land for the convent."[220]

This reminded me of what my taxi driver told me about some Church leaders in different churches having slaves. Some had slaves even after many Popes, including Pope Gregory XVI who in 1839 had condemned the slave trade in an apostolic letter, *In Supremo Apostolatus Fastigo*.[221] Pope Gregory XVI denounced slavery in these words:

We do. . . admonish and adjure in the Lord all believers in Christ, of whatever condition, that no one hereafter may dare unjustly to moles Indians, Negroes, or other men of this sort; or to spoil them of their goods; or to reduce them to slavery; or extend help or favor to others who perpetuate such things against them; or to exercise that inhuman trade by which Negroes, as if they were not men, but mere animals, however reduced into slavery, are without any distinction, contrary to the laws of justice and humanity, bought, sold, and doomed sometimes to the most severe and exhausting labours.[222]

There was no difference between what was happening in the society and what was happening in the Church in the business of slavery. Indeed, most of the Church hierarchy could not condemn the trade because they were gaining from it. Dolan in his book, *The American Catholic Experience* points out that the first Catholic Bishop in the United States Bishop, John Carroll, had "two black servants—one free and one slave."[223] It is also on record that in 1815, DuBourg was made bishop of Louisiana diocese, which included St. Louis and New Orleans. He was not only a slave owner; he also supplied the Vincentians in Missouri their first slaves and helped them to purchase more.[224]

Justification of Slavery by Some Catholic Theologians

Many Catholic theologians and clergy gave moral and theological justification to slavery, using many arguments from both Bible and canon law to prove that blacks were inferior to whites and so should be subjected to slavery. Zanca asserts, "American Catholics, regardless of region, supported slavery and regarded the black as their social inferior."[225] Some bishops also used their apostolic letters to argue in support of slavery, for example, Bishop Auguste Marie Martin, the bishop of Natchitoches in the northern part of Louisiana: "For Bishop Martin, slavery is really a disguised blessing for Africans, 'children of the race of Canaan,' for through slavery they have received the faith and other advantages."[226] Bishop Martin's use of the word *children of the race of Canaan* for blacks, reminded me of the story of my taxi driver about a bishop who called his slave, *son of Ham*, in his funeral service.

Bishop Martin's pastoral letter on slavery was condemned by Rome because of the report of Vincenzo Gatti O.P., who was sent by Rome to review Martin's pastoral letter to evaluate the doctrinal validity.[227] After his review and evaluation, Gatti's recommendation was that Bishop Martin's pastoral letter should be placed on the index of Forbidden Books as condemned literature and before doing so, Marin should be allowed to amend it. Gatti's recommendation was accepted by the Congregation of the Index, and in December 17, 1864, it was made known to Pope Pius IX who approved the condition given to Bishop Martin.[228] However, the prevailing Catholic argument about slavery was the view of Bishop Francis P. Kenrick of Baltimore who argued that "if slave owners minimally respected the physical and moral rights of slaves by providing food, shelter, and opportunities to practice their religion, then slavery was neither repugnant to natural law nor inconsistent with the exercise of the true faith."[229]

Some bishops were both condemning slavery and supporting it at the same time. To please John Forsythe, the secretary of state, who criticized Pope Gregory XVI for condemning slave trade, John England the first bishop of Charleston, South Carolina, argued in his public letter to Forsythe that "Pope Gregory XVI's letter condemned the slave trade rather than slavery."[230] England's argument was that slavery can continue indefinitely as far as masters handled slaves according to Christian principles.[231] Davis points out that England based his argument on history, Scriptures, canon law, and the Roman law, to prove that slavery has been an acceptable trade. He forgot that the slavery practiced in the Old Testament, which was recognized by the Roman law and the teachings of some of the Popes, recommended some rights for the slave. These rights include rights to marry and raise a family, freedom from sexual abuse by their slave owners, and the right to own some belongings. Davis still argues that the slavery practiced in the South of United States never allowed the slaves to marry and raise stable families.[232] Moreover, the women were sexually abused by their owners. Slaves never owned properties but worked for the enrichment of their masters. The worst was that they were not allowed to practice their Catholic religion freely. "According to Stephen Ochs, "Many Catholic masters refused to allow their slaves to attend Catholic services off the plantation for fear that their slaves would run away."[233]

Perhaps, John England simply was afraid of offending many officials of the government of the United States, who were mostly Protestants and who expected Catholics to go the extra mile to prove that they can be *good Americans* and Catholics loyal to the Pope at the same time. In the words of Zanca,

> To prove that Catholics were "good Americans," the Catholic hierarchy practiced a studied noninvolvement in politics and political issues, especially the most controversial issue of the times, slavery. This noninvolvement, however, must not be mistaken for neutrality on the issue. Catholics were tolerant of state rights and slavery. Some of the brightest lights among the American hierarchy (Bishops John England, Francis Kenrick, and Martin Spalding) had written extensive theological justification of slavery. The Catholic press was also foresquare behind the legality and morality of slavery.[234]

Phelps gives example of a bishop who both supported and condemned slavery, at the same time, but later repented his support of slavery. "Bishop Verot whose diocese included the states of Georgia and Florida, supported the southern institution of slavery, using the prevailing arguments. At the same time, he called for the reform of the inhumane form of slavery that existed in the south."[235] Verot showed his repentance and good will for the blacks by recruiting European religious sisters and establishing schools in various parts of the country. For example, he established schools for blacks in Savannah, Jacksonville, Fernindina, Palatka, Mandarin, and Key West.[236] Verot went to the extent of "carrying his concern for them to the floor of the First Vatican Council in 1870."[237] While at the council, he advocated for the condemnation of those who argue that Negroes are not human beings and have no souls.

Pastoral Ministry and Evangelization of the Black Slaves

Like most Protestant churches, the Catholic Church also converted slaves not necessarily for their salvation, but to encourage them to be obedient to their masters. Quoting *The Theologia Moralis* of Francis Patrick Kenrick (1796-1863), the archbishop of Baltimore, Davis, reveals how some bishops felt about the black slaves and their salvation. ". . .

The slaves, informed by Christian morals, might show service to their masters, venerating always God, the supreme Master of us all; so that in turn the masters might show themselves gentle and even-handed and might lighten the condition of their slaves with humanity and zeal for their salvation."[238] This was a moral theology lesson, which archbishop Kenrick composed for his seminarians who might be evangelizing slaves. This was also a racist preparation for future priests trained in American seminaries for pastoral ministry.

However, there is evidence that some efforts were made pastorally to evangelize the slaves in some regions. Zanca testifies to this in these words:

> In 1791 the Sulpicians in Baltimore began to work among the blacks, teaching catechism and administering sacraments. In the 1820s Bishop England of Charleston celebrated a second mass and preached a sermon every Sunday exclusively for blacks. He opened a school for freed black children with the help of the sisters of Mercy. In 1829 Archbishop Ambrose Marechal of Baltimore endorsed the founding of the first community of black nuns, the Oblates Sisters of Providence. In 1842 Archbishop Anthony Blanc of New Orleans gave permission to Henriette Delille to found the Sisters of the Holy Family, a second group of black women devoted to serving the needs of blacks. In 1859 St. Francis Xavier Church in Baltimore became the first parish established exclusively for black Catholics. Bishop Augustin Verot of Florida brought the Sisters of St. Joseph to his diocese in 1866 to work with black children. [239]

About baptism of the slaves, Bishop Manuel de Barcelona, the auxiliary bishop of Havana and the Episcopal visitor of the Florida and Louisiana made some recommendations for the evangelization of the slaves. The slave owners were given conditions to make sure that slaves are baptized after receiving proper catechetical instructions. They were also threatened with excommunication and a fine by the secular authorities if they do not see to the baptism of their slaves within at least six months after purchasing them.[240] Davis gives an example of such baptism of slaves in St Augustine, Florida, the first Catholic parish in what is now the United States. "On January 13, 1788, Don Miguel O'Reilly baptized three children—two girls, one seven and the other ten, and a one month old baby boy—all described as slaves of Maria Beatrice Stone. Their parents were slaves of Francesco Sanchez."[241]

In some parts of America, pastoral ministry among African Americans was not flourishing. "Most religious orders, with a few notable exceptions such as the Josephites, shied away from ministry to African-Americans for fear of alienating their white constituency."[242] Why was it that in some parts of United States, the pastoral care ministry among African Americans seems to have received better attention while in some areas it was not treated as something important? Generally speaking, there doesn't seem to have been any formal pastoral care plan laid down by the Church for the African Americans. It was only after the Civil War, precisely in 1886, that the Plenary Council of Baltimore discussed something about a formal African American apostolate.

> Bishop Martin Spalding, serving as apostolic delegate, took a deep interest in the African American apostolate, suggesting that special prefects apostolic be appointed for African-Americans. His proposal did not carry the day, but nine decrees were adopted which focused on a new outreach to African American community. The question of segregated parishes, however, was left to the judgment of local legislation. Unfortunately, little in fact came of these decrees as racism both among clergy and laity vitiated their intent. Bishops in the Southern states appealed for workers and funds, but their calls largely went unanswered. [243]

In situation of pastoral difficulty due to lack of priests or lack of finance, the pastoral needs of white Catholics were granted before the pastoral needs of blacks. "Archbishop James Whitefield of Baltimore clearly showed that the needs of white Catholics took top priority when he wrote that though the slaves presented a golden opportunity for apostolic labor, he could not even meet the needs of whites, who felt deprived of the succors of religion, and that he therefore could not attend to blacks."[244] This is exactly how things are still considered in the wider American society till today. The needs of the white American population take top priority over the needs of Americans of color. There is no difference in this case between church and state.

Abolitionism and Civil War

When many radical Protestant groups like the Quakers and the Mennonites attacked the institution of slavery, most Catholics did not support the abolitionists and had ignored the condemnation of slavery by Pope Gregory XVI. "The Catholic hierarchy basically distanced itself from the abolitionist movement and only a few individual Catholics took a strong anti slavery position."[245] Phelps adds that the Catholic bishops did not initially join in the public debate to stop slavery. Officially, they preferred to be neutral and silent.[246] There was a strong clash of opinion between the abolitionists and most Catholics about the institution of slavery, as Rice indicates:

> Most Catholics—including most bishops—viewed abolitionists, who proclaimed that holding slaves was "a sin against God," as insurrectionists who were a threat to the "safety of the country." Their ideas were thought to be in conflict with the basic ideals of Catholic ethics. Abolitionists, in turn were publicly anti-Catholic. They generally looked upon Catholics as ignorant, pro-slavery, foreigners at odds with the ideal of social equality.[247]

As already mentioned, Bishop Augustine Verot, the Bishop of Florida, earlier supported slavery and opposed abolition before changing his mind later. "Verot charged the abolitionists with causing the present strife by their charges that slavery was evil. He then proceeded to show that 'slavery has received the sanction of God, of the church, and of society at all times, and in all governments'."[248]

However, many Catholics did not accept the on-going American way of looking at slavery and racial equality.[249] There were some Catholic bishops, pastors, and laity who opposed slavery and supported the freedom of the slaves. An example of a Catholic bishop who came out boldly to speak for the freedom of the slaves was John Baptist Purcell (1800-1883), the archbishop of Cincinnati.[250] He did not hide his feelings or play a double game in making it public that slavery was evil and had become a stigma on the Catholic Church in the United States until it is finally rooted out of existence.

There were some Catholic priests also who were very strong in opposing the continuation of slave trade. Father Claude Pascal Maistre was French by birth but later migrated to the United States. "By 1856 he was in the archdiocese of New Orleans and later became the pastor of St. Rose of Lima Church in New Orleans. Father Maister already had the reputation of being an abolitionist."[251] His anti slavery position brought about a clash between him and the archbishop of New Orleans who saw him as an untruthful man and stubborn for refusing to stop his public rhetoric in support of the abolition of slavery. When Archbishop, Jean-Marie Odin heard the compliant that Father Maister was preaching against slavery in 1862, he ordered him to stop. Father Maister refused to stop speaking publicly against the evil trade, and the archbishop in 1863 suspended him from ministry.[252]

An example of a lay Catholic who also opposed slavery and called for its abolition was William Gaston (1778-1844). He was a member of congress and later became a Supreme Court justice in North Carolina. "He spoke out publicly against slavery. In a commencement address delivered in 1832 at The University of North Carolina, he challenged the students in calling for the 'ultimate extirpation of the worst evil that affects the Southern part of our Confederacy."[253]

The abolition of slavery remained a controversial one in the Catholic Church. As we saw in the case of the Protestant Churches, the issue of slavery brought divisions among many of them, but the Catholic Church did not split.[254] However, it was "as the Civil War threatened the union and the stability of the social-political order previously legitimized by law, bishops who had maintained an official silence on slavery began to speak out."[255] It was after the war that bishop Verot and Lynch abandoned their support for the continuation of slavery. When the freedom of the slaves became a reality, both of them made plans for helping the newly emancipated slaves.[256]

Segregated Parishes

In terms of organization, "the vital element in the development of American Catholicism was the parish."[257] The parishes were formed along ethnic lines. As the immigrants were coming from Britain, France, Germany, Spain, Portugal, Ireland, Poland and other parts of Europe, the Catholic Church established parishes to take care of the pastoral or spiritual needs of these groups. According to Dolan,

> Each of these groups had their (sic) own national parishes. Based on nationality as well as language, these parishes became the hallmark of urban church. A city neighborhood could have several different national parishes within its boundaries. Like separate galaxies, each parish community stayed within its own orbit. The Irish did not mix with the Poles. The Germans never mingled with the Italians.[258]

Inside such churches the cultural heritage of each nationality was preserved as language, national festivals, and feasts were observed. St. Patrick's Day, for example, was well observed in all Irish churches in the United States. It may have not been a mistake for the church to have provided for the spiritual needs of Catholic immigrants by considering their nationality and language. At the same time, this segregation of parishes compartmentalized the Church. Each national church was a world of its own, and any one who was not Irish or German or Italian did not feel accepted.

This ethnic separation was hard on African American Catholics who though they spoke English were not always very welcome in such national churches. In all these churches, blacks were asked not to mix with whites during worship. The African American Catholics were forced to stay at the back of the churches or in the galleries during worship. MacGregor asserts, "Bowing to the social conventions, most Catholic churches segregated their black communicants restricting them to separate sections of the church and teaching their children in separate Sunday school classes."[259] It was well and good for the Church to comply with the government policies even when they went against justice, human rights, and the demands of the gospel.

Though it was the immigrants that may have contributed a larger portion of the money for the building of such national parishes, it was not easy for the African Americans who were very poor due to the marginalizing effects of slavery and segregation laws, and so could not easily build such churches with their money. The Catholic Church did not build many of such churches for them as may have been needed. However, it is on record that few parishes were established exclusively for African Americans in the nineteenth century (after the Civil War). "The year 1864 records the first church building for colored Catholics exclusively in the United States, St. Francis Xavier's."[260] In 1865, St. Augustine, Washington D.C. was the second parish built exclusively as black parish. The third parish probably was St. Monica Chicago which Father Tolton started in 1891 and which was not completed before he died, because he had not enough funds to finish it.[261]

It was in the 1900s that more black parishes were established especially in New York and in Chicago. Most of the churches, however, were not originally and exclusively planned and built for blacks. In most cases, they were abandoned or left over parishes by white Catholic communities who left the cities and fled to the counties as African Americans started migrating to the cities in large numbers. In the words of Koren,

> In Chicago, St. Monica's parish was merged with St. Elizabeth's formerly an Irish parish that was given to the Society of the Divine Word in 1924. St. Elizabeth became the center for black Catholic activity for an ever-increasing black population on the South Side of Chicago. The parish had a black Catholic elementary school and high school as early as 1922. In New York the traditional black Catholic parish was St. Benedict the Moor in lower Manhattan on West 53rd Street. In 1925, as Harlem had become the center of a growing black population, the church of St. Charles Borromeo became a thriving black parish. In 1912 the Spiritans took over St. Mark in Harlem as a black parish.[262]

Most of these parishes were remarkable for their very poor conditions. About the administration of these black parishes, "the Church's black apostolate relied on the individual efforts of interested white clergy."[263]

In most cases, they were handed over to religious priests to manage as most diocesan priests did not want to live in very poor conditions along with their blacks parishioners. Describing the way the church handled the pastoral needs of the African Americans, especially in the nineteenth century and in the earlier parts of the twentieth century, Father Charles Hart OFM, the supervisor of pastoral care at Forest Park Hospital St. Louis, describes the American Catholic Church as a mother that had many children but decided to provide food, clothes, and shelter for some and left one to suffer without enough food, enough clothes, and enough shelter as if he or she was not equally a human being and so did not need equal care.[264]

Segregated Church Schools

It was not the intention of the slave masters both in the church and in the society to expose their slaves to education due to fear that they may know the truth and their rights and fight for them. Gillard supports this claim in these words:

> After the nineteenth century began, however, there was a reaction against permitting Negroes to learn reading and writing because of a growing fear of insurrection on the part of the Negroes who were learning too much from the French Revolution and too frequently emulating the example of the revolutionists on the French Islands.[265]

The first recognized effort to formally educate Negro children was made providentially by Josephine Alicot, a French lady who came to United States to visit her Ursuline sister in New Orleans. She made a promise to dedicate her life to helping the Negroes after her life was saved from drowning by a Negro man when she accidentally fell off the ship. She fulfilled her promise in 1825 by first establishing a school for children of free slaves in New Orleans.[266] The Ursuline sisters took over the management of the school and engaged in teaching colored children. Further efforts made to open schools for black children were not encouraged. "In 1835 England opened a school to teach black boys and girls of free black families. The school raised such opposition from the white people of South Carolina that there was a riot, forcing England to close down the school. A further attempt was never made."[267] Mary A. Ward's estimation of the rate of illiteracy among blacks after the Civil War was 95 percent. [268]

However, later in the nineteenth century and the beginning of the twentieth century, more Catholic schools were opened exclusively to educate colored children.

Despite the effort made to open more schools for colored children, the Catholic schools like the Protestant ones up till the middle periods of the twentieth century were segregated. "Not all Catholics welcomed blacks, even black Catholics, into the parochial schools."[269] According to Joseph B. Connors, "In 1887, Fr. John Slattery, in an article published in the *Catholic World*, stated that he knew of no Catholic college or seminary in the country that admitted African Americans."[270]

According to Monsignor Frank Blood, it was Cardinal Ritter who started breaking down the racial barriers in St. Louis Archdiocese by integrating the Catholic schools system in 1947 even before the American government ended the public school segregation in the 1950s and 1960s. It was a prophetic action in the Catholic school system that inspired some other bishops to do like wise in their dioceses. However, his action to integrate the schools met with swift resistance by some wealthy and well known Catholics to the extent that he threatened to penalize some of them who resisted his good will of making the blacks feel accepted in the Catholic school system. [271] Pawlikowski, O.S.M., also asserts in agreement with Monsignor Blood, "A major breakthrough on the racial front in American Catholicism did not occur until 1947. It was in that year that Cardinal Ritter of St. Louis ended all racial segregation in the Catholic schools of his archdiocese. Ritter's action was duplicated the following year by Archbishop Patrick O'Boyle of Washington."[272]

Rejection of African American Vocations

One of the major problems the African Americans experienced in becoming Catholics was that "most dioceses were reluctant to accept African Americans as candidates for the priesthood."[273] In my discussions with Monsignor Frank Blood, he told me the story of how difficult it was for the first African Americans to become Catholic priests in the

American Catholic Church in the late nineteenth century. He told me about an African American man whose name was Augustus Tolton.

He was born in the state of Missouri, but because he was African American, he was not allowed to enter the seminary to become a Catholic priest in America. "Despite the rejection, the disappointment, and the repeated refusals, Tolton persevered in the desire to become a priest, and his dream became reality in a rather dramatic way." [274] Through the help of Father Michael Richardt, OFM, he got in contact with the Congregation of the Propaganda in Rome and got admission to study for the priesthood in Urban College under the Congregation of the Propaganda. Tolton became ordained to the Catholic priesthood on April 24, 1886, in Rome, at the age of thirty two. [275]

When he came back to this country, as a priest, he was rejected by many of his fellow priests and bishops who were whites. Monsignor Blood states, "It is not unreasonable to hear that African Americans see the Catholic Church as *a white man's or a racist Church*. It was because of such unfortunate events in the history of the Catholic Church in this country that such impressions were created." [276] Stephen Ochs also asserts,

> The resistance of church authorities in the United States to the ordination of black priests damaged both blacks and the institutional church itself. Black Catholics were deprived of almost any visible position of authority. The lack of black leadership, in turn, seriously compromised the church's claim to universality and convinced many non-Catholic blacks that the Catholic Church was the 'white man's church. [277]

Why did the church authorities resist ordination of blacks to the priesthood? Mary A. Ward has the answer in these words. "Whites had ambivalent feelings regarding the ability of black men to fill the intellectual and celibacy demands of priesthood. Blacks who were courageous enough to seek a priestly vocation had to face loneliness, prejudice, and the stress of continually proving to bishops and clergy that they could measure up. Black priests struggled to find a bishop who would give them faculty to function in a diocese." [278] It was when some black men became Catholic priests in the dioceses that their white counterparts discovered that black priests are as intelligent as white priests and as for celibacy, it was also discovered that all human beings are the same. It was after the Civil War that "some quasi-systematic efforts were made to encourage black men toward priestly ordination, but social and psychological impediments affecting both whites and blacks kept the number very low until the 1970s."[279]

What was happening among the religious communities? It was not also very easy for African Americans, because the white religious communities of priests, brothers, and sisters were not very prepared to accept African Americans as members of their communities.[280] Ward also recounts how difficult it was for Henriette Delille and Juliette Gaudin to start a religious order for African American women called the Sisters of the Holy Family in New Orleans in 1842. They "struggled for many years against the constraints of poverty, segregation laws, and even an archbishop's aversion to seeing black women in a religious habit."[281]

The Catholic Church and the Segregation Laws

As already indicated the Catholic Church like the Protestant Churches complied with and applied the segregation laws of the governments in Church worship, to reflect what was happening in the society. Before the formal enactment of the discriminatory laws by the American government, there was segregation already existing in the Church against the African Americans. The humiliation of being forced to the galleries, the resistance of black vocations to the priesthood, and the non acceptance of blacks in parochial schools, all started long before the formal promulgation of the racial laws. We already saw how some church theologians and some bishops used arguments even from the Bible to work against emancipation of the blacks from slavery.

When the racial laws were finally enacted for the entire country in 1896, the Catholic Church like all Protestant Churches had no problem and qualms of conscience welcoming them and making them part of the church life. This, of course, took its own toll on black membership in the Catholic Church.

> The church made few inroads in the black community, and lost
> many of its black members in the nineteenth century, because
> it did not allow blacks to participate fully and freely in the

life of the church. Many congregations humiliated their black members by establishing segregated seating arrangements and by requiring blacks to wait to receive the Eucharist until all whites had done so first.[282]

However, many notable Catholics of color appealed to the Church hierarchy to speak and to act against racial discrimination in the Church. In 1931, Thomas Wyatt Turner wrote a letter to the American bishops asking them to see that the doors of Catholic schools, colleges, universities, or seminaries are not shut to blacks because of the color of their skin.[283] Turner was the leader of the Federation of Colored Catholics and a strong advocate for racial justice in the American Catholic Church.[284] He was active in appealing to the Catholic bishops not only to fight against racial segregation in the church but also to discipline those in the church who prevent black Catholics from taking active part in activities in their different dioceses as other Catholics. He also appealed to the bishops to speak out in condemnation of lynching of blacks and the forcing out of residents of color from cities.[285] Lynching, as already indicated, was the brutal killing of black people especially in the South, by burning or by hanging, in order to protect the racial purity of white women. Most times, these killings were done without trials, and church leaders kept silence over it. "From the year 1889, there have been 3,443 known mob murders, 54 of them the victims being women. American mobs murdered 54 persons in 1921, four of whom were publicly burned at the stake. In only a few instances has prosecution of lynches been attempted"[286] According to James H. Smylie, a Presbyterian minister, "Miscegenation was outlawed, but such laws did not prevent Christian whites from exploiting *Afer* women for pleasure."[287]

There were also some white Catholics who worked hard for racial equality and justice. George K. Hunton, was one of the most popular advocates of racial justice in the middle of the twentieth century.[288] Hunton was a very active leader in the Catholic Interracial Council. He not only worked as a team with black leaders but also worked hard to enable the Council to take a strong stand in support of the antilynching laws.[289] On the female side, through the leadership of Mother Katherine Drexel, many churches and schools in black communities were funded and the Catholic Church made some improvement in the area of racial justice in the middle decades of the twentieth century.[290]

Among the Catholic bishops, there were some who were prophetic in some of their actions against racial injustice even before the Civil Rights Movements. As already mentioned, the prophetic actions of Archbishop Joseph Ritter of St. Louis, Archbishop Patrick O'Boyle of Washington, and bishop Vincent Waters of Raleigh were actions which so many other bishops found very difficult to take until the challenge of the Civil Rights Movement of the 1950s and 1960s. Archbishop Ritter and Archbishop O'Boyle ended racial segregation in all Catholic schools in St. Louis and Washington respectively in 1947. In 1954, Bishop Waters of Raleigh followed their good example and ended segregation at different levels in the diocese of Raleigh.

The Catholic Church and the Civil Rights Movement

Like most Protestant Churches, the activities and successes of the Civil Rights Movement of the 1950s and 1960s became a big challenge to the Church to react positively to the winds of change.

In 1955 the blacks of Montgomery, Alabama, began a boycott of buses because of segregated seating. A young black Baptist clergyman, Rev. Martin Luther King, Jr., became the leader of the movement. The boycott was successful, and the African American community was galvanized across the nation.[291]

Initially, not many Catholics were seen at the fore front of this struggle[292] The American bishops responded in support of the movement after three years. "In 1958, the American bishops addressed racism as a moral issue and finally took an unequivocal stand. They stated for the first time that racial discrimination was immoral and unjust."[293] They presented a good address in support of racial justice but like some Episcopal bishops, they applied a little twist in their address that could be easily misunderstood as inaction, by their advising for a gradual process in ending racial discrimination. Before the group action of the American bishops, there had been individual actions by certain bishops. The actions of Archbishop Ritter, and Archbishop O'Boyle are good examples of some individual bishops who did something to end the evil laws. [294] Also "in

Washington, Baroni found himself working with a select group of white clergyman (sic) in alliance with the movement's local black leadership, especially Walter Fauntroy, Channing Philips, and Ernest Gibson."[295]

Father Baroni was a white Catholic priest of the archdiocese of Washington and a civil rights activist. Instead of receiving objections from his bishop, Baroni was surprised to find Archbishop Patrick O' Boyle as a strong ally in the struggle against segregation.[296] Archbishop O' Boyle was also a civil rights activist who used his office well as the archbishop of Washington to appeal to Americans to end all forms of racial discrimination. "In a series of sermons and statements in the early 1960s, he outlined a strategy for convincing Americans that social justice was a religious and moral issue."[297] Archbishop O' Boyle was the chairman of the Washington Interreligious Committee on Race Relations. He frequently addressed the D.C. Commissioners and other governmental bodies, in favor of the proposed ordinances to eliminate discrimination in housing and to ensure justice in employment.[298]

Due to the fact that many black priests were not in leadership positions, many of them were not at the leadership position in the Civil Rights Movement as were their Protestant counterparts. [299] However, there is evidence that many Catholics, white and blacks and clergy, took part in some of the massive demonstrations that brought about the removal of the laws in 1964.

> The massive demonstration by whites and blacks at the Lincoln Memorial in Washington, D.C., on August 28, 1963, did, however, include some Catholics of diverse backgrounds as well as some Catholics organizations, including religious communities. Archbishop O'Boyle was on the platform with civil rights leaders and delivered the invocation just before Martin Luther King began his famous 'I Have a Dream' speech.[300]

The response of many Catholic priests and religious including sisters to the invitations made by Martin Luther King Jr., especially the invitation to all the nations' clergy to come to Selma, Alabama in 1965, was very encouraging and supportive to the black cause. Solidarity to the movement also gave rise to the formation of the Black Catholic Clergy Caucus which also put pressure on the Catholic bishops to respond to the winds of change and to lead the American Catholic Church to a new era of integration of the African American Catholics.[301] Though the Catholic Church, like most Protestant Churches, supported the Civil Rights Movement, this question remains: what has happened since the removal of the laws and what is happening now? We shall look into this question and similar questions in the next chapter.

CHAPTER FIVE
THE CATHOLIC CHURCH AND RACISM FROM
THE 1960S TO THE PRESENT

The support of the Catholic Church to the Civil Rights Movement--whether due to pressure from the civil right activists or as a matter of conscience--was encouraging to the struggle for equality and racial justice in America. The support, however, did not necessarily mean a victory over racial inequality at all levels in both church and state. The answers to the following questions would help us to find out what has happened and what is happening now in the Catholic Church since the Civil Rights Movement of the sixties.

1. Does the removal of the Jim Crow laws mean that the Catholic Church is presently committed to speaking for equal opportunities and equal conditions for every American citizen regardless of color?
2. Is there still racism in the Catholic Church? If yes, what forms is it taking now?
3. How prophetic has the Church been addressing the greatest effect of racism, which is poverty, through its pastoral ministry among the people of color, in the 20th and 21st centuries?
4. What can the Catholic Church still do to continue the fight for the total eradication of racism in both church and society and to change the impression by many African Americans that the Catholic Church is a white man's church?

The Recent Developments

Since the Civil Rights Movement of the sixties, many Catholics, white and black, have denounced interpersonal and institutional racism. They do not see racism in any way compatible with the teachings of the gospel about love, justice, and peace. Some church leaders also have started to see things differently and have started to do certain things that could help to continue the efforts to work for love and justice. According to Jamie T. Phelps,

> Concrete evidence of some bishops' intellectual and moral conversion on the matter of racism is manifest in numerous ways: · by the publication of *Brothers and sisters to Us: U.S. Bishop's Pastoral Letter on Racism in Our Day and Economic Justice for All: Pastoral Letter on Catholic Social Teaching and the U.S. Economy;* · by the promulgation of the Black bishop's pastoral letter *What We Have seen and Heard,* which calls for African American Catholics to assume leadership roles in the continued evangelization of Black Catholics and unchurched members of the African American community; · by encouraging liturgical inculturation; · by adequate support, funding, and staffing of the Secretariat for Black Catholics and diocesan Offices for Black Catholics; · by pastoral planning that ensures the continued active and developing growth of churches and schools in African American communities; · by encouraging religious communities and seminaries to attempt to identify and nurture religious vocations from the African American community; · by supporting and providing for the development and inclusion of African American Catholic leadership in parishes, schools and diocesan offices; · by developing and sponsoring programs to help white Catholics undergo a conversion from racist attitudes; and · by public denunciation of racist acts and situations.[302]

Some dioceses have also initiated efforts to make Hispanic Catholics feel cared for pastorally. According to Fr. Gene Morris, "There are offices opened for Hispanic ministry in many dioceses and parishes. We now have Hispanic Lectionary, Bible, Sacramentry and so on."[303] While acknowledging the above efforts, Phelps also observes that these efforts are not general, and that there is still the historic silence of many church leaders to racial issues.

Some American bishops and other Catholic religious leaders still seem to avoid the public debate and action on racism in America. Many seem to lack the sensitivity, passion, and moral fortitude of a John

Marcel Augustine Verot, who having experienced intellectual conversion, continued to manifest this conversion by bold actions on behalf of justice toward African Americans.[304]

Phelps recorded these observations in the nineties. To obtain current information on recent racism in the Catholic Church, I interviewed some members of the Catholic clergy and laity in different dioceses in this country. Some of the people I spoke with allowed me to mention their names and publish what we discussed, and some did not want me to mention their names, but allowed me to use the information they gave me anonymously.

The Interviews

Some of the information from these interviews confirmed information already discussed in this book, while some of them reflect new developments in the racial history of the Catholic Church in this country.

Interview with Father C. Eugene Morris

Father C. Eugene Morris

The first Catholic priest I interviewed was Father C.Eugene Morris. He is the only active African American diocesan priest in the whole of the St. Louis Archdiocese and teaches at Kenrick seminary.

"Father Morris, as an African American Catholic priest, you may have noticed that some black Catholics still complain of racial attitudes during church worship and during some church activities in the parishes. Do you believe that racism still exits in the Catholic Church as it exists in the secular American society?"

"Racism exists in the Catholic church as it exists in other churches, as far as white and black people are members, though it is not as it used to be in the past when blacks were formally not allowed to sit together in the same pews with whites. There are still other forms of racism existing in the Church today across the country even as we speak."

"Before I ask you about the different forms it is taking now, let me first ask you this. I have noticed that African Americans seem to have this impression that the Catholic Church is *a racist church or a white man's church.* Can you tell me briefly what led to such impression?"

"At a period in the nineteenth century when the movement to abolish slavery was going on, to free the slaves, there was the perception that the Catholic Church in America did not do much to speak for the freedom of the slaves as some other religious groups did. The period after slavery led to African Americans becoming Baptists, and joining other Protestant denominations though the issue of slavery and racial prejudice divided the Baptist church into factions and conventions. However, African Americans felt more welcome in the Baptist Church despite the Baptists' own racial problems. Even though white Baptists did not welcome blacks Baptists as members on equal grounds, the black Baptists were allowed to build their own churches, have their own pastors, and manage their own affairs. It was not like that in the Catholic Church. So instead of the Catholic Church speaking out forcefully and identifying with the oppressed slaves, many bishops and religious groups or congregations were still keeping their slaves as the abolition movement was still going on."

"Actually, I heard it first from an African American taxi driver. It was really surprising to hear that. I felt like asking a person like you. Could you please tell me more about this?"

"When slavery was finally abolished and also formally condemned by Rome, there was a push from Rome encouraging the bishops in this country to reach out to the freed black slaves and also to create super jurisdictional dioceses which would cut across geographical boundaries. Many bishops in this country resisted that idea simply because a number of them were bigots who did not want to lose control in their dioceses."

"What about vocations; were African Americans accepted into the seminaries?"

"Vocations from African Americans were rejected and some of those who were ordained were sent to Rome or other foreign countries to study for the priesthood. Catholic priesthood was perceived as a white man's vocation only. Black Catholic children were not admitted into Catholic schools until Cardinal Ritter integrated the schools in St Louis Archdiocese. This is the history behind the feeling by African Americans that the Catholic Church is *racist or a white man's church*. The Church did not do much to provide for the spiritual needs of the black people because many of the church leaders were racist and did not accept the black people as human beings and as members of their flock.

"What was the consequence of this?"

"The Church through such mistakes lost its opportunity to get the minds and the hearts of most African Americans. However, there are some areas such as Baltimore, Philadelphia, Virginia, and Washington DC, where you have many African Americans who are Catholics. You have a few in St. Louis and other areas but the greater majority of African Americans did not see the Catholic Church as a comfortable place where they were made welcome. Though there have been some apologies rendered by some dioceses to African Americans, which have not made much impact."

"Father Morris, thank you for sharing this information with me. Let me ask you a little more about the present. As the only active African American diocesan priest in this diocese, how are you treated in the midst of a white majority?"

"Some people like to deal with me, not because I am first a human being or a priest but because surprisingly they say that I am intelligent, articulate, and dedicated. You are not seen as a human being first like every one else. People have to determine you are the type of black man who possesses those qualities that indicate that you are reasonable to deal with. The color of your skin for some people is what counts first."

"Have you recently had any direct experience of racism from your church members as an African American priest?"

"Yes, I can tell you about one. I was assigned to go and celebrate Mass at a white dominated parish. While I was sitting down on a seat near the entrance of the church before the Mass started, one white man came in and looked at me in a very mean way, without greeting me or saying a word to me. The man's mood changed and he called some people inside the church and was asking them in my hearing whether this *Nigger* priest was going to celebrate the Mass. He told his fellow parishioners that it was time they stopped all these black priests from coming to celebrate Mass here."

"I am sorry for that, Father Morris. How did you feel about that?"

"I heard what he said and I was deeply saddened by the man's comments. The worst was that he was telling his friends that black priests should go to black parishes if they want to celebrate Mass. When Mass started, I used the experience in my homily to let the people know that the color of the skin has nothing to do with the sacrament of the Eucharist."

"Do you feel that the Catholic Church in America is doing enough to eradicate racial prejudice both in the church and in the state and also doing anything to appeal to the government to get the racial problems of this country discussed at all levels?"

"There have been some verbal condemnations, pastoral letters and apologies rendered to the African Americans by some dioceses for the mistakes of the Church in the past, but there has not been enough done in the practical sense to appeal to the government to get the racial problems of this country discussed at different levels. After verbal condemnations, things continue the way they have been both in the church and in the state, without a meaningful change. Many of our church leaders prefer keeping silent to what is happening in the society, and by so doing racial inequality continues."

"Thank you so much, Fr. Morris, for talking with me."

Interview with Monsignor Frank Blood

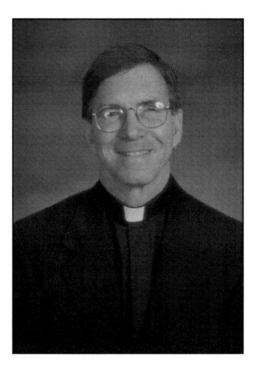

Monsignor Frank Blood

After hearing from Father C. Eugene Morris, I spoke with Monsignor Frank Blood, a Caucasian priest, from another perspective. Monsignor Blood is in charge of Society for the Propagation of the Faith for the St. Louis Archdiocese.

"Monsignor, as a white pastor, do you believe that there has been racism in the Church and that has made the African Americans see the Catholic Church as *racist and as a white man's church?*"

"Yes, there has been racism in the Catholic Church. Unfortunately, the attitude of the Catholics even in this archdiocese followed the attitude of the general population in this country. There was a black man who wanted to become a Catholic priest. He was born in the state of Missouri and his name was Augustine Tolton. This was in the 1800s, but because he was African American, he was not allowed to enter the seminary and he actually had to go to Rome to study. Through the help of the Congregation for the Propagation of the Faith, he was ordained and came back to serve in different parts of the country but was not welcomed by the archdiocese of St. Louis."

"Do you have some personal experiences about this problem?"

"From my experiences of the African Americans, having served among them in a black parish, many of the older parishioners were telling me about their experiences in the past, how they were not welcomed to worship in many parishes because of the attitude of the whites. At that time, they were only welcomed in the old St. Elizabeth in a black neighborhood evangelized by the French sisters and administered by the Jesuit priests."

"Could you please tell me more?"

"There is an old friend of mine who told me how she attended mass at Visitation Parish many years ago, and she was told that she should not sit in front with whites because blacks were not supposed to sit in front with whites, but at the back. This was the situation of things until Archbishop Ritter, who later became Cardinal Ritter of St. Louis Archdiocese, started to break down these racial barriers by integrating the Catholic school system. This move was sharply opposed by many well-known Catholics in the archdiocese to the extent that he threatened to excommunicate many of them for opposing his welcoming attitude to African Americans."

"I remember having read about the prophetic action of Cardinal Ritter. I think his action was an inspiration to the government also to know which way leads to justice. It is true that the government is secular and is not associated with any particular religion. At the same time, one may say that the government is made up primarily of Christians, and sometimes they expect the religious leaders to take the lead in morals and justice. When that leadership is not coming, justice could take centuries to come. I was so happy when I heard about the prophetic action of Cardinal Ritter. I think that should be a leading example to other Church leaders and other Catholics in this country. Do you think, Monsignor, that the example of Cardinal Ritter is being followed by other Catholics today?"

"Apart from the move of Cardinal Ritter, which was opposed, the general attitude of other Catholics, especially in some neighborhoods of St. Louis, has not been very welcoming, and it is not unreasonable that African Americans tend to see the Catholic Church *as racist and a white man's church*. However, I do not agree with those who say that there are very few African Americans who are Catholics in St Louis, because the population is about four percent, which is about one out of every twenty five Catholics. There was even an African American bishop appointed as Auxiliary Bishop of St. Louis Archdiocese. His name is Bishop J. Terry Steib S.V.D. He was extremely popular through out the archdiocese because of his great personality and personal warmth. He is an outstanding preacher. These are just a few of his fine qualities which endeared him to the hearts of the people of the archdiocese. He was auxiliary bishop here until May, 1993 when he was appointed bishop of Memphis, Tennessee. "

"I understand that some efforts are being made by the Catholic Church in the United States of America to change this impression by African Americans that the Catholic Church is a racist church or a white man's church. What can the American Catholic Church still do to correct the mistakes of the past?"

"The appointment of African Americans to leadership positions in the Catholic Church is very important because that will give them a stronger sense of belonging. For example the human rights office of the archdiocese is headed by an African American woman, Leodia Gooch. She is very capable and a great role model. There is need also to promote vocations to the priesthood and religious life among African American youths. This is very important and remains a challenge to the Church in America. For example in this archdiocese, there are still so far only two African American priests. One is retired, while one is active."

"Monsignor, thanks for these suggestions. I learned that some of the predecessors of Cardinal Ritter were very racist against African Americans in this archdiocese. Following Cardinal Ritter's prophetic action, what do you feel the Archdiocese is doing now to make the Catholics of color in St. Louis to feel that the Catholic Church is also for them and is concerned about what is happening to them both in church and in American society?"

"I have already told you about the appointment of an African American woman as the head of the human rights office of the archdiocese. The archdiocese also does a lot to encourage education among African American youths. For example, the archdiocese spent millions of dollars to build the Cardinal Ritter College Prep school in an African American community to encourage African American youths to have a better education."

"What else do you recommend?"

"There should be more of what we call twinning of parishes. This helps black parishes and white parishes to worship together, to promote understanding, and acceptance. This also could be an opportunity for rich parishes to help the poor ones financially."

"Thank you, Monsignor, for your time and for the valuable information you gave me."

Interview with Father Grenham John Patrick. (JP)

Father Grenham John Patrick (JP)

Having interviewed two priests from St. Louis Archdiocese, I decided to go to other dioceses to get more information. Hurricane Katrina attracted me to New Orleans. I wanted to know more from the perspective of the Church about what really happened, since some people suspected racial mishandling of the problem. I wanted to know how, pastorally, the crisis was handled by the Church. So my next discussion was in New Orleans with Father Grenham. Father Grenham is the pastor of St. Hubert's Parish in the Grayville neighborhood of New Orleans. His home was one of those completely destroyed during the flooding. He did not leave his parish throughout the crisis because so many people took refuge in his parish, and he stayed with them to feel with them, give them hope, and to minister to them. I was happy to talk with him because of the racial overtones in the government's handling of the crisis.

"Father Grenham, I must commend you for being there for the victims of the Hurricane Katrina who flocked to take refuge in your parish during the flooding and after. New Orleans, where your parish is located, has been in the news for some weeks now. There has been much criticisms against the government for the late response to the victims.

Some are saying that this was due to the fact that most of the victims were black. What have you to say about the response of the government?"

"When you say the government, do you mean the local or state or the federal government?"

"Any one blamed for the delay."

"The local and state governments tried to get many people out of the city but the number was too much, to the extent that many people were not able to get out. There were different types of stranded people: the very old people, people of very low income, and the helpless people in the city, mostly the younger children. So when the storm came, and the federal government's response was not forthcoming, the local community was unable to do much and their ability to do the whole job was exhausted. Then the city started to flood and people who did not have the means or money to get out, flocked to the Super-Dome as a place of last resort."

"We saw that over the television. Tell me more about this, Father"

"There was no communication, no food, and no water for some days. What was thought was going to be a federal response according to the plan never came. So because of that, we had a concentration of people at the Super-Dome. Some people said that it was an economic question, but if you look at the places that were flooded, the poverty of the city, it is ninety percent African American communities. We also had other communities, such as the Hispanic community, the Asian community, the Central American communities and some members of the white communities, most especially the old white people who had been pulled out of the nursing homes.

"What have you to say about the media coverage of the crisis?"

"What happened was that the media was showing only the African American people acting in very bizarre ways. What really happened was that when people were left for days without food, water, and other needs, a lot of criminal minded people took advantage of it and started doing things outside the law. However, most of those things started to happen when the help was not coming as expected and the local authorities could not handle the number of people any more."

"So are you saying that things would have been much better handled if the expected help from the federal authorities had come faster?"

"Yes, the federal government was expected to come in by Monday evening, but the federal government never showed up until Friday morning."

"So what do you think was the cause of the delay? Was it really a racial issue as some people were saying?"

"I may not say that it was preplanned as a way of neglecting people because of their race, but underneath the delay, was a feeling of the fact that it wasn't important. Some people say that if the victims were mainly whites, it would have been seen as more horrifying. That may be true in its own way, but I think that apart from the delay from the federal authorities, there was no cohesion in decision making between the local city authorities and the state authorities. The confusion was compounded due to lack of communication and other problems. Apart from that, there seems to have been lethargy in decision making. They needed to have woken up earlier to make better plans because they needed to have known that they were dealing with human beings. To an extent, I do agree that if it were mainly a white community, there would have been a better response. In that sense, I would say that there was a sort of racial bias in the whole thing, because the importance was not placed on it as it would have happened if it were a white congregation. No body wants to talk about that and no one wants to hear that."

"There seem to have been a lot of lawlessness during the crisis. We saw a lot of people looting. This was also presented as something racial."

"Yes, as I have already said, a lot of criminal minded people took advantage of the whole thing to do all sorts of horrible things. Some were breaking into any store they saw and looting because they needed food while some were looting for the sake of doing that. There was looting everywhere and the looters were not only black people but all kinds of people. Unfortunately, the media pictured only the blacks looting, but the fact was that most of the lootings were not carried out in New Orleans. I tell you, some of those lootings were done in the gulf coasts like in Long beach. There were lots of mysterious deaths in the hospitals and homes. Some of these deaths would have been avoided if the help had come faster enough."

"Father, looking at the problem of poverty in New Orleans and in the whole of United States, most of the blacks are very poor, as exposed by Hurricane Katrina. Some people seem to dismiss any sympathy for their poverty by blaming them for being lazy. Do you feel that their poverty is due to laziness and that they should be one hundred percent blamed for their poverty?"

"No, I do not think it is laziness. I think it is a long term process that has gone on in this country. The social and economic structure of how we handle people in this country, most especially those who are not very educated is to make them dependent on the government. So people, instead of being self reliant, they depend on what the government would give them. This actually made the horror of the storm worse, because you have a lot of generations that depend on government subsidized life and housing. So when the subsidies were not forthcoming or the housing flushed away, such people would have no where to run to."

"Some blacks complain that they are not given loans for their own businesses on equal conditions as others are given. Is that true?"

"They are given a limited kind of loan."

"Is that justice in America, Father?"

"No, there is no equal opportunity in doing that. It is economic marginalization."

"Thanks a lot, Father Grenham; I am happy you were able to help the poor victims pastorally when they needed a pastor like you. However, pastoral letters of consolation from the spiritual fathers or leaders of different denominations in this country, broadcast over the television and radio, would have been a great source of hope for the victims."

"Thanks, that is true."

"Okay, let me go to the area of racism in the Church. Many black Americans see the Catholic Church as racist and as a white man's church. Do you believe that there is racism in the Catholic Church in America?"

"I think there is racism in the Catholic Church but not by design. It is due to the culture from which we come. I think in the Church itself, racism comes out of the American mindset from the clergy who grew up in middle class American society where you have a lot of racial fears, and these racial fears are increased by the media coverage and that has gone into a lot of people's minds for many years."

"Does this happen in your own parish?"

"My parish community now is a mixed parish of black and white members. They get along well and carry out social functions together but outside the church they do not go to each other's neighborhood. So there is a mindset that this side is a black community and the other side is a white community. This is happening in 2005."

"Is the problem only from your white parishioners or also from your black parishioners?"

"In some cases, racism could come from a black person also. For instance, I went to a store to buy milk the other day. The black lady that sells things there behaved as if she did not see me and was attending to others for a long time. When I called to her attention, she expressed surprise as if she did not know that I was there. It is like a total neglect as if the other person does not exist. It also happens in white communities."

"Any one can be racist, and there is nowhere racism is a virtue no matter who does it. Since it is clear that racism is still a problem in the Catholic Church, what do you suggest should be done by the Church to improve the race relations?"

"I think the first thing is to get honest with each other, cherish, and accept our diversity. Secondly, we need to practice the love we preach which knows no color or race or any other condition. Every human being is a child of God and we are all equal before God."

"What do you suggest for the government to do, to help solve the problem of poverty in the black communities?"

"I think I will make a million dollars if I answer that. Well, I think the government has to start consistently to think of how to give back people their dignity, not worried about who is to blame but to help people learn the skill to achieve their self esteem and acceptance. It needs to be emphasized that to be a black person is a very wonderful thing. Unfortunately, that is not the view of most black people about themselves. The white people also need to appreciate the importance and equality of the blacks instead of seeing them as a bunch of lazy people. So the government can make more effective laws that can prevent racism and inequality from continuing. Another thing is that there is need for a dialogue at all levels about the racial problems and their effects in this country."

Interview with Ms. Jessie Thomas

Ms. Jessie Thomas

To hear from the side of a lay Catholic woman, I interviewed Ms. Jessie Thomas. She is a mental health administrator and a nurse. She is also a lay catechetical minister at Our Lady of Sorrows Parish in Monroe, Ohio.

"Ms Jessie, as a lay minister in the Church, you may have heard of some accusations that there is still racism in the Church. From your own part of the country and from your own experiences as one who has been active in the Church; do you believe that there is still racism in the Church?"

"I appreciate this opportunity to speak with you. I believe that there is racism in the world and thus in the church. I believe that racism exists in very different forms than in days of slavery and during the period of segregation laws. As for the church, something that has been noticeable for me is the lack of education and training opportunities for parishes situated in African American communities. It was especially noticeable to me when I attended seminary classes. I would often overhear my classmates, all of whom were Caucasian, mention that they received tuition assistance from their parishes. I did not receive tuition assistance from my parish because there was no money to do so. Due to urban flight, many people have moved to the suburbs, leaving those who are the working poor and impoverished to provide for larger churches that need money for operation. In the future, there is a plan for Lay Ecclesial Ministers who are trained at the Master's Degree level. I have concerns that many of our African American brothers and sisters will not have the opportunity to become leaders in their own parishes. Individuals who are trained will be assigned to work in the inner city parishes where many African Americans are in attendance. I am concerned that there is no empowerment, but only caretakers who believe that they have a hand on the needs of all ethnic groups."

"You are talking from experience. Is there any other form of racism you are experiencing in the Church?"

"I do have some concerns about the number of urban parishes that are closed due to lack of money or the absence of a ministerial complete staff. Many churches are closed or often merged together with very little recognition that people of color do not all come from the same backgrounds and some times, they speak different languages. If more people could be trained from the community, the churches might be more sustainable. I have concerns also that the teachings of the church are often not portrayed in such a manner that the congregation understands that all people, disciples of Christ belong to one Body. If this is what we teach and believe, why is there such disparity?"

"What advice can you give to the Church to help eradicate the racism that exists now?"

"I don't know if racism will ever be eradicated. Changes have to be made in one's heart. We need cultural diversity education and enlightenment. However, there must be action steps. The action steps could be more fellowship with individual parishes. This would allow for opportunities to understand and appreciate the diversity of a culture that is not your own."

"In what ways can this cultural diversity education be carried out?"

"It can be done first of all through preaching, identifying that God is within all of us. It could also be the focus of seminars, workshops, and RCIA gatherings. In the seminars and workshops, people could be made to know that racism is still in our midst and is not acceptable to the Church in any form it takes, whether inside the Church or in the society. The real meaning of love could be taught so that people will get to know that love is not limited to one's own race or people. I see the Church organizing workshops and seminars to help people know the evils in abortion and sexual abuse of children. Racism is not a lesser evil."

"What do you think that the Church currently is doing to help people to understand that racism is not in keeping with our faith?"

"There are pastoral letters and documents written by the United States Catholic Bishops Conference. They are nice reading; however, how are they implemented in the church? Many churches seem to have little knowledge of the documents on racism."

"Thank you for spending your time with me. I do appreciate all the information you have given me. I feel that they will go a long way to help me make meaningful suggestions that will help to solve the problem."

Interview with Ms Leodia Gooch

Ms. Leodia Gooch

The second Catholic woman I interviewed was Ms Leodia Gooch, the director of Human Rights Office of the Archdiocese of St. Louis.

"Ms. Gooch, I am happy that we have a Human Rights Office in this Archdiocese, and I believe there are such offices in other Catholic dioceses across the country and in other Christian denominations. Could you please tell me a little about the origin of this office?"

"The Archdiocesan Commission on Human Rights was established in 1963 by Cardinal Joseph Ritter to let Catholics and non Catholics know the position of the church in St. Louis on the matter of race relations. Through this Commission, Cardinal Ritter put the Catholic Church at the forefront of racial progress in the metropolitan St. Louis area. In the entire country, he was the first to desegregate the Catholic Schools in St. Louis in 1947. He was a leader who practiced what he believed in."

"I have read a lot about his exemplary leadership. Does this

Commission on Human Rights exist in other Catholic dioceses and in other Christian denominations across the country?"

"Yes, in some Catholic dioceses, it is called Social Concern Office or Office of Social Justice. They all mean the same thing, even in many other denominations. It was part of the church's response to the Civil Rights Movement of 1950s and 1960s when the Churches woke up to support the Civil Rights activists in the struggle against the segregation laws."

"As a foreigner, let me ask you a few questions based on some of my observations in the city of St. Louis and in other cities in other parts of this country. I have lived in St. Louis for about four years; I have also traveled to Chicago, New York, Washington D.C., and to no less than ten other American cities. I discovered certain remarkable things that show that there are still differences between the treatment given to black communities and white communities in most American cities. For instance, if you drive along the roads in East and North St. Louis, you discover that the roads are not well maintained by city officials like the roads in white dominated parts of the city and in surrounding counties. I have visited many black schools or racially integrated schools in the city and many white schools in the suburban areas. They are two different worlds in terms of funding, maintenance, and equipment. My question then is does your office have the power to dialogue with city officials or state government officials to address this clear inequality that still exists?

"No, we do not address such issues."

"I have watched over the television on so many occasions groups of policemen beating up black men along the streets. I know that in a society like this, it is right for the police to arrest any one who goes against the law; at the same time, I do not think that it is right for the police to punish any suspect without a fair trial. This is the type of picture we used to have about Apartheid South Africa. It does not tell well of the police of this country. Punishing a suspect without trial is a violation of the law itself. Does your office, possibly in union with similar offices of other denominations, dialogue with governments and police chiefs to reform the police force in this country to stop such public embarrassments and human right violation?

"No, we do not address such issues."

"I have heard reputable American politicians and media men making public statements against the blacks and some other races in this country. For example, a few months ago, one American statesman and broadcaster openly said that 'you could abort every black baby in this country, and your crime rate would go down.' This statement only increases hatred and racial tension. It is also against the Church's teaching on abortion. I was surprised at the silence from those who should condemn this statement. Does your office, in union with others, react to discourage such unhealthy statements on behalf of the Church officials and appeal to the government to make laws forbidding racial stereotyping of any kind?"

"No, we do not address such issues, but we can react to them if asked to do so."

"A lot of business people of color have complained that they are not given enough business loans as others are given by the banks, and in most cases they are given loans with different interest rates that keep them marginalized economically. Can your office carry out investigations to know the truth about this claim?"

"No, we do not do it."

"Then what are these offices established for, if you can not address such issues? Why call it Office of Human Rights or Office of Social Justice when injustice is seen as you drive along the roads, in schools, and along the streets?"

"Right now, we address more of global issues that affect human rights like the death penalty, health matters and so on. About the above issues you raised, we first of all meet with the bishop before we address such issues. We go to schools to teach the children about race relations when the schools request for it. The only problem we have with the schools is that most times schools do not request it, and we cannot go without their request. We some times go to parishes to talk about race relations. The only problem we have with going to parishes is that people do not respond well. We always educate people according to the position of the church on these issues."

"It is like you only respond to requests but you do not take initiatives?"

"Correct. Or to put it another way, we educate and advocate, to bring about an awareness that, hopefully, will move people to action.

"Is there a national union of Human Rights Offices or Social Justice

Offices of different denomination in this country that brings them together to handle certain issues as a team?"

"Yes, there are organizations whose mission is to address racism and bigotry. However, I have not seen any public demonstration or heard statements that specifically address the unequal treatments being currently experienced. For example, the public beating of black men by the police we see on televisions."

"How do you feel about the way the American Churches are handling racial matters that have much to do with inequality in this country?"

"The Churches rightly condemn racism as a sin but many Churches do not have laws to enforce equality and stop racism among their members. The government has such laws, but the only problem is that most times the laws are not well handled or enforced."

"Thanks, Ms. Gooch, for sharing this information with me."

The Story of a South American Priest

A black priest (name and picture withheld) from South America, told me the story of what happened to him the first time he served as a pastor in an all white parish, a few years ago in one of the dioceses in the south. When the bishop of that diocese assigned him to a particular Church, the parish council of that parish had a meeting with him. He thought that the chairman of the parish council was going to give him a welcome address. Contrary to his expectation, the chairman asked the new priest, "Do you see any of your brothers or sisters here?" He could not answer the question because he did not understand what the chairman meant. He told the priest to his face, "Go back to whoever sent you. We know that it was the bishop that sent you. Our parish is not a black parish and so we would prefer going without a priest to having a colored priest." The priest was so surprised that he did not know what to say.

The parishioners then sent words to the bishop that they do not have any room for a black priest, only a white one. The bishop went to them in person and told them, "If you reject this priest because of the color of his skin, I will automatically close down this parish until further notice." When the people saw that the bishop meant what he said, they allowed the priest to stay. Still, the decision of the bishop took its own toll as more than half of the people left that parish and started to attend mass in a nearby parish with a white pastor. On Sundays, the black South American priest would see very few people in the Church, and he would go ahead to celebrate the mass, not minding the number of people that came to church that day. Although the attitude of the people demoralized him, he gathered courage to continue with the few white parishioners that showed up for church activities.

It happened that this priest has a great gift of preaching and can attract crowds with his sermons. When the few people who attended mass listened to his preaching, they were amazed and some would go home to tell the other parishioners that the black South American priest was a wonderful preacher. The news about his preaching continued to circulate in the whole town, to the extent that many who left the parish returned. His preaching also attracted youths in the town, who began coming to church, taking part in some of the church activities.

One day, a young woman who so much admired the priest's preaching asked him to preside over her wedding. The priest agreed to do so. She made a second request and begged the priest not to say no to it. She said to the priest, "I would like you to attend my wedding reception after the church wedding." The priest agreed. Before the wedding day, the priest drove to the reception hall to acquaint himself with the place.

When the priest got to the reception hall, he was surprised to see the notice posted by the door: *Blacks are not allowed.* The priest quietly drove back home in shock that such a thing still exists in the present American society. He told the young woman that he was sorry that he was not going to attend her wedding reception. The lady asked him why he had decided not to keep to his promise. She begged the priest not to break his promise, since that would make her unhappy on her wedding day. When he told the young woman why he couldn't attend her reception, she replied, "Don't worry. My father owns the place, and I'll ask him to remove the sign."

Her father agreed to allow the priest into the hall, provided he wore his collar so that everyone would know that he was given the special privilege because of his clerical status. The priest refused the "privilege." He explained to the young woman that if he were not allowed admittance because he was a human person, then he preferred not to enter. Furthermore, he said that if other black persons were denied admittance, he would not enter. Finally, he told the woman that such a sign violated the principles of her faith and that she should go and tell her father that it was wrong to treat his fellow human beings unequally. The woman's father replied, "Go and tell your nigger priest that we can do without his presence."

The Story of a Lay Foreigner

One day I received a phone call from Mr. Osy Kokelu, a fellow Nigerian, living in the St. Louis area. We arranged to meet and get acquainted. After some small talk, I asked him about his experiences with the Catholic Church in the United States. He said that when he first arrived, he went to a Catholic Church near his home in Little Rock, Arkansas. He was the only black person at the Mass he attended, and he noticed that he invariably sat alone in a pew, even when the church was crowded. He also noticed that, at the greeting of peace, no one offered him a greeting, though when he extended his hand, the greeting was returned.

Finally, one Sunday, the pastor asked him if he was comfortable at this church. He assured the pastor that he appreciated the liturgy he found there. The priest, nevertheless, suggested that he transfer to another church and gave him the name and address of a church about a twenty-minute drive from his home. The congregation at this church was entirely African-American. Stunned at the blatant racism, he became so angry that he never went to a Catholic church again in Little Rock, Arkansas until he came to St. Louis to live. He started going to Catholic Church again when he got married and his wife kept persuading him to go for Mass and not to mind the ugly experiences at Little Rock, Arkansas.

My own Stories and Experiences

In my first year of stay here in the United State, I did not experience any direct act of racism. The priest I was living with was Caucasian; He was very nice to me and some of the parishioners were nice to me also. Where is racism, I asked my self? Well, I told my self, there may be racism but it depends on whom you meet. Not every person is racist. I know that there are two types of racism, individual and institutionalized racism. Some people may not be racist as individuals but they keep to the racist policies of institutions they belong to and see it as normal, while some people by nature hate any one who is not of their own color and do anything it takes to make the other feel inferior and less human.

I received the best act of generosity, acceptance, and tolerance since my stay here from a white couple that took me as their son, Ed and Marge Meiners, from Bopp Des Peres St. Louis.

Ed and Marge Meiners. Good Example of Love that Knows no Color.

They invited me to their home, and they celebrate my birthday every year. They gave me the car with which I go to school and visit the sick in the hospitals. I call them my American dad and mom, and they are very happy to be my dad and mom in the United States. They are a good example of Americans who love and care for every one they meet regardless of race, color or nationality.

They are life members of St. Vincent De Paul and have contributed significantly to their parish, St Clement of Rome, helping many orphans and the poor in the United States, Africa, Asia and South America. I am so grateful to them and pray for them always not just because they are good to me, but mainly because they are good examples of what it means to love as Christians. My experiences with them, the priest I was living with, and some other white family friends, made me at first think that racism was a fairy tale, but as the taxi driver told me, a few months in the United States was too soon to feel immune to racism.

My First Unexpected and Surprising Experience

My first experience of racism came when I did not expect it, at a church dinner. I arrived a little late, and sat at a table with a group of two white women and two white men, whom I supposed to be Catholics. We greeted each other, and I listened for a while before I joined their conversation. After a few minutes, they left the table, and I assumed they left because they had finished eating. Soon after, a woman from another table, came to me and whispered in my ear, "Father, how is it that as soon as you sat at the table to eat with those folks, they all left the table for you? Are you sure you washed your body before coming to this ceremony?" I was amazed, speechless. She bent low to hear my answer. What came out of my mouth was "What do you mean by that?" She tried to calm me with "Don't mind me. I was just kidding, okay?"

She smiled an unnatural smile, and I asked her, "So you take what you have just told me as a joke? If I had made this comment to you and claimed it as a joke, you would have taken it as abuse and made a case of it." At this, she ran away and joined her companions, who had been watching us. They laughed loudly. I then knew how a victim of racism feels, as I left the place in annoyance. It could be that she was really joking but to have made me know why those racist men and women left me to eat alone and adding an insult to it was the same as doing what they did. What surprised and hurt me most was that my first experience of racism came from a white woman. I know that white women in the United States are champions of emancipation of women against discrimination and unequal treatment from men. Many other women's groups in other parts of the world are taking their lead from them.

I have been a sympathizer of their cause, but I get so disappointed and discouraged when I hear and notice that many of them are also racists and treat others unequally because of color, in working places, government offices, schools, church meetings, and even in convents. If American women are struggling against inequality based on gender, at the same time treating others unequally based on color, they are making a big mistake and may find it difficult to get the type of support they need. I feel that all women whether white or black who are fighting against inequality in both church and state should first purge themselves of any kind of prejudice and treat all human beings the way they would expect others to treat them, for their war against inequality to be more meaningful.

My experience at the church dinner party also made me start comparing the way we treat white people in Nigeria when we see them and how these two white men and two white women treated me. I was the pastor of Mater Misericoridiae Catholic Church, Port Harcourt Nigeria for four years before coming to the United States to study. Port Harcourt is a Nigerian Southern city rich in oil and natural gas. There are many white oil men and women living there and working in the various oil drilling companies, oil servicing, and marketing companies, such as Halliburton, Shell, Agip, Schlumberger, Mobil, Elf and so on. We used to be very friendly to them. We also used to make sure that they were given special places to stay at ceremonies and served them well with special food and drinks. We enjoyed eating at table with them and discussing some important issues as friends. There was no issue of feeling superior or inferior to them or their feeling superior or inferior to us. I felt it was going to be the same. I was disappointed that here in America it is different.

I know that not every person would behave the way they behaved, at the same time, their attitude made me start comparing the difference between the way some people treat their pet animals and how they treat their fellow human beings who are of a different color. If the pet cats and dogs of those four people came to stay with them at table, or in their living rooms, or even in their bed rooms, they may not have walked away or chased their pet animals away. Does it mean that there are some people here who would prefer to love and treat their pet animals better than they would treat blacks who are their fellow human beings? That experience made me start wondering if this is possible.

My Hospital Experiences

My second shocking experience of racism occurred while I was ministering to the sick. The Chaplain on call at a nearby hospital paged me to respond to the request of a Catholic family to have their father anointed. When I arrived at what I assumed to be the patient's room, I asked the assembled family members if I were indeed at the right room. I received no answer. I mentioned the patient's name, and still received no answer. Disturbed, I inquired at the nurses' station, and the nurse assured me that I had the correct room number. I then called the chaplain to confirm the name of the patient. He asked me what had happened, and I told him. He explained that the family had asked for a white priest. I could not understand what color of one's skin has to do with the Sacrament if we really believe that it is Jesus who administers the Sacrament through the priest. Is the color of the skin stronger than our faith for some people?

On another occasion, I was making a routine hospital visit to a Caucasian man in his seventies, a cancer patient. When I entered his room, I noticed by his mood that he was feeling uncomfortable. When I began to speak to him, he ordered me out of his room and shouted, "Who brought you into my room?" I apologized and left quickly, wondering what offense I had given. I did not immediately think of racism, but considered his pain, his age, and the possibility of some bad experiences that had soured him against the Church. However, his African American nurse apologized to me for his attitude, saying that he does not want a black man or woman to touch him. I was shocked, and was tempted to doubt her, but I remembered my earlier experience with the family of the other dying man.

At midnight that night, I received a call to come to the hospital to anoint a dying patient. I rushed there, and was astonished to find that the patient was the man who had ordered me out. Unfortunately, the man died shortly before I could anoint him. I blessed his body, and did what I could to comfort and feel with his family members who did not know about my earlier experiences with him.

Comments:

The above research and interviews show that there is still racial inequality in the Catholic Church in the United States of America. Though the interviews do not account for what is happening in all the Catholic dioceses in America, it gives us an idea of what could be happening in the Catholic communities in other parts of the United States. The question remains: What are the measures that could be applied to fight against racial discrimination of any type in the American Catholic Church?

CHAPTER SIX
FINDING OUT THE TRUTH ABOUT RACISM IN THE AMERICAN JUDAISM FROM THE 1600s TO THE PRESENT

In my effort to investigate the truth about the role played by American early religions in the racial crisis of this country as reported by my African American taxi driver, I decided to include Judaism. In this chapter, we look at Judaism, which came as early as Christianity in this country, to find out how far discrimination in the synagogues is affecting the lives of Americans who identify themselves as Jewish. We attempt to answer the following questions.

1. How did Judaism come to America?
2. Who were the early members of the Jewish communities that brought Judaism to America?
3. How were they treated initially by the dominant white Christian Americans and did that affect the way they treat each other in the synagogues today?
4. Is there discrimination currently going on among Jews in the American synagogues and communities?
5. If there is discrimination, what measures could be applied to fight against racism in the American synagogues?

The Coming of Judaism to America

Historians believe that some Jews were among Columbus' crew when he first set foot on American soil. Organized Jewish life in the New World began, however, in the 1600s when the descendants of Jews expelled from Spain in 1492 settled in what would become The United States.[305] These settlers formed the first Jewish community—Congregation Shearith Isreal—in the British colony in Newport, Rhode Island. In 1763, they built the first synagogue in America, Touro synagogue.[306]

Jewish immigration to the United States from Europe continued to increase, especially in the 1800s, until Judaism, "developed from a tiny minority to the point where, along with PROTESTANTISM and ROMAN CATHOLICISM, it has become one of the country's three major faiths."[307] The first Jewish immigrants were mainly Sephardic; from Spain, but later in the nineteenth century thousands of Ashkenazim Jews migrated from Germany and from other part of Europe. Initially, all worshiped together in the same synagogues, following the Sephardic rites.[308]

By the end of the nineteenth century, and the beginning of the 20th century, there was mass immigration of Jews. Calvin Goldscheider and Jacob Neusner, estimate that from 1880 to 1920, more than 3.5 million Jews came to USA from Russia, Poland, Rumania, Hungry and Austria.[309] The need to respond to the new social and cultural challenges of the American society brought about reformations within Judaism, and divisions into Orthodox, Conservative, and Reform Judaism as it is today. Another division of Judaism in America includes Sephardic, Ashkenazi, and Black Jews.

The Sephardic Jews

The Sephardic Jews refers to a group of Jews in Diaspora. "*Sepharad* is the Hebrew name for Spain, where most of the Sephardic Jews lived before their expulsion in 1492."[310] Some Sephardic communities were also found in places like the Mediterranean Basin, North Africa, and the Middle East. After their ejection from Spain, and Portugal where they were not allowed to practice their religion in 1496, many resettled in the domains of the Ottoman Empire, which gladly welcomed them. Some relocated to the New World, the Middle East, North Africa, and Erets Isreal.[311]

They can be distinguished from the Ashkenazim Jews by the holiday customs, liturgical rites, pronunciation of Hebrew words, and the cuisine.[312] They used Hebrew or ladino for prayers and used Judeo-Spanish or Judezmo, which was a mixture of Hebrew and Spanish as their daily language.[313] Many of them are now settled in South Africa, Canada, Mexico, Latin America, England, and in the United States. The greatest Sephardic communities are found in Israel since the creation of Israel as a state.[314] The term *Sephardic* is now used in a more inclusive sense, to include all Jews who follow the Sephardic rites of worship, traditions, and customs, even if their fore fathers and mothers never lived in Spain.[315]

Ashkenazim Jews

The Ashkenazim is another Jewish group in Diaspora. The word Ashkenazim refers to "the name given to the group of Jews who were originally from Germany and France (and their descendants). The word Ashkenazim is the Hebrew name for Germany."[316] As Sephardic Jews were expelled from Spain in 1492, Ashkenazim Jews were earlier expelled from England in 1290 and from France in 1306 and in 1394. After their ejection, many of them resettled in other European countries, but mainly in Germany, Poland, and Austria.[317]

These groups are "distinguishable from Sephardic and 'Oriental' Jewish communities by virtue of their folkways, outlook, cultural heritage, and religious traditions."[318] They spoke Yiddish. They constitute a greater percentage of world Jewish population, despite the fact that many of them were killed by the Nazis during the Second World War.[319] Many are now settled in the state of Israel, different parts of Europe, Latin America, South Africa, and in the United States.

Black Jews

The third group of Americans who identify themselves as Jewish are the Black Jews. "The term *Black Jews*, or *Hebrews*, refers to several African-American religious movements that proclaim Judaism as the true religion of African Americans and claim a racial connection with the tribes of Israel through either descent from Queen of Sheba and the Ethiopian Jews or the 10 lost tribes of Israel."[320] Many black Jews also migrated to the United States of American from some African countries such as Ethiopia, Uganda and South Africa. Some black Jewish communities, especially those that migrated from Ethiopia, worship comfortably in the synagogues with other Jews, particularly in the reformed congregations. Some others have their own brand of Judaism, with doctrines that could be described as "a syncretistic mix of black nationalism, Judaism and Christianity."[321]

The Division between Sephardic and Ashkenazim

As already indicated, the Sephardic Jews migrated to the United States first, while the Ashkenazim migrated later and more so in the 1800s.[322] The Sephardic Jews and the Ashkenazi Jews initially got along very well and worshiped in the same synagogues despite the fact that they had different rites of worship.[323] However, as many immigrants continued to arrive, from northern and eastern Europe, the Ashkenazim outnumbered the earlier colonial settlers who were mainly Sephardic. "The increase in number and in diversity of background created strains within the Jewish community."[324]

There was resistance of Ashkenazim to the Sephardic system of conducting the rituals. This led to the formation of new Ashkenazim congregations and establishment of different synagogues that followed their own manner of worship.[325] In the words of Robert M. Seltzer, "Acculturated native American Jews found the newcomers alien, abrasive, and uncouth, while immigrants found their Americanized fellow Jews lax in religious observance."[326] Ashkenazim Jews, influenced by German language and culture, felt more enlightened than the Sephardic and brought reforms to American Judaism, which challenged many of the traditional practices. For example, the German speaking Jews arrived in the United States with some practices such as the introduction of organ music, the rabbi delivering a weekly sermon, and the translation of certain prayers from Hebrew to German language.[327] These reforms were foreign to Sephardic Jews.

Discrimination against the Jews in the United States

Discrimination against the Jewish immigrants in the United States, like that against the blacks and the Indians, started as far back as the foundation of this country. "As members of discernable minority groups in American society, both Black and Jewish Americans have been and are the recipients of prejudice and discrimination."[328] Unlike the blacks and Indians, however, Jews were not subjected to slavery, but they were subject to the same type of racial discrimination that was common. There were discriminations against Jews in admissions to colleges and universities, and many hotels and restaurants refused services to them.[329] The worst was that "entire industries declared themselves off-limits to

Jewish employment."[330] In many American states, such as Arizona, New Hampshire, and Maine, overt discrimination against Jews was manifest till 1948.[331]

On the religious side, in the 1800s, and in the early 1900s, Protestants discriminated against both the American Jews and Catholics. Thus, Jews initially saw their stay in America as that of visitors in a strange land dominated by Anglo-Saxon Protestants.[332] The common image of Jews by some Christians, as Christ killers, helped to bring about hatred for Jews by hate groups like the Ku Klux Klan who also claim to be "Christian people defending the Christian way of life."[333] In the 1920s, the American Jews suffered so much in the hands of Ku Klux Klan who described them as a parasitic race of businessmen, communist conspirators, and the damned."[334] The Klan not only attacked and lynched blacks, but also Jews. "Both Black and Jewish Americans have experienced the extreme forms of animosity in America—lynching in the first instance and mob violence in the second simply because of their discernable differences from the majority populace in the United States."[335]

An example of lynching of Jews was the case of Leo Frank in 1913, a Jewish manager of an Atlanta pencil factory. He was accused and convicted of killing a teen-age white girl who was one of his employees."[336] As Frank was being tried, crowds outside the court were shouting "Hang the Jew!" He was first condemned to death without enough evidence, but later the sentence was reduced to life imprisonment after lots of appeal to save his life. Despite all the efforts to save his life, a vigilante group abducted him and hanged him in 1915.[337] However, after the Leo Frank case, there was a decline in anti Semitic activities in America. Polls carried out between 1937 and 1962 record a remarkable decline in anti Semitism.[338] This, however, does not mean that discrimination against the Jews has finally stopped in America. Some hate groups or white supremacy groups such as the KKK if given the chance would still see them and the blacks as subjects of attacks.

However, some of these Neo-Nazi groups are still operating openly and having their meetings. Their websites are still full of hateful statments against Jews and blacks. Occasionally we hear about the burning of black churches, especially in the south by members of such groups. Some black residents living in some all-white neighborhoods where the members of such groups are concentrated are constantly being terrorized to abandon or re-sell their homes and go for safer and more tolerant neighborhoods. I have some family friends who are presently being threatened by some members of these hate groups living in their neighborhood in west county of St. Louis. They told me how many times they have alerted the police to help them, but the help has not been effective enough to stop these groups from terrorizing them to leave the neighborhood. They have put their newly bought house on sale.

From what we have seen earlier in this book, many of these supremacy groups have a long history of intimidating and killing blacks, Jews, and whites who support freedom and democracy for all. Some pastors both whites and blacks were afraid of allowing me to publish my interviews with them because of fear of attacks by members of these groups. I was warned by some friends that writing this book and publishing it may expose me to their attacks. Though there may be a sort of surveillance over them by security agents, it is still hard to understand why they have not been formally classified under "terrorist organizations" and included in the war against terror. I like and support the war on terror. I also believe that all sources of terror whether from inside or from outside should be fought against and rooted out in order to protect all Americans. Even if some of these groups are no longer allowed by law to attack people physically, their continued existence and use of the media to make public hateful comments against other Americans is enough intimidation to people. It is against democracy and freedom. I wonder how people do not see terror threat in using the media to suggest the killing of all black babies in the womb. We shall revisit this issue in the next chapter to see how it should be a concern to the American churches or religious institutions. Terrorism is evil whether from white supremacy groups, or from black gangs or from Hispanic gangs or from any foreign groups. It does not deserve a lighter attention. Neither the identity of the attacker nor that of the victim justifies it.

The Jews and Civil Rights Movements of the 1960s

The civil rights movements of the 1960s also involved many Jews who became political allies to African Americans. The alliance between African Americans and the Jews in the 1960s was largely because of common interest in social justice and for the fact that both were seen and treated as the minority and inferior to the Anglo- Saxon white majority. According to Hubert G. Locke, "Given the historic Jewish concern with issues of social justice, traceable to Biblical times and the common experience of Jewish and Black Americans with rejection by the larger American populace, it also is not surprising to discover the emergence of a common set of interests between the two groups."[339]

The alliance between African Americans and Jews in the fight against injustice and oppression suffered in the late 1960s and in the early 1970s. This was created mainly due to the political development in the Middle East.

> The Six-Day war of 1967 made many Jewish Americans fear for the state of Israel and strengthened their interest in it. At the same time many African Americans identified their struggle for civil rights as part of a wider movement against European hegemony within the developing world. They tended increasingly to support the Palestinian and the Arab states in their conflict with Israel.[340]

Another blow to the relationship between the Black and Jewish leaders in the 1970s was the costly meeting between Andrew Young, Jr., the first Black United State Ambassador to the United Nations, and representatives of the Palestinian Organization. "For Jewish leaders, Young had committed the unpardonable political sin, while in Black circles Young had been made an unwitting victim of excessive and misplaced Jewish sensitivity."[341] Since then, the relationship between African Americans and American Jews has not improved significantly especially in the New York area where there had been physical clashes between blacks and Jews.

Since the middle of the twentieth century, American Jews have seen economic and social progress, especially since the "abandoned practice of setting quotas for the admission of Jewish applicants to colleges, universities, and professional schools."[342] The government post war affirmative actions of the 1940s, 1950s, and 1960s such as the GI, FHA and VA mortgages, which were disproportionately administered to favor only European immigrants, also helped many American Jews to achieve economic progress up to the middle class level, and they are now assimilated into the class of white majority of this country.[343]

Discrimination against Jews of Color by White Jews in the synagogues

Recently also there have been many reports of white Jews discriminating against Jews of color. As we shall see in the interviews, in some synagogues, a black Jew may not be prevented from entering the synagogue, but he or she may not be surprised when a white Jew turns and asks him or her "Are you also Jewish?"

Outside the synagogues there have been reports of white Jews not wanting to live in the same neighborhoods with blacks and other people of color. One Jewish woman told me what happened when she moved into the house where she is now living with her three bi-racial children. Her next-door neighbor was also a Jewish woman in her seventies. When the Jewish neighbor saw the bi-racial children, she called her landlord, who was white, and asked him why he allowed this woman to move into the building with these *Nigger* kids. She threatened to get the other whites who live in the same neighborhood to sign a petition accusing her fellow Jewish woman of criminal acts so as to throw her and her children out of the place.

Inevitably, the innocent children heard their mother arguing with her neighbor about the color of their skin. They asked her, "Mom what is wrong with the color of our skin?" Of course, there was nothing wrong with the children's identity as colored Jews. To get to know more what is happening in the Jewish synagogues and communities and why, I had to engage in serious discussions with Jewish rabbis from different parts of the country. I present here the ones that allowed me to publish the details of our discussions.

Interview with Rabbi Carpers Funnye

Rabbi Carpers Funnye

The first Rabbi I had the privileged to interview was Rabbi Carpers Funnye. He is the Rabbi in charge of the Ethiopian Synagogue in Chicago.

"Rabbi Funnye, I have heard complaints from many Jewish friends that the Ashkenazi Jews who see themselves as white Jews do not like worshiping in the synagogues with the Jews of color—the Sephardic who look more Mediterranean and the black Jews. Is it true?"

"That may be true, but it depends on the Ashkenazi community. That feeling is not common with all Ashkenazi communities. There are some Ashkenazi communities that are welcoming and encourage people from different denominations. One of the things that seems to happen is that, for instance, if I go into an Ashkenazi Synagogue and I have not been invited there, and maybe they were not expecting a black Rabbi to come and speak, ultimately some one in the congregation may come to me and ask me if I am Jewish, although I wear my little skull cap or yamica and have all the other things Jews use in praying, including the Jewish prayer book. Some one may still come and ask me if I am Jewish. Yes, one can see racism in that question, because the person who asks that question is assuming that if you do not look like me who am white, you can not be Jewish."

"I agree with you, Rabbi. That question is not only embarrassing but also racist. As you said, it means that the person who asks that question believes that to be Jewish is to be white, and if you are not white this synagogue is not for you. This confirms what some one complained about. The overemphasis on the color of the skin which is a problem in most Christian churches, as it is a problem in the wider American society, is also a problem in American Judaism. Do you now believe that there is racism in Judaism?"

"Unfortunately, yes."

"Is there any marked physical attribute that differentiates those who see themselves as white Jews from the others?"

"Particularly here in America, the Ashkenazi community that came from Eastern and Western Europe tend to see itself and labels itself as white, although in the history of Europe, Jews have never been considered as white. That is a new phenomenon with the Jewish communities that are coming to America from Europe. It is not more than a hundred years since this started to happen. The Sephardic communities have the physical qualities of people from the Mediterranean, North Africa, Algeria, Palestine and other places. They have dark hair, dark eyes, and even darker skin. The African communities are from Ethiopia and other parts of Africa, and are just like any other African."

"Is there any national body that unites the whole of Jews in America regardless of color and other differences? If there is such a body, what is it doing to help make the Jews in America understand themselves better and welcome each other better regardless of color?"

"There is the Jewish Federation here in Chicago which tends to treat all Jews the same. Then there is also the Reformed Movement, which is also a National body. They have a more welcoming attitude to non-white Jews, though it may not be the same everywhere. I do not know if it is the same in St. Louis, because I know that there is a reformed movement there."

"Are these national bodies doing any thing to help solve the problem of racial divide in Judaism?"

"Nothing is being seriously done. However, there is another well known organization in San Francisco called the institute for Jewish and Community Research. This institute is working very hard to let the white Jewish communities know that we have brothers and sister who are Puerto Ricans, Chinese, Cubans, blacks, that may look a bit different physically, but are still very much part of our community and we need to be interested in opening the doors of our institutions, of our hearts to these other Jews that do not look like us. This institute is a nationally known organization that travels round the country, speaking to other Jews of their inclusion."

"What do you recommend as measures to be able to overcome racial prejudice in Judaism?"

"We all have to realize that Jews come from every color of the human family and that when we see this stranger that comes into our midst, we can not assume that they are not one of us. We need to be more welcoming and tolerant as Jews. The administrators of synagogues, and Rabbis, need to understand that people are on a spiritual journey, and Judaism is the natural place for people to go because it is the mother of Christianity."

"Is there any other measure that could be applied?"

"People need to read more and be aware or be more enlightened about the diversity of the human family. It is a big mistake for a people to think that one color or one race is the ultimate and every other one is not important. I will also recommend having some enlightenment programs like seminars, workshops, and other activities that could bring people together to know each other the more and appreciate the diversity of cultures."

Interview with Rabbi Randy Fleisher

Rabbi Randy Fleisher

My second interview was with Rabbi Randy Fleisher. He is the Associate Rabbi in the Central Reform Congregation in St. Louis.

"Rabbi Fleisher, in our Christian churches, we sometimes experience the same discrimination that is unfortunately experienced in the society. The same problem is being reported among Jews of different background. Some Jewish Americans who look Mediterranean, Asian, Mexican, Latin American, and black complain of discrimination by some Jews who now identify themselves as white. Does this truly happen?"

"Yes, I think that is probably true in some communities. It depends on the community. For instance, here in our own synagogue, we work very hard to make sure that it is a place where every one can worship comfortably. We have a number of Jews of color. Most of them are African Americans who converted to Judaism from Christianity. Here we also have bi-racial families. We also have children of color who were adopted by white Jews who are part of us. We work very hard to make sure that such ugly behaviors of racism don't occur among us. We had a whole lot of programs last year to address racism. We emphasized the fact that white Jews need to be conscious of the fact that Judaism is multiracial and that we at the same time work on issues of racial justice in the synagogues. It is as important to address issues of racial justice within the general community. We also need to ensure that there is racial justice within the synagogue."

"Tell me more, Rabbi. I want to hear more."

"You can see in this office some posters that depict our multiracial nature and the fact that Jews come from different colors and are all part of our synagogue."

"I hope it will be like this in all American synagogues, especially the very conservative and orthodox ones."

"So we try to make people know that Judaism is multiracial. We do not deny the fact that, in America, racism is still a serious problem. I do not think that there is any community in America that is free from it. So we try our best to make people feel free to worship with us, though we may not be perfect. Our goal is to make Judaism as diverse as possible."

"In the history of the world and in this country, the Jews have suffered so much from racism just like the blacks. Now some Jews are white. Do the white European Americans in this country accept them as white?"

"I know that this country has a history of anti-Semitism. There are some Anglo-Saxon whites who still hate Jews for being Jewish. I think Jews in this country have been successful. So this is a tricky question; I think that there is still racism against Jews in this country but not as intense as the African Americans and other people of color are now experiencing it. There is a book I will like you to read; the title is *How Jews became White Folks*. I think what the book is saying is that there was a time when Jews in this country were not seen as white--not white in terms of skin color, but white in terms of social and economic construct. I think there is now an acceptance of Jews in this country as part of the majority even though they are in the real sense a minority by number. It is not the same with African Americans. So there is now a difference."

"That is true, Rabbi; there is really a difference. I will like to have that book and read it so as to see what happened and how the Jews who suffered racism with African Americans have risen from the former state in which they were kept with African Americans to a state of whiteness and to a different economic and social construct. I think that state of better economic and social construct will also be good for African Americans, and for other minorities, if whatever made their counterparts what they are can be applied equally."

"I think the way the Jews were taken as a despised race in Nazi

Germany is the way the African Americans are taken in the United States. I think the history is different now for the Jews."

"That is history, Rabbi. Thank you so much for talking with me."

Interview with a Jewish lay Woman (Name and Picture withheld)

My last interview was with a Jewish lay woman. It was good to hear from the perspective of a Jewish lay woman. I met her in one of the synagogues and she agreed to speak with me.

"Thank you for agreeing to speak with me. I heard that we have Sephardic Jews, Ashkenazi, and black Jews. How do you identify yourself?"

"That is my biggest problem and I feel I should tell you the truth about what is going on. The truth is that everybody has a problem classifying me under any of those categories. I am biologically Ashkenazi but in my family I seem to be a bit darker than every one. My family sees me as Sephardic because I look more ethnic as a Jewish woman. For my family, which is Ashkenazi, and for most Ashkenazi Jews in the United States, Sephardic is a negative term and it means black. I do not have any problem with Sephardic Jews because I look Sephardic. The black Jews, on their part, have a problem accepting me as black because I am light skinned. So I am in a purgatory of not knowing where to go and where to be accepted. That is my biggest problem with Judaism because every person wants to know what am I and nobody wants to accept who I am as a Jewish woman. I look like original Jew or ethnic."

"You made mention of your family and the fact that you are a bit darker than the other members of your family and so they take you as Sephardic or black by their own interpretation. Did this impression about the color of your skin affect the way your family treated you or is treating you now?"

"I am completely ostracized even from my own family. They made a lot of excuses but the truth was that I do not look Ashkenazi, which means that I am not white enough and with blond hair. For them, I was bad even by sight because I have darker coiled hair."

"How did you feel about your family not accepting you?"

"I grew up feeling like I am disgusting, even though when I look at my picture, I know I was really beautiful. They made me hate myself as if I was repulsive."

"Do you still relate well with your family?"

"They have absolutely nothing to do with me now. As I was growing up, nearing the age of being legally on my own, they hastily threw me out of the house.

In the part of St. Louis where I was born and grew up, there were no Middle Eastern people, and so it was either you are white or you are black. So since I did not fall into the white category, I was thrust into the black category, which I feel is a shame to my old blond mother who treated me as if I was not her child."

"Can you please tell me how you were treated by your mother?"

"She never liked to talk to me as her child, she never liked to wash me or touch my hair, and she never wanted to take me out in public like my other siblings. I grew up in West County of St. Louis which was a rich white area, without a winter coat, without gloves, and without boots."

"What was the reaction of your father to what your mother was doing to you?"

"He did not bother about me. He was afraid of fighting with my mother. He really did not do anything to protect me. Many years later, my father started sending me flowers at work. Each time, he would tell me not to tell any one that he sent me flowers.

One day he asked me what I needed for my birthday and I told him that I only needed him to hug me and openly tell me that he loves me as his daughter. He told me that he can't do it but that he can buy me electronics. He bought the electronics and secretly dropped it near my door. I saw it and threw it away. I called him and told him that if he was not proud to acknowledge me as his daughter in public, because I am not white enough, he should stop sending me gifts. I told him that I was no longer a child and that I know when someone is just trying to cover up just to satisfy his guilty conscience."

"I am sorry for all these ugly experiences. I know how bad such treatments can make one feel. In this synagogue, are you accepted to worship freely?"

"I am still shopping for synagogues to worship in without embarrassment. I stopped going to synagogues for a long time because of the hateful attitude of some white Jews in the synagogues. I specifically came to try this one. I heard that people of color are free to worship here. I can't say much yet, until I have started worshiping with them. In most synagogues I have visited in different parts of this country, especially the Ashkenazi ones, it is true that no one will tell you to get out of the synagogue because of the law, but people embarrass you by turning and looking at you as if you are a criminal or drug addict or prostitute that is missing her way and has come to worship with very righteous ones. After worship, you greet people; no one responds or talks to you. You leave the synagogue feeling unhappy more than you were before you entered to worship God!"

"I appreciate your spending this time with me and for being open to say your mind. I know that there may be other ethnic Jewish people or Jews of color in this country who are also suffering this type of color embarrassment. The information you have shared with me will help such people to know that they are not the only ones suffering from this short coming of the American society and the fact that all of us have to join hands to bring these ugly and uncivilized behaviors to a stop."

Comments

From the above research and interviews, it is clear that there is truly racial discrimination going on in and outside the American synagogues. Though these interviews do not account for what is happening in every synagogue in United States of America, they give us an idea of what could be happening in other synagogues and Jewish communities. From my observations, I have the following questions to ask: Why is it that many American white Jews who suffered discriminations along with blacks in the past are now discriminating against Jews of color whom they feel whiter than and against other people of color? Is discrimination (even against family members who look darker), the best way to express whiteness? What are the measures that could be applied to fight against discrimination of any type in American synagogues and communities?

CHAPTER SEVEN
PASTORAL CARE MINISTRY, RACISM, AND POVERTY IN AMERICA

It is the pastoral responsibility of any church or religion to listen to the complaints of its members or, in fact, to be concerned with whatever causes any human distress. Racial oppression is one of those causes of human distress, which religion should without reservation or condition respond to, irrespective of who is the oppressor or the oppressed. According to my taxi driver, the American churches are not listening enough to the people of color to help them out of what has been causing their distress for hundreds of years. It was his dissatisfaction with the way the churches handled and are handling the racial inequality in this country that attracted my attention to discuss in this chapter the pastoral response of the American churches to racial inequality in United States of America.

My intention is to find out if there are ways racism has, in our modern or post modern times, conditioned the type of pastoral care that is given to people of color in their long struggle against inequality and oppression. When people are disturbed and find it very difficult to handle their problems, they run to God. One of the visible signs of God's presence, where people could get some defense when they feel defenseless is the church for Christians and the synagogue for Jews. Other religions also have their own places of consolation and support. It is questionable and hard to understand when a people feel that they have suffered for centuries from oppression and are still not getting the required pastoral response from their religious groups in their painful struggle, especially when racial oppression is continuous in diverse ways or when past racial oppression is still affecting millions of lives.

We have already seen from the racial history of all the American mainline churches that Negro slaves were allowed to receive baptism as Christians, hear the word of God, and receive some limited pastoral care only after so many years of deprivation, based on the fact that the institution of slavery needed to be justified and protected by most of the churches. When they were allowed to receive some pastoral instructions, it was rationed out to them with conditions. As L. Richard Bradley observes, "One should note that the idea of religious education for 'the colored people' was determined by what Scriptural material would make the Negro a good slave and not by what would make him a good Christian."[344]

The pastoral attention given to the people of color has, however, improved since the removal of segregation laws in the 1960s. Blacks are no longer forced to sit at the back of the churches and in the galleries, though there are still some Christians from different denominations who would get up and leave their seats just because a black person is sitting next to them during church worship. In the past, blacks were not allowed to become pastors, but now the story is much different. Many all-white parishes of different denominations now accept black pastors to minister to them, though there are still some all-white parishes or churches that do not want black pastors to minister to them or black seminarians to do their vicarage trainings in their parishes as we saw in the interviews and recent incidents. In the past, most white patients in the hospitals did not want black pastors to touch them or to anoint them, but now many white patients do not mind the pastor's color, though there are still some white patients, as we saw in the previous chapters, who do not want black pastors to touch them or to minister to them.

However, pastoral care is not limited to what happens in the church premises or in the hospital or school premises, as we shall see. So the following questions are yet to be answered.

1. How attentively have the American churches listened to the stories of the people of color to know what their real problems are and how to prophetically speak out for them?

2. How effective have the pastoral ministry of the American Churches been able to respond to the greatest effect of racism, which is poverty, in the 21st century?

3. How do we identify the poor in the present American society?

4. How can the American churches join hands with the government to address the roots of poverty with the intention of helping the poor minorities in American society to be more economically self reliant?

Our discussion in this chapter is not limited only to the mainline churches which have been under discussion, but also to other churches which used to be part of these mainline churches or which were formed later in the twentieth and twenty first centuries, for example, United Church of Christ, Salvation Army, Apostolic Church, Seventh Day Adventist, Pentecostal Churches, and all the new Evangelical denominations.

Pastoral Care Ministry and what it involves in the Twenty First Century

Pastoral care ministry according to Alastair V. Campbell, "is that aspect of the ministry of the church which is concerned with the well being of individuals and of communities."[345] Individuals and communities in the American context could refer to blacks, whites, Hispanics, Indians, Jews, and Asians. Taking care of people pastorally is not limited to just celebrating the Word and the Sacraments inside the church on Sundays as some conservative people see it. Clifton E. Olmstead, the author of *Religion in America Past and Present,* observes, "To the impressive number of church members whose social and economic views were of conservative bent, the task of organized Christianity was to provide instruction and worship; for the more unfortunate elements in the community there was the obligation to grant charity and evangelization, since in order to rebuild society one would first have to rebuild men."[346] Emmanuel Y. Lartey recommends that, "pastoral care has to do with the whole well-being of the whole person."[347] The whole person refers to any person, created in the image and likeness of God irrespective of color, class, race, age, and sex.

Pastoral care ministry could take place in the church office, hospital, prison, industry, school, and even in the black ghettoes. David Hogue recommends that pastoral care could take place not only outside the church premises, but also should involve listening to people's life stories anywhere possible. "Stories are at the heart of ministry, whether they are told or heard in the sanctuary, the hospital room, the prison, or the counseling office."[348] Listening to stories in this situation does not refer to listening to the stories of a particular racial group or of some people more than the others, but giving equal listening to all.

Serious Omission in American Pastoral Care Literature

Sharon G. Thornton in her book, *Broken yet Beloved*, observes that recent American literature of pastoral care fails to offer the needed ideas to address the particular anguish of people in America of the 21st century. While acknowledging the efforts made by the American pastoral experts in some other areas, she criticizes them as having conceived and practiced their theories within academic settings among persons who are mainly white, middle class, and normally male. She argues that "the historical context and social and economic realities that contribute to the hardship and misery of people were rarely discussed. And the political conditions that militate against wholeness were not talked about at all."[349]

Thornton wonders why "the special circumstances of people who are poor and marginalized were largely absent from their writings."[350] Does it mean that those who are not white, middle class, and male are not human beings? In this context, one is right to point out that racism is one of the major causes of this shortcoming in American pastoral theology. Racism can also hinder experts in pastoral care from being sensitive to human suffering, especially when it does not affect the pastoral expert either by race or sex.

With this shortcoming, the American church leaders may not be getting comprehensive advice from their pastoral theologians on how to give equal pastoral attention to all the moral evils that affect human persons in both church and society. Church leaders are rightly fighting a war against abortion as a moral evil. I have not observed that same amount of effort being made by church leaders to fight against racism or racial inequality in America. I do not see racism or racial inequality as a lesser moral evil than abortion, because the worst genocides in the history of the world have been caused by racism. The killing of six million Jews during the Second World War by Hitler and his Nazi white supremacists is a good example. No person was able to calculate the number of babies in their mothers' wombs who died along with their adult mothers in those gas chambers. Racism can affect the life of both the adult and the child in the womb.

I am pro-life myself and I believe in the rights of the unborn child. I do not mind the color of the unborn child, for he or she is a human being made in the image and likeness of God. I also believe in the rights of adult human beings to exist on equal conditions regardless of their color or race. Whatever affects the life of the child in the womb should be fought against and whatever affects the life of an adult human being should be given equal attention. It may be right to argue that the child in the womb is defenseless. There are so many adult human beings who have been defenseless against inequality and the oppressive structures that have caused their poverty for centuries in this country, as we shall see when we shall discuss the revelations of Hurricane Katrina.

I believe that the church leaders in this country have always received good advice through the writings of pastoral theologians on how best to fight against abortion. I am always happy when I see young men and women of all colors from different Christian denominations and even other religions, travel to Washington D.C. on every 22nd of January to carry out a peaceful march in protest against abortion. The pro-life groups are able to mobilize thousands of white youths and youths of color in this country to peacefully protest against abortion as an evil that should be condemned by persons of all colors. I have been so happy with the number of pro-life organizations formed at the parish levels, diocesan levels, and outside the churches to help defend the rights of the unborn child.

Many of these pro-life organizations rightly spend a lot of money to support whatever it takes to fight against abortion. I have taken part in the conferences of so many pro-life groups and I do appreciate the efforts they are making. Though these efforts have not stopped abortion in this country, at the same time one can count on the positive effects of the efforts being made. To be honest, these efforts are helping to form the consciences of millions of people in this country, especially the youths, to respect life. I was shocked when I heard that "over 1.5 million babies are killed every year through abortion in America alone." I love the effort being made to calculate the number of lives that are being affected through abortion every year.

All these efforts to check and control or stop abortion are godly. As already indicated, I have not observed the same type of attention either from the churches or the state in fighting against racism, which for centuries has affected millions of lives especially the lives of the people of color. I have, however, observed and read about how racism has evolved and has been modified from human enslavement to segregation laws and from segregation laws to racial inequality, as it exists today. I have not observed the mobilization of millions of American youths of all colors by church human rights commissions to travel to Washington D.C. on Martin Luther King's day to peacefully protest against discrimination and inequality, which is still "big news." I only observe African Americans in good numbers with a few white sympathizers march along the streets in some American cities like St. Louis. The small number of white participants in such peaceful protests may give one the impression that fighting for racial justice is mainly the black person's business. The impression is different when one sees large numbers of people of all colors protest against abortion. I wonder if any one has been interested in calculating yearly how many people die of poverty or poor conditions due to long periods of neglect and unequal treatments. No one knew the magnitude of poverty in just one American city, New Orleans, until Hurricanes Katrina struck. Sociologists and economists may know how many other millions are living in other American cities in similar very poor conditions, but this may not be known to the general public.

I observe Pro-life groups respond to any rhetoric or argument in favor of abortion from politicians and from media men and women. On the other hand, I observe some lack of interest and neglect in responding to racial stereotyping made against the lives of innocent black babies in the womb. For example, I was shocked on the 28th of September 2005; there was a radio broadcast by Bill Bennett, a well-known American statesman who has served this country in different capacities. He said, "You could abort every black baby in this country, and your crime rate would go down."[351] I was so disappointed to hear such an open and hateful broadcast. This is the most ridiculous statement I have ever heard a human person make in my life. It is wrong to use the media to threaten the lives of innocent black babies in the womb. This reminds me of how wrong it is to use the same media to threaten the lives of innocent Americans by terrorist groups. I was worried about the impression such an open broadcast will make in the minds of the younger white Americans about their black friends and class mates in the schools and churches. I expected a swift reaction from church leaders, church human rights commissions or social justice offices, and reputable Americans in condemnation of such broadcast that can only create more racial hatred and tension.

I also expected the very active church pro-life groups in this country to defend the rights of black babies in the womb to live and also defend them from the implications of such obnoxious broadcast. That broadcast was simply an open encouragement to kill black babies in the womb as if they are not human beings and to blame the whole of crimes in America on one racial group. I did not hear any of these church pro-life groups talk in defense of black babies and condemn such an open invitation to harm the unborn child in the womb. It made me ask a question: When these pro-life groups are talking about defending the rights of babies in the womb to live, is there any color that should not be defended? Do they mean only white babies?

I was very happy to hear that the President called Bill Bennett's statement an *inappropriate* statement. It is not enough to call his statement an *inappropriate* statement, but it is time to make laws against any form of racial stereotyping before it causes more problems. I love freedom of speech, at the same time, any hateful public statement against a particular individual, or group, which is capable of demonizing an individual or causing prejudice against the individual or group, should be highly discouraged. This is because some white American children, who heard that statement and grow up with that idea, will think that to kill a black baby or any black person is an option to stopping crime. If such children grow up to become policemen and women, they will not only hate black people but also see them as criminals who should be subjected to brutal beatings before trial as we often see caught on tape and aired over the television. Unfortunately, many people do not see this shortcoming of the American police as a serious violation of human right.

If such children grow up to become sales men and women in shopping malls, they will see any black person that enters the shopping malls as a thief who should be followed around to make sure that he or she doesn't steal any thing. There was an incident that took place in Chesterfield Missouri, which I heard from a friend. A white woman went into a shopping mall to buy groceries with her five year-old bi-racial daughter. While she was selecting her stuff, her child was dipping her hand inside her bag to search for candy. The woman knew that her daughter was searching for candy but allowed her. One of the workers in the shopping mall picked her cell phone and dialed 911 to alert the police that a black child was stealing something from the bag of a white woman. When the Police came to arrest the five year old black child, every one was embarrassed when it was found out that the child was the bi-racial daughter of the white woman and that the woman had allowed her daughter to take candy from her bag. When the sales woman was asked why she called the police to arrest a five year old girl, she replied, "I am just doing what I was asked to do and because the child is black."

I have been embarrassed by some sales men and women in my innocence, while shopping in some parts of St. Louis. I have never stolen in my life. I wonder if I will start learning how to steal in a shopping mall just because I am a black man. I may not blame such sales men and women because they are doing what they have been told to do by their employers, who have with statements like Bennett's, created the wrong impression about all black people.

His unapologized[352] statement alone could increase the number of abortions of black babies in a year or even encourage medical students to use black babies as specimen for laboratory experiments. This is because instead of condemning Bennett's comment, on the 3rd of October, 2005, one pastor or religious leader defended him. "Defending Bennett's comments, Rev. Peterson cited alleged violence at Superdome to claim that most blacks 'lack moral character'."[353] If the impression is being created by some religious leaders, that blacks are the only people who commit noticeable crimes in this country, I strongly disagree. I accept that sometimes the media makes it look as if being black is being more naturally prone to evil than being white. The American media seem to recognize and broadcast more the crime of the minorities, making it look as if crime is a racial or color issue.

If I had not interviewed Father Grenham who lives in New Orleans, I wouldn't have known the truth about what really happened in New Orleans during the Katrina crisis. After discussing with him, I realized that hunger due to lack of food for many days, contributed much to the lootings while negligence and whatever weakness, contributed to not planning well and the delay in bringing the much needed food and other supplies. Which one is a lesser crime or a more recognizable crime? Which one gave rise to the other? The lootings show that a hungry man is an angry man. In a state of hunger bad things can happen. Hunger can also elicit animal behaviors. However, it is not only black Americans that looted. I have watched over the television, the arrests of serial killers, armed robbers, sex offenders, child abusers, drug barons, top government embezzlers, corrupt celebrities, internet predators, high profile bribe givers and takers, and murderers of all colors for the past four years. Crimes are of different kinds and any person could be prone to any, depending on the person's state of mind and some environmental forces that act on the individual. All human persons share a common link with animals and so, aggressive and harmful behaviors are evident through out the animal world.

One of the fastest and most enduring means of triggering off the animal behavior in any human person is to treat the person as if he or she is an animal. This was the problem of slaves in the American plantations during slavery. Their masters beat them with whips, used hot irons to give them identification marks on their bodies, forced them to work so many hours every day under harsh climatic conditions, and removed all their rights and freedom. The master still blamed the slave for reacting and called his reactions violence. The master did not first see his own actions against the slave as enough violence. Religion did not help matters because the slave master sometimes was a religious leader. The master did not expect the slave to react because he did not think that the slave was a human being, who needed love and the good things of life like himself. Do you pierce a person's body with a pin or a sharp knife and not expect the person to react? If you keep the pin inside the person's body without considering him or her human, how do you expect him or her to be happy and keep cool when the cause of his pain is continuous? When injustice or unjust treatments continue in any form, to any extent, and in any period, they trigger off consequent animal behaviors commensurate to them from the victims. It is justice only that brings peace and normalcy in any strained human relationship. It is justice that proves love, respect, and care. However, I do not support voilence, but I support dialogue no matter how hard it comes.

I have seen the crime of the rich and the crime of the poor. I have seen the crime of the more privileged and the crime of the less privileged or even that of the deprived. I have seen the crime of the powerful and the crime of the powerless. I have seen the crime of the mentally disturbed and the crime of the smart ones. It is not right for people to talk about others without considering these issues and considering themselves as not even better. The crime of the ghetto man or woman may not be the crime of the congressman or woman of any color or class. At the same time, the crime of the congressman may not be less noticeable and less harmful because society has placed him higher or treated him better than the ghetto man. If the congressman was in the same environmental condition as the ghetto man, he will not be different. If both of them are criminally minded, neither of them is going to be less dangerous than the other, due to the difference in their color or class. However, all crimes are evil no matter who commits them. Later in this chapter, we shall discuss the particular crime that sends the greatest number of young men and women to prison in America, to see if there is racial justice in enforcing some of the laws and in determining how many people are sent to prison. We shall also examine whether there is any church pastoral response to the way some laws are enforced and the way some people are targeted more than the others by the police and other law enforcement agents.

Apart from Bill Bennett and Rev. Peterson, I have also observed some other top politicians, especially from the South; make unhealthy and hateful statements about the African Americans, which indicate that there is no empathy in some people about what the African Americans have suffered in this country from slavery and segregation laws. If given the chance, such people would still like to subject them back to slavery and segregations laws and even genocide. By making such statements, they are trying to repeat history and may like to provoke the whole nation into another civil strife. No matter how powerful such individuals are in this country, the American government should be strong enough to make laws that can control such individuals. These people believe that America belongs to them more than it belongs to other Americans or that they are more American than others. For a person or some people to suggest the killing of all the babies of a particular race is suggesting genocide. If all the babies of the black race in America are killed, it will be the end of the black race in America. Silence from religious leaders and pastoral theologians in this country when such people talk and act could mean it is not important to caution people about the statements they make, or that religious leaders do not care, or what they are saying is true and acceptable. Such people should be watched always because, out of the abundance of the heart, the mouth speaks (Matthew 12: 34-35).

This reminds me of what happened in the 1930s and 1940s, before and during the Second World War. Hitler did not kill the six million Jews from no where. He started by making similar destructive statements against the Jews. He was taken for granted even by some churches or religions that should have spoken out strongly in condemnation of Hitler's *ideology of hate*, until he was able to use his powerful rhetoric to convince most of his subjects (religious and non religious people alike) to see nothing wrong in taking part in one of the worst and one of the most regrettable crimes of humanity, (the Holocaust). It is true that some churches and some church officials or members made some statements to express their disagreement with Hitler's ideas. Some even suffered heavily for disagreeing with him. At the same time, the actions and words from the churches and church officials were not seen by some Jewish leaders as strong enough and unanimous enough to stop Hitler. Stuart E. Rosenberg and many Jewish writers still blame Christianity for not doing enough to save the lives of their brothers and sisters.[354] According to Rabbi Randy Fleisher, "the way the Jews were taken as a despised race in Nazi Germany, is the way the African Americans are taken in the United States."[355] We need to learn from history. I strongly suggest that American churches and church officials need to be more vocal and more united in condemning such statements that are motivated by similar *ideology of hate*. It is better to avoid evil than to apologize for it because apologies do not bring back the dead.

The usual reactions of some black leaders to such statements are not always taken seriously and may not be enough to discourage the making of similar provoking remarks in the future. African American leaders do not have the power to make laws forbidding racial stereotyping. They do not have a strong back up or a strong support system from the churches. In the face of this unresolved racial crisis, the best pastoral advice which pastoral theologians need to give to their religious leaders is that they need to listen more attentively to the concerns of the oppressed minorities and speak out more effectively against racial injustice in the society irrespective of who is involved, whether individuals or institutions.

The Churches need to engage in more Attentive Pastoral Listening

Listening to the stories of those whom Thornton describes as *broken in history* so as to know how to help them is a crucial aspect of active pastoral response expected of the churches. Charles V. Gerkin, the author of *An Introduction to Pastoral Care*, recommends, "Pastoral care at the turn of the twentieth and the twenty first century must find new ways to give equal emphasis to concern for the individual and concern for the larger social environment that surrounds the individual."[356] Gerkin goes on to talk about the importance of giving a listening ear to people pastorally, at all social levels.

> Listening involves more than simply hearing the words that people say. It means being attentive to the emotional communication that   accompanies the words. It means listening for nuances that may give clues to the particular, private meanings that govern a person's inner life. It means listening for hidden conflicts, unspoken desires, unspeakable fears, and faint hopes. . .What in the social situation of the people receiving our care may be causing or exacerbating people's distress? Are the social structures that surround the lives of those under our care providing the social support that people need in order for their lives to flourish?[357]

It is very important for the churches to really listen to the oppressed minorities in this country because that is part of their God-given responsibility to humanity and because the churches are historically implicated in the racial crisis that is still affecting millions of people in this country. In support of this claim, Thornton asserts, "Pastoral theology, as a child of North American Protestant liberalism, has participated in trusting insight with its pretense to possess the truth. This has been a major source of much suffering imposed by one group on another."[358] In view of this, G. Lee Ramsey, the author of *Care—Full Preaching* then advises, "The caring thing to do is for the church to identify with the poor among us, raise the cry of justice, and seek the welfare of those whom society (and the church) continually use and abuse."[359] The motive behind proper pastoral handling is love and "love is a thoroughly social phenomenon. Not only does it impel us into relationships with others, it also enables us to recognize injustice and do something about it."[360]

A Wonderful Personal Experience through Listening

In some hospitals I visited, especially in St. Louis, I observed that most people who frequented the psychiatric sections of these hospitals were African Americans and Hispanics. This is not to say that there are no white patients that come to the psychiatric sections of the hospitals. They are very few in number comparatively. Sharon G. Thornton also made the same observation while describing her ministry experience as a chaplain in the emergency room of a community hospital, where she lived.

> Many of the men and women who were admitted to the psychiatric unit were street people. They were the ones who held out their paper cups to moviegoers at the entrance of the local theater. They were those who aimlessly roamed the sidewalks whispering, 'Spare change?' as they looked for temporary places to lay their heads. A disproportionate number of these people were African Americans or Hispanic. Many were women. Too many were children. Without exception, all were poor.[361]

In my own experience, I observed that many of these poor people of color, especially African Americans, in their thirties and forties, have the habit of repeatedly coming back to the psychiatric units of these hospitals at least once every two weeks for the past two years I kept track on them. Because some of these hospitals are charitable and so do not turn back any patient, some of these people of color see these hospitals as their second home. Having observed some of these patients come and go, only to return to these hospitals after some days, I decided to listen to their stories. The majority of them had similar stories. I present in this book my discussion with one of them who happens to be almost the same age as me. I will call him Mr. Jones. When I entered his room with his permission, I greeted him and said,

"Hi, Mr. Jones"

"Hi, Sir," he replied. Smiling at him and looking into his eyes, I introduced myself to him.

"My name is Father Cajetan. I was just passing and I decided to come and express my concern about your being here." He did not return my smiles. He looked unhappy. I felt unhappy myself.

"Why do you want to express your concern about my being here? Did I ask for it?" he replied.

"You are right, Mr. Jones. There is no other reason why I wanted to visit with you apart from the fact that I am concerned about you and I do care. I am sorry that for a long time I have been visiting this hospital, I have not been able to talk to you. I have been visiting mainly Catholic patients and patients of other denominations who needed my attention. Today, I felt like expressing my long time desire to spend some time with you."

"Oh man, do you mean that you really care about me?" he asked.

"Yes, I really do care about you." I could see his mood changing for the better.

"Thank you for caring to visit with me."

"It is my pleasure. Mr. Jones, I can observe that you have been here for so many times this year and I have always wondered what could be wrong; at the same time, I can see that you are a good looking young man in his thirties or forties. Did I guess right?"

"Yes, sir, you are correct; I was forty two, a few months ago."

"Oh my goodness, you are almost the same age as me. If you had invited me to your birthday party, I would have come with some gifts. If you are celebrating next time, please invite me and I will surprise you."

"Do you mean it, sir? No human being has ever told me to celebrate. What do I need to celebrate? My life has been a disaster and I have ever regretted the day I was born.

"Mr. Jones, you will be doing me a favor if you tell me what makes your life a disaster. I am all ears for you, if you do not mind."

"Why do you want to know?"

"I want to know because I care for you." He took a deep breath and bent his head down. Raising his head up he looked at me and said,

"It is a long story and I do not know where to start."

"Start from somewhere, Mr. Jones; I am listening to you and I am a good listener."

I fixed my attention on him and looked directly inside his eyes. I could see his eyes getting wet with tears. I was uncomfortable myself, but I pretended to be calm.

"My life has been a disaster because I regret every thing that has happened to me since I was a teenager. I had no father to direct me on the right decisions to make and so I made terrible mistakes that have helped to ruin my life. The only father I knew was a street cleaner who was too poor to take care of my mother and me. He was a veteran of the Korean War. When he and the other veterans came back to this country after the war, he could not get a meaningful job and could not go to school. He regretted being a street cleaner because he did not go to school and so could not do any meaningful job to provide for us. I asked him why he did not go to school, and he told me that he could not pay for schooling after the war and more so, his own parents were illiterates and did not encourage him."

"Sorry to interrupt you, Mr. Jones. I thought that having served his country in such a deadly war he could have been given an education loan to go to school because I know that veterans now do get some help from the government. Was there no education loan in the 1950s and 1960s?

"I do not know because I did not know what education loan meant by then, so I could not ask him about that. So my father became so depressed that he started taking so much alcohol to cool off, because he had no health insurance and money to go to a psychiatrist or a psychologist for treatment as I have in this hospital. Alcohol became his only option. At a point, he started misbehaving like someone insane and we could not understand him again. He was unlucky one day as he was crossing the road, he did not look well, and he was knocked down by a hit and run driver and he died on the spot."

Immediately he said that, he broke down and cried. At this time, I could no longer pretend to be a strong man. Tears filled my eyes. He continued.

"I was with my mother one evening; the police came and told us what happened. His death devastated my mother and me."

"Sorry for that, Mr. Jones. I feel so sad that such a thing happened to your beloved father."

"We mourned him for a year and my mother remarried to a man who did not take me as a son and never did anything to help direct me because I was not his blood son. I did not equally see him as a father since he was mean to me. My mother herself could not help me much either. I got fed up with my stepfather's meanness and left the house to manage my own life. When I left home in 1979, life was not so easy for me. I became unhappy and depressed like my father. I had some friends by then that introduced me to taking and dealing on drugs. I could not resist taking it because I remembered my father taking something of that nature to cool off. I thought it was the best way to get over my distress, but I did not know that I was making a huge mistake."

He stopped talking and tears rolled down his face again.

"I was arrested, charged with drug felony, and convicted. I went to prison for my offence. Life in the prison was not a lucky experience and I regretted ever getting connected with drugs. I came out of prison a few years ago only to find out that I cannot get a meaningful job due to background check. I am just grounded; I am depressed, homeless, poor, and my life is a very miserable one. I am left with three decisions, either to commit another crime and go back to prison where I will get free food, clothes, and shelter; or to be coming to this hospital frequently since this hospital is so charitable that those who work here do not turn back people; or to commit suicide and leave this miserable world."

I felt so sad and sorry for him.

"I do not want to die like my father because the accident that claimed his life looked suicidal. I do not want to commit another crime because I regret the one I already committed. If my father had been educated and had a more meaningful job, he wouldn't have ended the way he did and I would have had a more responsible father to guide me and direct me. I would have gone to school like others and be more responsible to manage my own family. I was just acting like a stupid young man. So instead of committing another crime or taking my own life, I decided to be coming here as a psychiatric patient when ever I am depressed, because they take good care of me here."

"Oh my brother, I feel so sad for all these things that have happened to you."

"So you can see with me, sir, that there is nothing to celebrate in my life."

"I understand how you feel and why you feel that way. I am happy that you have realized that drugs never helped you and happy about your decision not to take drugs again. I am also happy that you know the worth of life and happy about your decision not to take your own life. I am grateful to this hospital for helping you and the others. I do not mean to argue with you about whether there is anything to celebrate in your life or not. If I am not going to upset you, I would like to let you know that there is something still to celebrate."

"What do you think I can celebrate?"

"You are loved."

What do you mean? Who loves me?

"God loves you."

"God!" he shouted, "Does God know my name? How can you prove to me that He loves me?"

"He loves you because I am here and because I do love you."

"Come on man, I am not gay!"

"No, Mr. Jones; that is not the type of love I mean."

"What type of love do you mean?"

"I mean the love that does not reject you because of your past mistakes, the love that is not limited because of sex, color, race, age, and class. It is the love that made me to come to you, to listen to you and to feel with you. It is the love that God expressed by creating you in His image and likeness. That is the love of God and that is the love we are going to celebrate on your birthday."

"Oh my God, no person has ever talked to me like this and no person has ever told me that he loves me outside my family. If that is the case, there is God and I have to celebrate my birthday for the first time in my life. Thank you for visiting with me, and for talking to me as a friend."

"I am glad to be your friend."

"Can you please pray for me now?"

"It is my pleasure."

I did pray with him before I left him. I had a few follow up encounters with Mr. Jones and I believe that he received healing from the hands of God. His comments, "If this is the case, there is God," and "No person has ever told me that God loves me," really struck my heart. I felt like following up with his case and see if I could be of more help to him. This has made me to start thinking that many people have not known God because they have not been given the true picture of God as a loving Father, who loves and favors all. With the doctrine of divine election still influencing ministry here, God has been presented as a Father who favors some people while some people are without much divine favor. The causes of their poverty and suffering, including the historical aspect of it, are seen as part of divine purpose or plan made for them and so, not much can be done about it. This also made me to start thinking about the limitations of the many church crusades and revivals I watch over the television being organized by some of these Tele-evangelists of the Evangelical and Pentecostal groups.

These crusades and revivals are good but most times they do not reach those whose lives really need to be revived and those who really need a spiritual crusade against the evil that has kept them in bondage of poverty and drug addiction. These revivals and crusades are held in hotels and stadiums where people like Mr. Jones cannot reach. It will be good also if these revivals and crusades are taken to the black ghettoes and to the psychiatric units of the hospitals. The people who live and frequent these places also need to hear that God loves them. They may not give millions of dollars during church offertory donations, but they will encounter God in their lives and their lives will change, because whatever is keeping them in bondage will be addressed.

This also will help the society in no small measure to combat crime. The millionaire evangelists who organize these crusades and revivals can also speak for the American poor and abandoned. I believe that the aim of pastoral ministry is to win the hearts of both the poor and the rich for God. Jesus did not only preach to the rich. His message was more to liberate the poor, the oppressed, the ostracized, and the abandoned and to make them have hope in life (Luke 4: 18-19). Any theology of prosperity, which does not address injustice in the society and does not care much about what is happening to the poor needs to be seriously reviewed and modified to be more Christ-like.

For Mr. Jones, I decided not to stop my pastoral response in the hospital room by just telling him, "God bless you and bye." I decided to follow up and give him proper pastoral backup by finding out why he had no family, why he is or was a drug addict, why he is poor and homeless, why he is not educated, what caused his family poverty cycle. My intentions were to help him have a restored or revived life, to find a way of helping him break his family poverty, to help him to stop crime and to become a more law-abiding and productive citizen of America. If it means speaking out for him and addressing all the causes of his and his family's problems, I will do it. If I am able to address the causes of his problems in any way I can, I believe I am doing the prophetic work of the church. This I feel is what the churches are supposed to do for Mr. Jones and millions like him in the American society of the twenty first century.

Finding out and addressing the Immediate and the Remote Causes of Mr. Jones' Problems

Mr. Jones' story is one among so many of such stories in this country and mostly among African Americans and Hispanics who frequent the psychiatric units of many American hospitals. According to Gerkin, "to care deeply for persons is to inquire with them, question with them about what the events of their lives mean at the deepest level."[362] From his story, I felt that the immediate cause of his crisis was that he made a very wrong decision as a young man by going into drugs. Thinking that he would make life worth living by taking and dealing in drugs was a huge mistake that has crippled his life as it has crippled the lives of so many youths. He not only went to prison, still he finds it very difficult to get a reasonable job to take care of him. No matter the family background of any young man or woman, taking or selling drugs can never be a better option but a devastating one. A young man or woman whether white or black needs to have a purpose in life, take his or her education very serious, and finish from college or university as an expert. At that level, one can then comfortably raise a family and then life is full of enjoyment.

I made more inquires about Mr. Jones' life and how to help him. I had to seek information with the Missouri Department of Corrections. I got the information that "in 2003, the Missouri Department of Corrections implemented the Serious and Violent Offender Re-Entry Initiative (SVORI), known in Missouri as Project Connect."[363] Through this program, offenders could be helped to be accepted back into the community. I made more inquiries if Mr. Jones could benefit from such a program. I discovered that "in order to participate in Project Connect, male and female participants must meet the following criteria: be between the ages of 17 and 35; have a poor criminal history; have a poor work history; and lack of vocational and educational skill."[364] Mr. Jones at this point in time was forty-two years old and could not benefit from such a program. I wonder why he was not taken to a correction home when he came out of prison. Is there any disparity or discrimination in sending ex-convicts to correction homes after their prison sentence? This is a subject for more research. Mr. Jones told me that he did not know anything about going to a correction home to get some help after he came out of prison.

I also made inquiries if Mr. Jones could at least get food stamps. I went to the Missouri Department of Social Services to get information about how to help Mr. Jones get food stamps, at least to be able to eat. I got the information that "anyone convicted in a federal, state, or local court of trading benefits for controlled substances, illegal drugs, or certain drugs for which a doctor's prescription is required shall be barred from the food stamp program for 2 years for the first offense and permanently for the second offense."[365] The question is what happens to the person for the two years after coming out of prison when he will find it difficult to get a job due to background check and he can not get food stamps? Is the prison sentence not enough punishment?

What does the state want to achieve in making it difficult for the person to get food stamps for two years after coming out of prison? Is hunger not going to lead the person to the same crime of selling drugs only to be arrested again and then be thrown into prison for the second time, where he will be worse and when he comes out, he will be banned for life without food stamps, a job, and an education? This policy will only create more street people when they come out of prison. It neither helps the individual nor the entire American society because one unproductive person in the society whether black or white is a set back to the entire society. If this policy was made to help the individual, it needs to be reviewed because depriving the person a means of getting food to eat when the person is jobless may put the individual into the same temptation of committing the same crime again, if the individual has no other option than to do anything to avoid dying of hunger.

However, I was happy that Mr. Jones was eligible for getting food stamps since he has not been convicted of a second drug offense and it was more than two years since he came out of prison. I wondered why he did not know that he was eligible for food stamps after two years of coming out of prison. It could be that no one told him that after two years he could get food stamps. Mr. Jones is getting food stamps of about 150 dollars a month now. Has that broken the cycle of poverty he inherited from his family? Food stamps are not the solution to his problem because a man at forty-two may not depend on that for the rest of his life. It means that he will continue to be economically dependent or be a beggar for life.

At forty-two, he can still have a career, get married and even go to school to make his life more meaningful. How can he do all these with about 150 dollars a month? If Mr. Jones had been educated, he would have been making about 3,000 to 4,000 dollars a month. We shall later examine why he was not educated, and this will help us to know if the food stamps of about 150 dollars a month is justified. So I did not stop at the food stamp level because that is not real solution to his poverty. Food stamps is a temporary help but at the same time a permanent economic slavery, especially when the individual is capable and can still be helped to be more self reliant.

How do we find out the major cause of the cycle of poverty Mr. Jones inherited from his family? Gerkin recommends not only listening to the personal histories of the individual, but also "examining them for what was faulty, the historical root causes of present difficulties."[366] I remembered that Mr. Jones told me that his father was a Korean War veteran. Did the Federal government not have any plan for those who defended the country during that war? Is the origin of the cycle of poverty, which contributed in no small measure to Mr. Jones' present regrettable life, historical? Is it what Sharon G. Thornton calls "historically rooted suffering?"[367] I needed to find out if Mr. Jones' personal and family suffering falls within what Christine Smith said about suffering in her book *Risking the Terror*. Smith asserts, "There is suffering that comes as a result of the natural flow of life and death, and then there is human suffering that is inflicted . . . there is suffering that is systematically intended for particular groups and individuals."[368]

To get to know if the origin of Mr. Jones' miserable life is historical, I had to start making inquiries about how the government handled those who defended the country in the Second World War and the Korean wars in the 1940s and 1950s. From Mr. Jones' story, the cycle of poverty of his family started from the time of his father. The only father he knew was a poor, depressed street cleaner who regretted that he did not go to school, could not get a meaningful job, and a government business loan to take care of his family. He later ended up an alcoholic due to frustration, and died disappointed with life. Why was it that Mr. Jones' father did not get all these benefits after defending his country in the Korean War in the 1950s? Karen Brodkin in her book *How the Jews Became White Folks and what that has to say about Race in America,* gives us the reason why Mr. Jones' father did not have the above opportunities and so remained and died poor and handed over the poverty to his son, which exposed him to a miserable life of drug addiction.

In trying to explain how the Jews and the other European immigrants were helped by the Federal government to achieve some economic progress up to becoming middle class Americans, Brodkin argues that the economic progress of her people (Jews) did not come mainly because of their love for education, hard work, smartness, and the culture of sticking together. She does not deny the fact that these good qualities may have contributed to what she calls "Jewish upward mobility."[369] She argues that Jews and other white ethnics' *upward mobility* was due to programs that allowed them to float on a rising economic tide.[370] The Federal government in the late nineteenth and twentieth centuries through affirmative actions opened the doors of economic progress for the southern and eastern European immigrants including the Jews to come up to the middle class status and so are now considered whites. Unfortunately, the African Americans who were not European immigrants were purposely deprived of any privileges.

She gave examples with the GI Bill of Rights, the Federal Housing Administration (FHA) and the Veteran Administration (VA) mortgages. "The GI Bill and FHA and VA mortgages, even though they were advertised as open to all, functioned as a set of racial privileges. They were privileges because they were extended to white GIs but not to black GIs"[371] The GI Bill of Rights started after the Second World War and the Korean War in the forties, fifties, and sixties, as "the Serviceman's Readjustment Act."[372] The purpose for this economic package was to create the required labor force for the booming post war economy in America and to compensate those ex-service men and women who served this nation during the Second World War and Korean Wars. Brodkin explains that the GI benefits that were extended to 16 million GIs (of the Korean War as well as World War II), "included priority jobs—that is, preferential hiring, but no one objected to it then—financial support during job search, small loans and educational benefits, which included tuition and living expenses."[373]

Brodkin sees this program as the most extensive affirmative action in the American History because it helped so many Americans.[374] Micheal J. Benneth agrees with Brodkin by saying, "With the help of GI Bill, millions bought homes, attended college, started business ventures, and found jobs commensurate with their skills. . ."[375] Unfortunately and sad enough, Mr. Jones' father, and millions of African American GIs, and female GIs of all colors who served to defend this country, were deprived of the above privileges given to their white counterparts. Though it was supposed to have helped all American GIs, Ira Katznelson observes that "Its administration widened the country's racial gap. The prevailing experience for blacks was starkly differential treatment."[376] Only Euro-Origin GIs gained from it.[377] Brodkin explains in detail how the injustice against African American GIs was carried out:

> The military, the Veteran Administration, the US Employment Service (USES), and the Federal Housing Administration effectively denied African Americans GIs access to their benefits and to new educational, occupational and residential opportunities. Black GIs who served in the thoroughly segregated armed forces during World War II served under white officers. African American soldiers were given disproportionate share of dishonorable discharges, which denied them veterans rights under the GI Bill. Between August and November 1946, for example, 21 percent of white soldiers and 39 percent of black soldiers were dishonorably discharged. Those who did get honorable discharge then faced the veteran Administration and the USES. The latter which was responsible for job placements, employed very few Africans especially in the South. This meant the black veterans did not receive much employment information and that the offers they did receive were for low-paid and menial jobs.[378]

This explains how and why Mr. Jones' father got only a menial job of cleaning the streets as his own benefits after defending his country, while his white male counterparts got educational loans, business loans, house loans, technical training, and better job opportunities. They were able to "take advantage of their educational benefits for college and technical trainings, so they were particularly well positioned to seize the opportunities provided by the new demand for professional, managerial, and technical labor."[379] The problem of not giving black GIs meaningful employment was not because of lack of professional training. In the words of Katznelson, "In the South, virtually no black veteran was given access to skilled employment by the USES, despite having had occupational training and work in the military."[380]

Mr. Jones' father was not dishonorably discharged and so his sacrifice for his country was rewarded with a low paid menial job of cleaning the American streets while his white counterparts benefited. Many of the black GIs who mustered courage to complain about this injustice and who spoke the minds of over a million other black GIs were discharged without a hearing.[381]

How did the above deprivation and injustice affect the Future of Mr. Jones?

Mr. Jones' father was a veteran of the Korean War and as a citizen of this country was supposed to have benefited from the above GI, FHA, and VA benefits. Mr. Jones' father could not go to school because he was not one of "the 8 million GIs who took advantage of their educational benefits under the GI. Bill."[382] His father did not take advantage of the above educational benefit under the GI Bill because he was not allowed to take it because he was not white. He, therefore, could not go to school after the war as a young man; he had no educational culture to hand over to his son. J. Nash explains how the above GI Bill also helped the next generation to have better education, in these words:

> It has been well documented that the GI educational benefits transformed American higher education and raised the educational level of that generation and generations to come. With many provisions for assistance in upgrading their educational attainments, veterans pulled ahead of nonveterans who had fewer opportunities.[383]

Mr. Jones, therefore, could not go to school because his father was not given equal opportunity to go to school as his white counterparts and so handed over to his son illiteracy, poverty, depression, and addiction before death struck. His sudden death may have been because of the condition in which perhaps this injustice kept him. Mr. Jones' father had indulged in alcohol addiction so as to cool off the frustration this injustice had inflicted in him. He behaved like any other abused person. Most sexually abused persons end up being drug addicts or alcoholics. Even if the abuse occurred fifty years ago, it requires justice to reconstruct the lives of such people and their descendants who are affected by what happened in the past. Mr. Jones had no one to direct him in life. Like any other young man without a guide, he started making the mistakes of lots of young men and women. The absence of his father helped to expose him to bad gangs and selling and taking of drugs.

Mr. Jones' cycle of poverty, illiteracy, and miserable life was not a result of inherent laziness or inherent addiction. What happened to him could have happened to any other young man or woman irrespective of color. It could have happened to me if my parents and grandparents hadn't the opportunity to go to school in Nigeria in the 1930s, 1940s and 1950s before I was even born. My father was a teacher before he became elected to become a traditional ruler. My mother was a trained nurse and later became a school teacher. If they had not gone to school, I would not have gone to school or even if I had gone to school, I may have ended up a school drop out. There were so many occasions when I refused to go to school. As a child who did not know the worth of education, my father with his big voice said to me, "Hell no! You must go to school." Mr. Jones had no father to encourage him to go to school and to command him with a big voice, "Hell no! You must go to school."

As a child, if I grew up to observe my father and mother rise up every morning to go and clean the hospital rooms, hotel rooms, and government offices, I may have thought that the world means being a house or street cleaner. I may have not had enough to inspire me to become a medical doctor, engineer, pharmacist, pilot, governor, pastor, and the president of a nation like America. I know that there are some people who came from such poor families, who have made it; at the same time, it is a fact that the profession of a person's parents can influence that person and can determine what that person may turn to be. I interviewed a Caucasian medical doctor (name withheld) who works in the hospital where I go to anoint the sick. I asked her what inspired her to become a medical doctor. She told me that it is like a culture in her family. Her great grandfather was a medical doctor, her grandfather was a medical doctor and her father also was one. In her family now, two of her siblings are medical doctors, as well as herself. That culture was maintained because each generation had someone to inspire and encourage its members to keep to the family's tradition. Mr. Jones had no tradition because of government's unjust policy against his people and no one to inspire him. Unfortunately, religion did not adequately defend his father and millions of others against this evil.

The white GI families and their future generations who had benefited from the government economic packages have a better standard of living as middle class Americans, better jobs, and better education. Brodkin acknowledges that her own generation has also benefited from the above privileges. She asserts, "The Federal housing Administration (FHA) was key to buyers and builders alike. Thanks to FHA, suburbia was open to more than GIs. People like us would never have been in the market for houses without FHA and Veterans Administration (VA) low-down-payment, low-interest, long-term loans to young buyers."[384]

Civilians also gained from the GI package, as far they were not blacks. She goes on to state how the GI benefits which her parents received have continued to help her. "Today I own a house in Venice, California, like one in which I grew up in Valley Stream, and my brother until recently owned a house in Palo Alto. . ." Both of us are where we are, thanks largely to the postwar benefits our parents received in the 1960s as a result of affluence and the social agitation that developed from the black Freedom Movement."[385] The economic fallouts from the Black Freedom Movement did not even benefit blacks. Brodkin sympathizes with her friends whose parents received fewer or none of the American postwar benefits and may not be able to own a house, despite their considerable academic achievements. Some of her colleagues, who are a few years younger than she, also "carry staggering debts for their education, which they expect to have to repay for the rest of their lives."[386]

Mr. Jones' father could not benefit from the above FHA and VA privileges and so could not buy a house but had to live in the ghettoes with Mr. Jones and in very poor conditions. If Mr. Jones is going to have children and grand children, they will all be living poorly. "Those racially skewed gains have been passed across the generations, so that racial inequality seems to maintain itself 'naturally' even after legal segregation laws ended."[387] The historically inflicted poverty of millions of families of color such as Mr. Jones' has continued till today as exposed by Hurricane Katrina.

The above Economic Exclusion still affects People of Color

According to Morris J. MacGregor, ". . . As the World War II came to an end, nearly one million black men and women had served in the armed forces during the conflict."[388] If about two million African American GIs had served in both World War II and the Korean War, the above deprivation has crippled the chances of education, job opportunities, technical trainings, loans for business, and loans to buy houses in decent neighborhoods, for two million African Americans and their next generations. Their next generations or dependents could be several millions of blacks presently facing poverty and without having a reasonable number of properties and business ventures like their counterparts. The Jim Crow laws have been removed but their effects have not been removed as millions of those deprived African Americans GIs have not been compensated by the past and present American Administrations. This has generally affected the economic status of African Americans in this country as we are going to see.

When I first came to St. Louis, my Caucasian friend and mentor at St. Louis University took me to many restaurants to eat. I discovered that among many restaurants and snack shops we visited, there were hardly any of them owned by a black person. I saw many black youths as sales men and women, waiters, cleaners, and dish washers. I asked my friend why blacks do not own some of the restaurants we had visited. The answer he gave me was not satisfactory. I then felt like studying the effects of past economic exclusions of the early and middle 1900s, (the Second World War and Korean War GI Bill and others), on the ability of African Americans to having properties and business ventures like their white counterparts.

I started with the restaurant business because it is one of the fastest growing businesses, may not require a huge amount of money to start and every one is eating. To know the number of restaurants owned by blacks in St. Louis, I decided to visit the AOL yellow page website for St. Louis. According to the AOL yellow page website, there are 4,053 restaurants in the city of St. Louis and in St. Louis County within a 25 miles radius. Among these 4,053 restaurants, 304 are Chinese; 167 are Mexican, and only 4 are African American. I assume that the Chinese restaurants are all owned by the Chinese or Asians while the Mexican ones are all owned by the Mexicans. According to the American census bureau of 2000, the population of African Americans in St Louis city is 51.2%, the population of whites is 43.8%, and the population of Latinos is 2%, while that of Asians is 2%. The population of African Americans in St. Louis County is 19%, the population of whites is 76.8%, and the population of Latinos is 1.4%, while that of Asians is 2.2%.[389]

More detailed studies prove that the majority of these restaurants were built between the 1940s and 1970s, showing that the GI affirmative action which benefited 16 million white Euro-Americans between the 1940s and 1960s really helped them to rise economically and own more properties. The above figures may serve as a good demonstration of how the different races or groups are considered and placed economically. The white Americans come first, followed by the Asians; the Hispanics come next and then the African Americans are placed at the bottom. This order seems to be the way other things are structured in this society. African Americans having only 4 restaurants out of 4,053 is a disturbing number considering their population, when they came into this country, and the contributions they have made in the development of this country. The above figures also could demonstrate how the different groups are considered and trusted in the granting of business loans at present. We shall find out if this great difference in the number of properties owned by each of the races or groups is only in St. Louis or if it is the same in other American cities. We shall also in this chapter discuss about the use of racial stereotyping to confuse people to believe that the African Americans are lazy by nature and are not able to manage such businesses.

From the population and the number of restaurants owned by each group, one can also see the extent to which the economic power of the African Americans has been crippled by past government racist policies. These are people who came to this country early enough from its foundation and contributed to its development and growth even if with forced slave labor. I wonder why they are placed at the bottom of everything. There is no justifiable reason why African American GIs were deprived of their Second World War and Korean War benefits apart from the fact that the system did not want them to rise economically. The poverty of most African American families is inflicted and not by nature because I have not observed any difference between them and other Americans if placed in the same condition. It is true that affirmative action may be beneficial to every one who qualifies for it now; at the same time it should be noted that several of them that were in the past denied, African Americans, and which have not been compensated are still affecting millions of lives today. We shall get to examine whether the American Churches responded pastorally to this racial injustice or if they kept silent over it as if it did not concern them what the government was doing to blacks.

My findings with the restaurant business made me wonder, and start asking the following questions. How many gas stations, car shops, hotels and motels, industries, factories, shopping malls, insurance companies, banks and other financial institutions, sky scrappers, air lines, shipping lines, car producing factories, hospitals, universities, farmlands, and other business ventures are owned by black people? People can visit the internet to find out how many of the above business ventures are owned by blacks in other American cities. This is not to say that there are no African Americans who have made it rich despite all odds through sports, music, and even business, but a greater majority is still to find its footing in the economic life of this country. If there was no economic marginalization, there would have been millions of the people of color in a better standard of living who would have also been the owners of big shopping malls, air lines, hotels, hospitals, and so on.

I am just using St. Louis as an example because it is where I live. However, when I traveled to New York, Houston, Chicago, Atlanta, Dallas, Los Angeles, and New Orleans, I observed that the condition of blacks is the same in most American cities. The economic exclusion did not start in the twentieth century. Kivel testifies to the economic injustice done to blacks in the nineteenth century in these words:

> For example, many of our fore parents gained a foothold in this
> country by finding work in such trades as railroads, streetcars,

construction, shipbuilding, wagon and coach driving, house painting, tailoring, longshore work, brick laying, table waiting, working in the mills, furriering or dressmaking. These were all occupations that Blacks, who had begun entering many such skilled and unskilled jobs, were either excluded from or pushed out of in the nineteenth century.[390]

Kivel rightly argues that this does not mean that "white Americans have not worked hard and built much."[391] In his honesty as a Caucasian, he goes on to stress how some past American governments in the twentieth century also unjustly favored whites and abandoned blacks. Kivel agrees that they (whites) have all these years worked hard and built much; at the same time he confesses in these words:

But we did not start from scratch. We went to segregated schools and universities built with public money. We received school loans, V.A. loans, housing and auto loans, when people of color were excluded or heavily discriminated against. We received federal jobs, military jobs, and contracts when only whites were allowed. We were accepted into apprenticeships, training programs, and unions when access for people of color was restricted or nonexistent.[392]

Kivel's confession, Brodkin's, Katznelson's, and those of other white writers are what Americans need to hear to know why some people are left to languish in poverty in the richest country of the world. Many African American children visit Mac Donald's and other snack shops, spend the last dollar they have buying snacks, but may not know why their parents do not own such multi million dollar snack shops. They go to shopping malls like Wal-Mart, K-Mart, Shucks, Shop and Save, Save a Lot, Wall-Green, Seven-Eleven, and so many others, but they do not know why their parents do not have any of these. Is it because their parents by nature are incapable of managing such big businesses? Of course, the answer is no! They were simply so many years ago deprived of equal opportunities of having such big businesses as we have seen and as we shall see when America had its post war economic boom.

One day, I interviewed an African American friend (name withheld) who works in a bank. I asked him this question, "Why is it that I do not see many African Americans who own such businesses as restaurants, hotels, shopping malls, car shops, big companies, factories, industries, and large farms and so on? I instead see many African Americans as housekeepers in hospitals, hotels, and shopping malls." He answered, "The minorities, most especially African Americans and Hispanics, are not given enough loans like their white counterparts, to do such businesses that could yield large sums of money. They are sometimes given very limited loans and most times with different interest rates that will make it very difficult for them to pay back and succeed in such businesses. Most times they are accused of not paying back and so, no further loans." I wonder if there are people monitoring what the banks are doing when people of color go to seek for loans and when whites go for their own. He also told me that most blacks who work in banks are marginalized and are not allowed to get up to the top level positions where such decisions are taken. He described the banks and some other financial institutions in America as the most effective means of marginalizing the people of color economically.

I do not doubt the truthfulness of this information; at the same time I do not know how exact this information is. I know that in one of my interviews, when we were discussing the poverty of minorities in New Orleans in particular and in America generally, after the Hurricane Katrina, Father Grenham of New Orleans told me that blacks are given limited business loans. Why are they given limited business loan with different interest rates? Why are they treated differently? Are they not citizens of this country? This is subject to investigation. I encourage the church human rights commissions of different denominations to investigate and know the exact truth and do something about it. The American churches, after condemning racism and inequality, should also follow it up with actions to find out more about such injustices still happening on daily bases.

How did the American Churches Respond Pastorally to the GI Bill Injustice in the 1940s, 1950s and 1960s?

When one reads or hears about the injustice of favoring a particular group of people at the detriment of the others in a country like America, one is right to ask, what were the churches doing to allow such injustice to go on for years unquestioned? Can the church authorities give excuses that there is separation of church and state and so prefer to keep silent and allow such glaring evil to go unquestioned? Shelton Smith and the others answered the above question in these words "Whatever concerns man and his welfare is a concern of the Church and its ministers. Religion has to do with life in its wholeness. While being patriotically loyal to the country within whose bounds it lives and works, the church does not derive its authority from the nation but from Jesus Christ."[393] This is to say that the church officials are not going to be accused of being unpatriotic if they call the government to order in some oppressive policies against anybody or any group.

Smith and colleagues argue that the Church should pay its supreme and ultimate allegiance to "Christ, its sole Head, and to His Kingdom, and not to any nation or race, to any class or culture."[394] America is also made up of other religions whose supreme heads or prophets or teachings do not support injustice. Racist government policies have survived for centuries in America because the government does not feel any strong and unified force of objection from the churches or religions. So the government can afford to treat the minorities any how it pleases. Most times in the past as we have primarily seen, churches cooperated with the government rather than defended the oppressed. Even when objections did come from the churches, they came either very late or as ineffective verbal condemnations without many actions. Actually I have not observed any clear seperation of church and state because both governing bodies seem to share power, especially when it comes to racial matters. I have not observed any clear disagreement between church and state on racial issues, as I have observed on other social problems like abortion, stem cell research, human clonning etc.

I have gone through available American Church documents, minutes of meetings, church general assembly proceedings, decisions of conventions, and decisions of bishops' conferences since the 1940s to date. I saw some documents that condemned racism generally, but I did not see any which mentioned specifically the above GI, FHA, and VA injustices against blacks and women GIs from the 1940s to 1960s. Does it mean that the leaders of the different Christian denominations were unaware that after the Second World War and Korean War, when African American GIs and women GIs were denied their rights that only white

Euro-American GIs got every thing they needed to live as middle class citizens? It was not a secret by then because local newspapers carried news about the injustice.

According to Ira Katznelson, "Two years after the passage of the GI Bill, Truman Gibson, Jr., Veteran editor for the *Pittsburgh Courier*, documented 'the sorry plight of Negro veterans and particularly those living in the South' in a story headlined 'Government Fails Negro Vets.'"[395] Gibson decried the injustice on how the whole veteran's package eluded the colored veterans.[396] Why is it that the injustice done to a people that staked their lives in defence of their country, was condemned in a secular newspaper, but silent in church newspapers and magazines? Why was it that religious leaders of that time felt that it did not concern them that the government dealt with African American GIs and female GIs that way? What will prevent the present American religious leaders from speaking for them since this injustice is still affecting millions of African American lives? It is one thing to condemn racism generally and it is another thing to name a specific instance and address or condemn the actions of whoever is responsible for what is unjust before God and humans. Majority of the members of those governments were members of churches or religions, as it is at present.

There may be or may not be a parity of power between politics and religion. In any case, the religious leader should not be afraid of asking for justice and calling the political leader to order when his or her decision is against justice and peace, even if the decision of the political leader favors the religious leader and his own people. For the religious leaders to ask government to compensate those African American and female GIs whose war benefits are still being withheld by the government is the right thing to do. It is important to remember that there are millions of Americans who are still suffering from the injustice of the past especially people like Mr. Jones. It is not late to show them justice. I have heard a lot about the effects of sexual abuse on the individual, but I have not heard much from American Psychologists, Psychiatrics, and Moral Theologians talk about the effects of racial abuse on the individual. From my experiences in the psychiatric units of hospitals, the effects of both are the same. If some people could trace the origin of their mistakes later in life to the sexual abuse they suffered earlier in life, about forty to fifty years ago, it is the same with racial abuse. It not only affects the individual but also generations after the individual. The poverty of an individual due to economic deprivation or marginalization, affects his or her dependants.

Church Human Rights Commissions and Social Justice Departments

It is a healthy development that church human rights offices or social justice offices were established in the different denominations after the Civil Rights Movement of the 1960s. In some denominations or dioceses, the name may be different. Some call it Office of Justice and Peace, while some others call it Equal Opportunity Office or Office of Social Concern. How effective are these church human rights offices in checking and responding to the unequal treatments still being observed in the society? Are these church based human rights commissions well financed by church leaders to be able to carry out their works? Since all the interviews show that racial inequality still exists in all the American churches, can these church human rights offices help their members to stop all forms of discrimination in both church and society? How many times can they organize seminars in schools and churches to teach children in schools and adults to be conscious of how they treat their fellow human beings, as all human persons are created in the image and likeness of God?

Can they be as active as the pro-life organizations in all they are doing to fight against abortion? Can they dialogue with city officials and find out why black areas of most cities in America are neglected and why the roads leading to black parts of most American cities are not well maintained like roads leading to where mostly whites are living? Can they visit public school districts and find out why there are disparities in funding by state governments? Can they dialogue with banks and find out how true it is that minorities are not given enough loans and when given, are given different interest rates that may not help them to progress in their businesses? Can they mobilize whites, blacks, Hispanics, Asians, and Indians on Martin Luther King's day to carry out a peaceful march or protest against inequality to show that fighting inequality is not only a black person's affair? Can they dialogue with government security officials about police brutality against black men? If these church human rights offices or whatever they are called are able to do all these and more, then their establishments are justified; if not, their existence may look like a cover up.

The Revelation of Hurricane Katrina and its Pastoral Challenges

The level of poverty among the people of color exposed by Hurricane Katrina in this country was a shock to every one in America and to the world at large. Though the experience was unfortunate because of the loss of lives and property, lessons were learned from it. According to Jonathan Alter of the *Newsweek Magazine*, "Katrina reminded us, but the problem is not new. Why a rising tide of people live in poverty, who they are and—what we can do about it."[397] According to the figures, "Only 8 percent of American whites are poor, compared with 22 percent of Hispanics and nearly a quarter of all African-Americans (in a country that is 12 percent black)."[398]

Alter goes further to describe the whole situation as "an enduring shame."[399] He is right to call it a shame because it is not supposed to be that way. We have already seen why the gap between the world of the rich and that of the poor is so wide in this country. The image of poverty in America exposed by Katrina was like the image of a people inside the ocean begging for water to drink. If America is the Promised Land as some people call it, it should be inherited by all its citizens. Looking at the images of Katrina, one can still argue that the Protestant doctrine of divine election may still be influencing the order of things here.

The world of the rich shows that there are some citizens who are treated in such a way they feel divinely called to inherit this promised land, while the world of the poor shows that there are some citizens who are treated in such a way they feel as if they are still in the wilderness, yet to enter the promised land. The American government and constitution are presented as not influenced by any religion, and so no religious doctrine should be suspected as directly or indirectly implied in the way some people are treated. The pastoral challenges are: What can the American Churches or religions still do to help these poor Americans, apart from simple donations or raising funds through their charity departments or social services? Can the Churches or religions appeal for a dialogue with the government to discuss the real cause of poverty in this country and effectively address it? Can the church leaders appeal to the government for those who were deprived of their GI rights to be compensated? Now that we have learned who the poor are and the extent of their poverty, before attempting to answer the above questions, let us first look at what

Americans say about the cause of their poverty and what effect it may have on the pastoral response by the religious bodies in the country.

Racial Stereotyping, Crime, Poverty, and Pastoral Response

In September 2005, I was in the house of a friend who is also a pastoral care giver. We were watching the television about the horrors of Hurricane Katrina. The horrible pictures made my friend say, "Why is it that these guys could not run away despite all the warnings?"

I replied, "Many of them look very poor and may not even have the means to get away and the places to run to."

He replied, "And who is to blame for their poverty? They have decided not to work hard and continue in their laziness."

The statement of my pastoral care giver friend reminded me of what I used to hear about African Americans when I was still in Nigeria. Some of those who came back from America used to give us discouraging information about African Americans, as lazy and poor because they do not want to work hard and go to school. It was when I came here and started seeing things for myself that I felt that what I used to hear before I came to America needed to be investigated to know the real truth. I see it more as racial stereotyping and as an unfair image or description of a people whom history has not treated fairly.

It is true that there may be some African American youths who do not have much interest in going to school such as Mr. Jones. A pastor who has the interest in helping such people needs to study the family history of such youths to know why they are that way. It was not until I sat down to talk with Mr. Jones that I noticed that his illiteracy, his poverty, and his drug addiction or criminality has much to do with what happened to his frustrated father who hoped to be better treated after defending his country in a deadly war, but was denied all GI rights and abused. His father was one among over two million African American veterans, whose descendants would be in tens of millions by now, languishing in poverty.

I challenged one of my class mates in a pastoral education class who told us about how some very poor African American women with their children came to beg for money in his church and how they made donations to help them. He complained that after giving them money this Sunday, next Sunday they would come again for more. After his interesting story, he said, "These people have no plans for their future at all, I wonder!"

To clear his wonder, I asked him, "Did you sit down with one of them and ask her to tell you her life history?"

He said, "No."

I told him, "Well, it would have been nice if you had sat down to talk with at least one of them or some of them. You may have gotten some information that could have helped you to see the missing links in their lives."

I am not trying to blame everything on the administrative system; at the same time, to use racial stereotyping to blame everything on the victim is not right. I wanted my class mate to talk with those women, to know what has happened to their husbands. If Mr. Jones had been married and had children before he went to prison, his wife would have been taking care of his children alone. No person would have believed that Mr. Jones' crime and prison sentence has much to do with the system or the administration. I was reading the commencement address of President Lyndon B. Johnson at Howard University, on June 4, 1965. He talked about the breakdown of the Negro family in these words:

> Perhaps most important—its influence radiating to every part of life—is the break down of the Negro family structure. For this, most of all white America must accept responsibility. It flows from centuries of oppression and persecution of the Negro man. It flows from long years of degradation and discrimination which have attacked his dignity and assaulted his ability to produce for his family.[400]

President Johnson's statement and honesty makes me think about millions of black and Hispanic women that are taking care of their children alone. What has happened to their husbands? Most of them are in prison. According to Virgil Elizondo, "The jails are still packed with an unusually high percentage of Blacks and Hispanics."[401] William Pannell, a Caucasian writer, accepted some degree of discrimination in the Administrative system, when he referred to the number of black males in American prisons. He asserts, ". . . A disproportionate number of black males are in prison even if you allow for a certain degree of discrimination."[402] Why must there be discrimination in the system in determining who goes to prison? What is the intention of putting some people in prison based on discrimination? No matter the degree, discrimination is evil and should not be found in any civilized system of administration.

There are evidences to prove that the "drug war continues to target racial minorities, especially African Americans."[403] In the words of Harrison Paige and Allen J. Beck, "Of the 265,100 state prison inmates convicted for drug offenses in 2002, 126,000 (47.53%) were black, 61,700 (23.27%) were Hispanic, and 64,500 (24.33%) were white."[404] I have not observed or read about any religious group in this country addressing the government specifically on the disproportionate number of blacks and Hispanics in the American prisons. It is, therefore, important to call to the attention of the American churches that discrimination in enforcing the drug laws is seriously affecting the family system of the minorities and something should be done about that. The discrimination in enforcing the drug laws, which has resulted in sending more blacks and Hispanic men to prison, could be seen as the post modern strategy of breaking down the family system of people of color as President Johnson confessed in the 1960s. According to Randall G. Shelden, "the effects on children have been dramatic, especially for blacks, as black children are about nine times more likely to have a parent in prison than a white child. The drug war is the main culprit here."[405]

When the men are in prison, their wives train their children as single parents and the children will not receive the love, protection, and guidance of their fathers. There is a limit to what a single mother can do. Children of such broken families may not really do very well, as many may end up having a moral break down. This moral break down is not because of color but could happen to any child irrespective of color. We saw how the absence of Mr. Jones' father contributed to his mistakes and how he ended up in prison. This has happened to so many black families for so many years, and still, some people use racial stereotyping to make it look as if blacks by nature commit more crimes than other Americans. Some studies have been carried out which demonstrate that blacks may not be using drugs more than other groups; at the same time, they are arrested and sent to prison more than the others due to discrimination. According to the federal Household survey,

> Most current illicit drug users are white. There were an estimated 9.9 million whites (72 percent of all users), 2.0 million blacks (15 percent), and 1.4 Hispanics (10 percent) who were current illicit drug users in 1998. And yet blacks constitute 36.8% of those arrested for drug violations, over 42% of those in federal prisons for drug violations. African Americans comprise almost 58% of those in state prisons for drug felonies; Hispanics account for 20.7%.[406]

Heather Ratcliffe of *St. Louis Post Dispatch* reported on April 6th 2005 a clear evidence of racial profiling which also has much to do with the unjust enforcement of the drug laws in favor of one race at the detriment of the others. "It is found that in 2004, blacks' cars were searched about 1.7 times more often than whites', but contraband was found in whites' cars about 1.5 times more often. . .The proportion of blacks stopped in 2004 was 34 percent higher than the proportion of blacks age 16 or older in the 2000 census. They were stopped 38 percent more than whites."[407] This indicates that racial profiling and the targeting of blacks or minorities by police is increasing, not reducing. Any police unit that is implicated as being discriminatory in enforcing the law may not be effective in transforming the society and the individual and so may require transformation itself. This is because the crimes of some people as we have seen may not be given enough attention and this is not helpful to the individual and to the society. I do not believe that any police man or woman is formally trained to be discriminatory in carrying out his or her duties. If any system does it, then it becomes a state sponsored discrimination. It is, therefore, a more serious problem that should require a more corporate attention.

Discrimination in enforcing the drug policies does not also spare minority women, as they are subject to drug laws that are prejudiced against them and have contributed to their over-representation in the American prisons. The incarceration rates of minority women show that there are racial and ethnic differences. "Black females (with a prison and jail rate of 359 per 100,000) were 2-1/2 times more likely than Hispanic females (143 per 100,000) and nearly 4-1/2 times more likely than white females (81 per 100,000) to be incarcerated in 2004."[408] It is estimated that "almost 80 percent of minority women in the prison system are mothers. . ."[409] What happens to their children? Sometimes they lose their children to foster homes where they may not get the required maternal care. The argument is not that people who break the drug laws should not be treated according to the law, but the problem is that people are treated differently by the same law, which is supposed to correct them, simply because of the color of their skins. A law that is unjustly enforced can not be a good means of correction.

It is estimated that about 90 percent of African Americans who are in prison are there because of drug offences.[410] Drug offense becomes the particular crime that sends the greatest number of people of color to prison. I do not support any person whether white or black who indulges in drug addiction or drug business. At the same time, we may like to examine the sources of these drugs since this problem is taking a very big toll. There are two possible ways these dangerous drugs get into this country, if they are not produced here. They are either imported or smuggled. We then need to ask these questions: Who are the importers of these drugs? Do they have import licenses? Are these drugs imported for medical use? How effective are the law enforcement agents in monitoring the distribution of these drugs if they are imported for good use? I wonder if those living in the ghettoes have import licenses to import such huge amounts of drugs used on a daily basis.

If these drugs are smuggled into this country, who are the smugglers and how effective are the law enforcement agents in monitoring them with the information they get from arrested drug suspects? I wonder if smugglers can satisfy the huge market already established for these drugs in this country. Smugglers can only bring in a small amount. America is a country that is very technologically advanced and can monitor the movement of so many things with its intelligence agencies and with all the advanced scientific equipment. What is the priority? Is it to arrest as many people as possible and put them in prison or to find those who are distributing the drugs before they get to the ghettoes? Law enforcement agents need to do a better job of finding out the true sources and the distributions of such dangerous drugs because drug addiction is at present affecting every body in this country directly or indirectly. However, discrimination in enforcing the drug laws or any other laws does not help this society but will only break down more families of color, produce more street people, and increase the crime of the poor and neglected. It has to stop unless the intention is to make sure that a particular people do not rise but continue to be marginalized. Using racial stereotyping over the radio, television, and internet to make it look as if they are the major problem of the American society is not helping either because truth can never be totally suppressed.

I often hear people say that black neighborhoods are dangerous and full of crimes, especially with the problem of drugs and theft. This makes many people avoid residing in them. Insurance companies charge you almost twice if your properties are in such places. Why is it so? Why are these communities not rebuilt or maintained to look like other parts of the cities? From my observations, these black parts of most American cities are abandoned, the roads are not maintained, the streets are not looking beautiful, and many of the houses are abandoned without windows and doors. These abandoned houses attract bad people and drug pushers as hiding places. Most of the business establishments in these areas are closed, making them less attractive to job seekers. There is not enough provision of security in these areas to lessen and discourage crimes. Security comes most times when a crime is already committed.

A good example of such places is North and East St. Louis. It is the same in New York, New Orleans, and most other American cities where only blacks live. The major reason why these areas are abandoned is because only blacks are living in them. Why is it that the government or city officials cannot maintain the roads like other parts of the cities, maintain the streets, and put more security in these areas? The abandonment and lack of care for these black communities only helps to increase crime. I see better parts of most American cities where the communities are mixed and the best parts of the cities where only whites are living. Why are things this way? Is it to perpetuate the stereotyping that blacks lack moral qualities as Rev. Peterson claimed?

Do religious leaders ever feel that it is part of their commitment to justice, to ask why many parts of American cities where a particular group of people are living are always abandoned and less cared for, while the tax payers' money is better spent on maintaining some parts of the cities where a particular group of people are living? I believe that one of the best ways to combat crime is to rebuild these black parts of the cities, make them attractive, and provide enough security. Instead of the abandoned houses providing hiding places or shelter for drug peddlers, they will be turned into beautiful apartments. If this is not done, there will be a time when every person including blacks will run to the counties where there are better houses, better roads, and better security. When this happens, the cities will be empty or some rich white business men and women may buy these communities over at very cheap rates and rebuild them and place their own prices on them, which may not be easy for the poor blacks to afford.

I see racial stereotyping in general as a way of escaping from the real issue and to calm the conscience as if nothing is going wrong in the system. What makes any person feel that African Americans and other people of color would not have done as well as their white counterparts, if they were or are given equal opportunities in the history of this country? I believe that those who indulge in racial stereotyping over the radio, television, internet, and newspapers, have not read the history. If they had known the history, they would have known that there are some statements that can only expose how uninformed they are about the history of their country. Racial stereotyping can only deceive those who are deceivable to believe that African Americans are naturally prone to crime and too lazy to progress economically. Those who use racial stereotyping to confuse or deceive the public from knowing the exact truth are obstructing justice. It is simply a propaganda war against the blacks and other minorities.

Any person could be lazy. I do not believe that laziness is a color issue. Any person can be a drug addict; I do not see it as a color issue. Any person can be a thief; I do not see it as a color issue. Any person can suffer from any type of disease; I do not see it as a color issue. Any child can do poorly at school if his or her school is not well funded. Most African Americans I talked to do not believe that they are lazy. Some argue that if their ancestors were lazy, slavery wouldn't have lasted for about four hundred years. They are not descendants of a weaker stock. How are they lazy when they do the most difficult, the most risky, and the lowest paid jobs in America of the twenty first century? Some argue that the foundation of the strong American economy was laid by the slave labor of their ancestors. Lefferts A. Loetscher, a professor emeritus of American Church history, agrees with them. Loetscher argues that the profits from slavery "remained as an economic foundation for generations after the traffic itself had been abandoned."[411] Unfortunately, it is the belief of most African Americans that they are placed at the bottom of the economy for which they helped to lay the foundation due to past and current unequal treatments.

However, the above stereotyping of my friend and what I used to hear in Nigeria about black Americans, tallies with the statement of Alter in *Newsweek* magazine, about the feelings of most Americans about the reason why most African Americans and Hispanics are poor. According to Alter, many people here believe that African Americans and Hispanics are poor because of their laziness. In the words of Andrew Cherlin of Johns Hopkins University, "Americans tend to think of poor people as being responsible for their own economic woes."[412] A Caucasian friend of mine told me that the problem of the African Americans is that they have "a culture of self defeat." I disagreed with her and encouraged her to consult the history. The history of this country tells me a different thing. The first and greatest step to solving the problem of poverty in this country is to accept the truth about the historical cause of it and to face the reality.

I believe that every African American, just like any person from any other group, has some personal efforts to make to improve his or her living conditions. At the same time, the continuation of discrimination in many aspects makes it more difficult for them. For instance, if the state government spends one million dollars to fund an all white-school in the county or in the suburban area in a year and spends just half a million dollars to fund an integrated school or an all black-school in a year, the results will differ. The 'much' you put in is the 'much' you receive. If any black child visits any of the white schools in the counties and sees the facilities and equipment in such schools, that black child may likely feel inferior but may not know where the disparity is coming from. If that child is not well directed, he or she may think that it is natural, while it is not.

This American attitude of blaming only the victim could make sympathy or empathy for the people of color more difficult and can also affect church pastoral response to their poverty. A pastor is a human being and could be subject to undue influences. Racial stereotyping can not only limit the sympathy of a pastor to the poor, but can also make him or her quote the Bible and say, "For everyone who has will be given more, and he will have abundance. Whoever does not have, even what he has will be taken from him" (Matt. 25:24-30). We saw how the Christian Churches used the Bible to support slavery and discrimination laws and applied them in church worship for centuries.

The argument by most Americans that African Americans and Hispanics are totally responsible for their economic woes is very wrong because I have not observed any difference between them and any other group of Americans. I have only observed a difference in treatment. From the 1800s, many governments had already started depriving people of color quality education which condemned them to the lowest menial jobs that never helped them to rise up economically. There are also records to show that black Americans made some efforts to rise economically after emancipation from slavery and after the civil war but were beaten down by past governments to remain poor. Stanley J. Kutler testifies to this in these words:

> After the civil war, African Americans improved their economic status as a whole, engaged in civil rights efforts to enforce new anti- discrimination laws, and became politically active. However, between 1877, when the federal troops were withdrawn from the south, and 1910, a new system of segregation and discrimination was imposed on African Americans. With each depression in the late nineteenth century, African Americans lost their hard-won rights, were deserted by liberals, and saw a number of rights eliminated or curtailed by U.S. Supreme Court Decisions in 1873, 1883 and 1896.[413]

It is clear from the above statement that the African Americans made many efforts after emancipation to improve economically, after centuries of slavery. They made these efforts irrespective of the fact that they had hard times during post slavery period when their masters who were not happy with the emancipation, especially in the south, left them without anything to start life. The above statement also makes it clear that there were deliberate efforts in the past to keep the blacks at the economic bottom of this country.

A second example that shows that blacks made efforts to improve economically but were beaten down during the era of segregation laws is the Tulsa race riots of 1921, which brought to ruins a thriving black business district of Tulsa, Oklahoma.

> Tulsa's Green Wood district is the site of one of the most devastating race riots in the history of the United States. Before May 31, 1921, Tulsa's black business district known as Greenwood flourished in spite of segregation. It boasted of several restaurants, theatres, clothing shops and hotels. Dubbed the 'Black Wall Street,' Greenwood was an economic powerhouse. After May 31, 1921, Greenwood would never be the same. The tension mounted between black and white communities over an incident that allegedly occurred in an elevator at Drexel building in downtown Tulsa involving Sarah Page, a 17-year-old white elevator operator, and Dick Rowland, a 19-year-old black man.[414]

There are different versions of what really happened that made the riot so intense that "airplanes distributing nitroglycerin, bombed the affluent community, and an angry white mob began the destruction of the Little Africa."[415] It is not clear why air planes were used to bomb only the black business district of Tulsa. The only explanation of who bombed the black business district was that "a former police officer, Van B. Hurley, gave a 31-page confession naming city officials who met downtown to plan the air attack on Little Africa."[416] Did the federal or state governments arrest the city officials for unauthorized air bombardment or even set up a commission immediately after the riot to know what happened? Did the churches ever think that it concerned them to ask what happened?

The government did not set up enquires to know what really happened until after seventy-eight years when most of those who would have given evidence had died or were unable to talk well."[417] This is not the normal American response to similar issues because I was so happy with the government swift response in setting up a commission to look into what led to the September 11th terrorist attack in 2001. I wonder what would have happened if a black mob destroyed an affluent white business district and bombed and killed hundreds of people. The investigation of the Tulsa carnage should not have taken seventy-eight years. The delayed government response to the Tulsa riot reminds me of the delayed federal government response to the Hurricane Katrina crisis.

One wonders why anything that concerns the lives of blacks, doesn't seem to be treated equally as something important.

According to the CNN report of the commission, "Experts now estimate that at least 300 people, and perhaps as many as 3,000 died."[418] Most of the people who died during the riots and after the bombings were blacks and were buried in mass graves.[419] All these examples are facts of history that can not be denied about how the blacks in this country have been beaten down, and neglected as if whatever happens to them does not matter. In addition, It was when Martin Luther King Jr. got to the point of addressing the poverty of his people that he was assassinated, showing that whoever killed him did not want his people to be freed from poverty, despite the removal of the segregation laws. The 40 percent of African Americans who are described as below the poverty line have the capability to work hard and would not like to remain in their present poor conditions, but the questions are: What plan and wish has any twenty-first century American governments for African Americans and other people of color? What are the plans and wishes of American churches for the American poor at present? We shall get to these questions later.

Church Pastoral Handling of Poverty and Social Services

Through social services, the American churches have tried to help the poor with material needs. There is a good record of how the Protestant and Catholic churches have tried since the 1800s to provide food and other material needs to the poor in American society and outside. This is why Olmstead asserts, "Prior to 1890, the principal activities of the Roman Catholic Church in the area of social betterment were along charitable lines. One of the most important agencies was the time-honored society of St. Vincent de Paul, a lay missionary movement which endeavored to bring both physical aid and spiritual sustenance to unfortunates."[420]

Another charitable church, which has played a prominent role in providing and serving the poor in the American society, is the Salvation Army. "The organization was possibly best known for the work of its Slum Brigade, which went into run-down sections of the cities, held services in saloons and halls, brought relief to the destitute, and preached against vice."[421] This is a good example of pastoral work, because it is important to go to where the poor reside, and experience the type of life they are living.

Here in St. Louis, the Catholic Charities of the Saint Louis Archdiocese have helped the poor by raising millions of dollars through the generosity of Christians and non Christians living in the city. I know that this could be the same in many other American cities in both Catholic and Protestant churches. The victims of Hurricane Katrina received great deal of help from these church-based charitable organizations. These questions still remain: Are the social services provided by these church based charitable organizations enough to fight against the problem of poverty among the minorities? Are the services provided by church charities solutions to poverty or the management of poverty? What do these poor Americans really need, the *fish* or the *hook* or both? What plans do the American Churches have to help these poor ones to be more self reliant and less dependent on others?

The American Churches Need to be More Prophetic

Without denying the efforts already made by the American Churches, there is the need to do more. The churches are called to be prophetic, as institutions representing the liberating power of God among His people on earth. We have to accept the fact that religion in America has in some cases, in issues of justice and peace, done well and in some cases failed regrettably. In the words of Sharon Thornton,

> Believers of all faiths expect their religious associations to interpret suffering and provide for its relief. For Christians, the church sometimes honored this trust and responded in effective ways. At other times it has failed miserably. Too often it has been a source of suffering itself, contributing to the hardship of people by aligning with unjust societal practices and patterns of living.[422]

The people of color whose poverty can not be simply dismissed as mere human laziness need the church institutions and individuals to speak more effectively for them, and address their poverty as soon as possible. Poverty is better eliminated or reduced than managed. The church based charities are trying their best to provide the *fish* for the poor, but it will be better to speak for equal treatment so that the *hook* will be given to them, to do the fishing by themselves, as given to others. This will make for self reliance, reduce begging, reduce crime, and improve the economy of this country. This is part of the ministerial responsibilities of the churches to their members and to humanity at large.

For the churches to be prophetic there is need to engage in careful listening to the stories of the poor. There can be no effective prophecy without story telling and the act of listening. God listens to His people and "His ears hear the cries of the oppressed" (Jas 5:4). God first listens to the cries of His suffering people before sending a prophet (Isaiah 6:8), to go and rescue His people. The prophet also listens in order to hear the complaints of the people. The people of Israel complained to Moses and Moses complained to God. (Ex.17:2-6) and the relief came. So since God listens, the churches, called to liberate the people of God, should also listen. The question remains, after listening to the cries of the poor, what are the American churches going to do to help the poor to be more self reliant? We shall get to the answer to this question after looking at the following acceptance speech by a representative of the American churches in the World Council of Churches that they have not done so well with being prophetic.

US Church Leaders Confess Prophecy Failures

The *Christian Century* magazine of March 21ˢᵗ 2006 carries an editorial captioned "US leaders confess church failures." The confession letter was read by Sharon Watkins, president of the Christian Church (Disciples of Christ), during the Ninth Assembly of the World Council of Churches held in Porto Alegre, Brazil. In the words of Richard A. Kauffman, reporting for Christian Century,

> Leaders of the U.S. denominations belonging to World Council of Churches created a small buzz at Porto Alegre by delivering a letter to the Ninth Assembly in which they confessed the complicity of the U.S. churches in actions and policies that are detrimental to the well-being of the world. They mentioned

three areas in particular: the Iraq War, the global environmental crisis, and global poverty.[423]

The signers of the letter used penitential terms to express their feelings.

> We lament with special anguish the war in Iraq, launched in deception and violating global norms of justice and human rights . . . We confess that we have failed to raise a prophetic voice loud enough and persistent enough to call our nation to global responsibility for creation, that we ourselves are complicit in a culture of consumption that diminishes the earth.[424]

I do appreciate their honesty in accepting some failures in these areas. I also do appreciate their concern about global poverty in particular; at the same time, I would advise that they start first by speaking out strongly in favor of addressing domestic poverty, as charity begins at home. The 40 percent of African American poverty, the 22 percent of Hispanic poverty and the 8 percent of white poverty is a thing of concern that needs to be immediately addressed. The image of poverty exposed by Katrina shocked the whole world and shows how concerned Americans are in helping poor people all over the world. It will be good not to forget that there are also millions suffering from severe poverty not just in New Orleans, but in many other American cities.

Something dramatic happened when I traveled to Nigeria last January to visit my former parishioners whose children died in the last plane crash that occurred on the 10th of December 2005 at Port Harcourt Nigeria. Most of the children that died in the crash were my former church school children. When I got to the parish, some children gathered to welcome me. They were asking me questions about America and about the Katrina victims, especially their fellow black children whom they saw over the CNN news network begging for food after the flood. They were surprised to see American children begging for food, because America to them is a very rich country and it was unusual to see its children begging for food like the children of Sudan, Somalia, Tsunami, and children of other war or disaster areas.

Some expressed their sympathy for their poor fellow children whom

Katrina rendered homeless and without food. A small girl of about five or six years old, got up from her seat and came directly to me and said, "I have something for those children who were begging for food over the television in America." I asked her, "What do you have for them?" She opened her small bag and brought out a packet of candy and handed it over to me and said, "Please, Father, give this candy to those black children and tell them that we are sorry for what happened and that we love them. When I get home, I will tell my daddy and my mommy to give me more candies to give them." The small girl's action made the other children burst into laughter but to me it was not funny. It really touched my heart and made me feel that Katrina has made people outside American now know that some people here also need help. Her action was prophetic to me and raised a lot of questions in my mind. She heard the voice of the needy; she listened and followed it up with action. She was ready to involve her parents to help.

Most people in and outside America see this country as the richest country and the most developed in the world. There is no doubt that America may be the richest and most developed in the world. I see America as a big family. The question then is: do all the members of this family benefit from its richness and development? How do you evaluate the richest and most developed country? Is it by considering part of the population or the whole population? Can the above claim be exact when you consider the poverty rates of 40 percent of black people, 22 percent of Hispanics and the 8 percent of whites? The above claim could be true when you consider the standard of living or the economic power of the majority of the white population and the development of where a greater percentage of them live, mostly in the rich counties. This does not mean that there are no poor white families, but the percentage is too small compared to others and considering the populations of the different groups.

When you consider the poverty of the majority of blacks, the neglect of their communities, (ghettoes and slums mostly in cities), without well maintained roads, schools, parks, street lights, and houses, the above claim may be subject to a serious argument. A developed country should be able to carry along all its citizens. It is not a question of some racial groups not wanting to come along, but history proves that it is a question of some racial groups are not allowed to come along on equal considerations.

The number of poor people in America may be as big as or even more than the number of poor people in other countries. Truth can never be hidden forever, because Katrina has exposed a fact that can no longer be ignored by the American governments and the churches or religions. Whatever may have contributed to the poverty of such a huge number of people in the richest country of the world needs to be well established and adequately addressed. It could be that the problem is from the individual or that something is still wrong in the administrative system; it needs to be talked about. The above confession of the American church leaders is a mark of repentance and true repentance comes with resolutions to make things better. If they have failed to raise prophetic voices in the past, as they confessed, it is not too late to start raising prophetic voices for a much needed dialogue to address the problem of poverty and inequality in this country.

American Churches to advocate for Dialogue with Governments on Poverty

My experience after visiting some other American cities is that the poor condition of the people of color and even some white families is the same in New Orleans, St Louis, Chicago, New York, Atlanta, Houston, Washington, Los Angeles, Atlanta, Boston, Philadelphia and so on. Millions of people are really suffering as we can observe in the case of New Orleans. Poverty makes the lives of millions of people very miserable and unbearable, and increases crimes as no person may be checking the number of poverty related deaths on daily bases in America.

This calls for an all out war on poverty, which should start with a sincere dialogue. This type of war, unlike the one in Iraq, is not fought with lives but brothers and sisters sitting at table over cups of coffee to dialogue on how to help one another and move forward in justice and peace. The religious leaders in this country are to act as catalysts to such a dialogue or are to appeal to the government to approve a dialogue with the help of "the United States Conference of Religions for Peace."[425] I am happy that "the United States Conference of Religions for Peace operates on the conviction that multireligious collaboration and common action can be powerful instruments in the quest for constructive social development, justice, reconciliation, and peace."[426]

Some top government officials are already thinking about the need for such a dialogue. The churches, acting as catalysts, will support their feelings and help to make the dialogue come faster. Responding to the poverty and the sufferings of the victims of Katrina, as reported by the *St. Louis Post Dispatch* of Saturday, September 17, 2005, President W. Bush promised an audience at the National Cathedral that "he would use the rebuilding process on the Gulf Coast to correct the poverty born of racial discrimination that left so many Hurricane Katrina victims vulnerable."[427] This is a promise that is not yet fulfilled as thousands of victims are still stranded. The billions of dollars already being spent are spent on reconstructing the levees that failed to protect the people. As the levees are being reconstructed, it is good to talk about how to reconstruct the lives of the people, as promised by the president. This dialogue should not be confused with the current discussions on what happened to the levees.

However, I love the President's remark because it shows that the government is now conscious of the fact that this is the time for the *Third Reconstruction* since the *First Reconstruction* and the *Second Reconstruction* failed to stop inequality and failed to make the African Americans fully part of the economic life of this country after slavery and segregation laws. Supporting the President's comment, a top government official, Sen. Barrack Obama, also said that the victims of Katrina "were abandoned long ago—to murder and mayhem in the streets, to substandard schools, to dilapidated housing, to inadequate health care, to a pervasive sense of hopelessness."[428]

It is important that the president and top government officials now acknowledge openly the sober truth that the poverty of millions of African Americans and other people of color not only in New Orleans but also in other parts United States has much to do with racial discrimination. This is clear with what we have seen above about the Second World War and Korean War GI Bill of Rights which was supposed to benefit all GIs but was disproportionately aimed and administered to help only Euro-origin GIs leaving African American and women GIs of all races and their families to suffer in poverty. "The record is clear. Instead of seizing the opportunity to end institutional racism, the federal government did its level best to shut and double-seal the post war window of opportunity in African American faces."[429] Katrina has exposed the fact that it is time to help African Americans and other deprived Americans to have their appropriate share of the American pie.

The Importance of a Dialogue to fight the Roots of Poverty in America

One thing is certain. If the churches and the government join hands to fight poverty not just among the people of color, but as it is affecting the lives of every American, the crime rate will certainly be reduced. According to Alter, ". . . Clinton initiatives and the boom of the 1990s pulled 4.1 million of the working poor out of poverty. (Good times don't always have that effect. The Reagan boom of the 1980s did the same for only 50,000.) Meanwhile crime plummeted in cities across the country, down to levels not seen since the 1950s. Few noticed that progress in fighting poverty stalled with the economy in 2001."[430] Since Clinton's initiatives helped 4.1 million people come out of poverty and reduced crime significantly, it means that one of the most effective ways of fighting crime is by fighting poverty.

Since the Democrats under Clinton could help 4.1 million people out of poverty and the Republican Party under Reagan helped only 50,000 people, it then means that any government that comes to power or is in power that decides to help about 8 million Americans, would not only be improving the lives of 8 million Americans but also reducing poverty twice more than it was experienced when Clinton's package helped 4.1 million people. These ideas call to mind the following questions: What is the wish of any American government that comes to power about the African Americans, the Hispanics, and the other people of color? Which of the political parties is more committed to the suffering of the American poor and is ready to start a dialogue to address the poverty that was inflicted due to long economic exclusion as President Bush acknowledged? Is it the sincere wish of any government that more or most minorities come to the middle class level through self efforts and through government help as was the case of the Euro-Americans? The above figures show that any government that comes to power in America can help any group it likes economically.

Is there anything like racial grading in this country in which there is a deliberate wish to keep some people at the lowest economic level and to keep the supremacy issue constant as Brodkin observes? "Those racially skewed gains have been passed across the generations, so that racial inequality seems to maintain itself naturally, even after legal segregation ended."[431] This was in reference to the GI Bill, the FHA and VA mortgages which functioned as a collection of racial privileges. Hilary Herbold, argues that "Race was contested terrain in the very inception of the GI Bill."[432] The result was a GI Bill that brought some people up and kept some people at the bottom economically and socially.

This deliberate government action is still affecting the lives of millions of colored people today. This question remains, how do the churches pastorally help these unfortunate citizens still languishing in historical poverty? As already indicated, there is no other way apart from the religious leaders of this country calling for an honest dialogue and an all out war against poverty no matter what it takes. If the churches can convince the government to come to round table discussions on this issue, then their prophetic efforts would yield a fruitful result that can change the lives of millions of citizens and also help to improve the society.

Can the government and the Churches Win a War on Poverty?

The answer to the above question is emphatically "Yes!" As indicated above, much depends on the wish of the government in power and the religious leaders that can speak for the poor. The United States of America is a blessed and rich country and can afford to fight a war on poverty as it is fighting a war on terrorism. Both evils are threatening the lives of citizens of America. I have no problems with spending hundreds of billions of dollars to fight wars overseas to protect American lives from potential terrorists. It is also good for the religious leaders of this blessed country to remind the government that poverty is also terrorizing and threatening people's lives at home and is worth spending for.

The question then is, can the government afford it. To answer this question, we may refer to the reports of Sar A. Levitan and Karen A. Cleary on how much the government spent on the GI Bill to rebuild the lives of 16 million American white GIs and their families after the World War and Korean Wars. "Between 1944 and 1971, federal spending for former soldiers in this 'model welfare system' totaled over 95 billion. By 1948, 15 percent of the federal budget was devoted to the GI Bill, and Veterans Administration (VA) employed 17 percent of the workforce."[433]

As the government could, in the 1950s and 1960s, help 16 million Euro-American former GIs and civilians to get up to a middle class economic status, it can also do the same now most especially for about two million colored GIs, including women GIs who were deprived of their benefits. It was revealed in the NBC news earlier this year, 2006, that about 200 billion dollars have been spent in Iraq only. On the 25th of April 2006, it was announced in NBC news that the president was going to use his veto to justify more spending on Iraq and for Katrina relief efforts. When interviewed by Brian Williams in New Orleans on 27th April, while on a visit to New Orleans, the president praised the economy as being strong and the best in the world. This shows that apart from the Iraq War, another war could be fought and that war should be on poverty, or if another war is going to be fought, it should be waged against poverty.

I believe that if the government can use just half of 200 billion dollars, at least 10 million Americans, especially those whose names are on record as having been deprived of their post war benefits can be helped. It does not matter if justice comes after 50 years. Those who were sexually abused 50 years ago are going to court to find justice even if not for themselves but for their dependents whose lives have been badly affected by what happened to them. The exposition of Katrina shows that something has to be done.

What will happen when 200 billion is spent on war against poverty? Most Americans irrespective of color will become middle class citizens. Is that the wish of every person in America? For some Americans, who want inequality to continue and look natural, it is not going to happen. For some Americans, who feel that what is good for the goose is good for the gander, it is a possibility and could be part of a government agenda for the first quarter of the century. The argument is not going to be if some people have the natural capacity to use the money well to be self reliant.

Every group in America is naturally endowed to succeed. God did not create some people to be at the bottom of everything while some people should be on top of everything. It is human made and unjust. I feel the government and the religious leaders can win an all out war on poverty, but it has to start first with a dialogue that should not be delayed or avoided or blocked any longer. I agree with Otis Turner who said that, "dialogue is central to constructive social change."[434]

I was surprised to hear Brian Williams, the NBC newscaster, say that some people are sending e-mails questioning why Katrina is still making big news when it is no longer a big story. When the corpse of another person's son or daughter is being carried along the road in an ambulance, it looks like a log of wood is being carried along. It becomes the body of a human being when it is your own son or daughter. Katrina is still making news because things are not yet in order there. Not only levees but also lives need to be reconstructed.

Representatives of the Proposed Dialogue and Items for Discussion

The dialogue to address poverty and all forms of racial inequality could involve federal and State government officials, representatives of the different religions or denominations, women's groups, related human rights agencies, and representatives of the different races. The proposed items for discussion in such a dialogue include the following:

1. How to fight against poverty in general as it affects the lives of Americans. In case of doubt about who the poor are, there could be a sincere reference to history to find out who the poor are and what has been the cause of their poverty. Strategies could be mapped out on what to do to help people to be more economically self-reliant. Decisions could be taken to avoid such strategies being disproportionately administered as happened in the past with the GI, FHA, and VA mortgages. Honest agencies could be established, if not yet in existence, made up of different religious groups and racial groups to monitor unequal treatments and do something to stop them.

2. Discussions could be held on well-documented affirmative actions that were disproportionately administered to help some people and deprive some people of their past rights like the GI Bills. There could be a review of why millions of African American GIs and the women GIs of every race were not given their rights after servicing their country. I believe that the well documented lists of the veterans who fought those Wars are still well preserved in the United States War archives. There could be a reference to such lists, to know those who were deprived of benefits. If there is any claim that anything has happened to the list of involved veterans, some of the veterans are still alive. If such veterans are dead, their children and grand children can prove that they fought such wars and then receive their benefits. The argument is not going to

be that affirmative action is now being administered to favor everybody who is qualified for it. This does not solve the problem because millions of African American Second World War and Korean War GIs and their families are still suffering from the ones they did not benefit from. It is like inflicting an injury on somebody and you're telling the person, "Sorry, I will not inflict such injury on you again." This does not remove the suffering of the injured person. The only way to show that one is sorry for inflicting the injury is to make sure that the injured person is taken to the hospital and is healed of the injury.

3. The dialogue will also look into how to end all other forms of inequality and discriminations. This will involve a review on job opportunities, educational funding, bank loans for business, residential issues, racial profiling, racial stereotyping, police brutality, and other related matters that have showed disproportionate handling in the past and in the present. Some institutions like the police, the banks, and the media and others that have been implicated as being discriminatory against some Americans are to be reformed and given a better orientation that will make for more tolerance. For the participants of the dialogue to handle all these, there is need for sincerity, openness to one another, and a matter of conscience to accept, tolerate, and be fair to one another in the name of justice and peace. Having dealt with poverty and its solution in this chapter, in the next chapter we shall look at the suggested measures which the churches can apply to eradicate racism among their members.

CHAPTER EIGHT
MEASURES TO FIGHT RACISM IN THE CHURCHES
IN AMERICA

It is one thing to identify a problem; it is another thing to offer some solutions to it, no matter how difficult the problem may prove to be. The wounds created by racism and long periods of oppression are still deep.[435] It is important to let people know that something could still be done to improve race relations in this country. Though racism may be difficult to fight against, at the same time, I do believe that racism can still be defeated if people can have a change of heart and treat others with fairness. Generally speaking, "Christianity and Christians will be judged by two criteria: how much we love God and how well we demonstrate that by loving our neighbor. This is Christianity in a nutshell."[436] Are our neighbors only white folks or black folks or brown folks? I do believe that if any person who had abused another person sexually can have true conversion and stop doing such evil, a racist can also repent and stop abusing others because of their race or color. It is individuals that make up the institutions, in the case of institutionalized racism. True repentance of the individuals that make up the institutions can also be a way out.

The people interviewed from the different Christian denominations and Jewish congregations testified that there is still racism or racial inequality existing in all the churches and synagogues in America, as it exists in the entire American society. The social scientist, Bob Blauner, describes racial oppression in America as "still the big news."[437] It is still the big news because the removal of the segregation laws and the passage of the civil rights legislation have not stopped inequality in America.[438] There is no doubt that the churches have been doing something, especially by issuing statements of condemnation and denouncement of racism; still they need to do more, be more sincere and take more practical steps. Otis Turner sees these statements of verbal condemnation and denouncement of racism as mere first steps of a long journey to fight this evil in both church and society.[439]

In discussing the solutions to racial inequality, I have decided to discuss them according to the existing order in this book, Protestant Churches, Catholic Church, and the Jewish religion. The measures may be the same but may be differently applied according to what is obtainable in each religion or denomination. It is possible that some of these measures are already being applied in some churches or synagogues, but from my observations, they are not generally applied. Some are weakly applied, while in some cases, they are not applied at all.

Protestant Churches

The Protestant Churches can comfortably apply the following measures, which I gathered from different sources including the interviews of some Protestant pastors and lay ministers.

1) A Greater Awareness about the Reality and Evil Nature of Racism

Protestant members through their pastors may need to be more aware of the reality of racism in their midst and the fact that it is not normal, but evil. Many Christians, due to the wrong impressions created in the society through racist theories, ideologies, and racial stereotyping, may think that the feeling of superiority to others due to the color of skin is normal and acceptable. Unfortunately, some Christian teachings and values were applied to defend racist behaviors among Christians. The Protestant Churches, therefore, have to be ready to purge themselves of any values or teachings from which racism "derives sustenance and nurture, many of which are deeply embedded in religious culture and traditions."[440] It can be very effective if members hear from their pastors during sermons that racism negates the teachings of Christ and that it "plagues and cripples our growth in Christ in as much as it is antithetical to the gospel."[441]

There may be need to organize seminars and workshops to re-educate the adult members on how to appreciate and nurture the important values for co-existing in a multicultural society.[442] Trained speakers from the different races and different churches could be invited to speak to the adult members of the churches in both diocesan and parish levels on how to "build bridges of communication across racial and cultural lines as they worship together and learn how to live into a vision of the beloved community."[443] Suitable dates in a year could be chosen to organize such seminars and workshops, especially Martin Luther King Junior's Remembrance Day.

2) Forming the minds of Young Ones in the Right Direction in Sunday Schools

Protestant children must be formed to have the right attitudes towards their fellow human beings and to relate well with children of other colors. Racism is a shortcoming of the adults. Children are innocent, and their minds should not be negatively formed by wrong teachings. People should be careful not to mislead any of these little ones (Mt 18: 5-6). During Sunday Schools, correct and helpful teachings could be given to them about the creation story and the fact that God created everybody in his image and likeness irrespective of color. They need to know that the difference in skin color does not mean inferiority or superiority over any one as the spirit and image of God is in everyone equally.

Children are often taught behaviors such as stealing, fighting, telling lies, and so on are among the bad behaviors they must learn to avoid. Discrimination against their friends in any form could be added to the list of bad behaviors. They need to know that they should avoid discrimination in their interaction with others because it is sinful.

3) Church School Curriculum to Reflect Race Relations

Most Protestant Churches in the United States have their private church schools; religious instructions in these schools could include lessons on proper relationships among the races. It could involve trained teachers who have a tolerant attitude towards people of other color to handle such topics.

In my interview with Reverend Dr. Dickinson of the Lutheran Church, he remembered and regretted how they were taught in segregated schools as children that "the black man is inferior to the white man and that the white man is the most evolved man, while the black man is the missing link between the apes and the white man."[444] Such teachings affected many of his friends psychologically to believe that they were inferior to their white counterparts. He hopes that teachers and parents do not presently give their children such false doctrines, as it does not help race relations.[445] Protestant children of all colors need to hear it from the mouths of their teachers, parents, and pastors of all colors, that the difference in the color of their skins and that of their peers of color does not mean superiority or inferiority. They need to get it right when they are still young with innocent minds.

Children need to learn about the evil consequences of racism. They could be told stories about the holocaust and shown pictures of wars and exterminations caused by racial prejudice. Movies dealing with the effects of hating their friends who are not of the same color as they are could be shown in classes or recreation halls. Activities that could involve interaction between the races could be encouraged. In such schools, teachers are to be careful not to make remarks or carry out any act that instigates racial feelings. Teachers who do that could be investigated, and if found guilty could be warned or disciplined if need be.

4) Cross Posting of Pastors to Serve in Integrated Churches

One of the scandals of racism in some Protestant Churches is the attitude of some members not accepting pastors who are not of their own race or color. Members are to be told how unacceptable it is for them to reject any pastor sent to them because he or she is the "wrong" color. Any parishes or communities doing that could be warned, and if they continue, could be disciplined by the church authorities.

5) Apologies should be Matched with the Required Actions

Many Protestant Churches and Conventions have rendered apologies to the victims of their racist pasts. These apologies may prove meaningless if they are not matched with the required actions that depict true repentance. There could be compensations either by appointments or by other considerations to the victims, in any way they may have been deprived of any rights or positions in their churches because of racial prejudice.

6) Policies to Counter Future Racial Scandals in American Protestant Churches

To counter issues and comments that could bring about disunity, laws and policies are made by a group, church, or community. Such laws or policies or rules and their penalties can help members to be conscious of what they have to avoid or else they may be disciplined for defaulting. One of the comments made by one of the interviewees was that most churches condemn racism verbally as a sin but they do not have laws to enforce equality and stop racism even among their members. If the protestant churches can handle racism as they handle other social evils, members may be more careful how they treat other members who are of different color or race.[446]

7) Condemnation of any Racist Act or Statement from any One in the Society

In American society, people frequently make statements or perform some actions that show hatred for other races. We hear about burning of black churches by some hate groups. We hear and see very often, over the television, police brutality, reports of racial profiling, and other forms of unequal treatment of others. Such actions and similar ones should not be greeted with silence from church leaders if noticed. In some Protestant Churches, there are human rights offices or offices of social justice or other commissions to protect the rights and dignity of persons in and outside the church. Such offices could react and speak out on behalf of the entire church or denomination against injustice in the society not minding who is involved. There should be no question of speaking out against some evils and keeping silent on others. For example abortion and racism or racial inequality should be given equal attention.

8) Joint Appeal to the Government for a Dialogue

This has already been discussed in detail in the last chapter. Dialogue is an act of love, and wonderful things happen when brothers and sisters come together for mutual understanding. It is the best way to create racial justice and fairness. The Protestant human rights agencies could form a team with those of other religious bodies in this country to appeal to the government to see the need for this dialogue which should not be delayed or avoided again.

Catholic Church

I do not believe that the Catholic Church is a *white man's* church, because the Catholic Church has never changed from being "One, Holy, Catholic, and Apostolic."[447] However, we must acknowledge that the Catholic Church in America has acted and failed to act in ways that made African Americans have such feelings about the Catholic Church. We have come of age in this generation to correct the mistakes of history and to put things right both in the church and in the society. This does not mean that we in the present generation are innocent of racism, as we saw in the interviews. "The sad story of racism and exploitation continues today in many ways—some quite open and others more subtle and unsuspected."[448] The following measures can be of help to fight against racism in the American Catholic Church.

1) To Create Awareness that the Problem of Racism Still Exists in the Church

One major step towards curing a disease is to be aware that it exists, where it exists, and the form it takes in the body. From my discussions with many Catholics across the country, I realized that there are different feelings and assumptions about racism in the Church. Some Catholics do not feel that racism exists in the Catholic Church, either because they are not victims, or because they feel racism is normal. From the interviews, I learned that some Catholics do not see anything wrong in asking black Catholics to go to black churches for Mass instead of going to any church that is near them.

A white Catholic does not know how painful a black priest may feel when he is posted to a white dominated parish to be a pastor or to say Mass and some of the parishioners reject him because he is black. Many do not know how a black or colored Catholic may feel when he or she enters the church to worship God and a white Catholic leaves the pew for the person to sit alone, while the church is full. These above examples are recent happenings. People need to be aware that these are happening, and that they are not expected of any Catholic.

The awareness could be created by pastors, occasionally instructing people how sinful it is for any one to discriminate against a fellow human being due to color or any other reason that is not of human making. Pastors can preach against racism and its bad effects on Sundays and weekdays when the readings from the American liturgical calendar are talking about how Christ handled the different races and also what some of the evangelists like Paul wrote about the races (Jn 4:7-26, Lk 9: 51-55, Romans 10: 12-13, 1Cor 1:24, Gal 3: 26-28). A local church can identify a local problem and adapt the readings and the instructions to fight against it. Catholics need to hear from their pastors that ". . . no form of racism can be reconciled with the fundamentals of our faith."[449]

Awareness could be created by organizing seminars occasionally at the diocesan levels and at the parish levels by the Church Human Rights Commissions or Offices of Social Justice. People who are well informed about the oneness and the equality of all human races could be invited to talk to people in the dioceses and in the parishes as is done in the case of abortion. Racist ideologies and theories are to be openly rejected and preached against as unbiblical. In such seminars, people should be made to know that the color of skin is not of human making and has nothing to do with one's disposition to God. I agree with Juanita Dick, a Caucasian Catholic woman from Collins Missouri who said, "If we were created blind by God, no one would be concerned about the color of our skins."[450]

2) Teaching Catholic Children Race Relations as part of Catholic Catechism

The Catholic Catechism could be a very effective means of teaching Catholic children how to relate to and treat people of other races. The catechism could be adapted to include among others, such topics as God's fatherhood and motherhood to all, the equality of all human beings from creation, God's creation of the human person according to His image and likeness, the love of God to every human person and Christ's new commandment of love. When children are brought up with the right impression about their peers who are of a different color, they grow to respect one another. Catholic parents also need to avoid any type of indoctrination in their homes that may make their children hate people of other races and form wrong impressions about others.

3) Catholic School Curriculum to Reflect Race Relations

In addition, the current school curriculum of Catholic schools should include race relation studies to teach children how to move along with everybody in a multiracial society with diverse cultures. Teachers should be careful to avoid teaching children racist theories that conflict with the Biblical teaching of God's creation and equality of all human beings. Racist lessons based on Social Darwinism should be avoided.

Students in the Catholic schools could also learn about the immorality and the evil consequences of racism. They need to know and hear about racist crimes which develop from racial hatred and could lead to murder. Stories of what racism has caused America and the world at large could be told. The Nazi atrocities against the Jews during the Second World War and the Tulsa Oklahoma race riot of 1921 could be told in the schools to help the young ones see the danger of prejudice and hatred against the other people who look different.

Special teachers could be trained to handle such subjects that deal with race relations. Catholic children of all colors need to hear it from the mouths of their teachers, parents, and pastors of all colors that the difference in the color of their skins and that of their peers of color does not mean superiority or inferiority. They need to get it right when they are still young with innocent minds.

4) Condemnation of any Racist Acts or Statements from the Public

As we have seen, some of my interviewees assert that Catholic authorities seem to prefer being silent and less concerned over national issues that have to do with race. One of the major reasons why African Americans seem to see the American Catholic Church as racist is that the Church has not been outspoken enough in its defense against past government oppressive policies, actions, and hate statements against them from individual politicians and the media.

To clear this feeling, which is still the feeling of many today, the Church Human Rights Commissions or Social Justice Departments could be empowered to respond on behalf of the hierarchy on certain racial issues, and take some practical steps to investigate some unequal treatments and report to the Bishop's conference. For example, police brutality, unequal funding and maintenance of schools, unequal maintenance of roads and other government facilities in black or colored communities by city officials, discrimination in business loans, making of hateful racial statements against any race, racial profiling, and other forms of racial injustice. The Bishop's conference could occasionally use pastoral letters to address some specific issues that have to do with racial injustice and inequality that are still affecting the lives of some people in this country. The pastoral letters have to be more specific and name the particular issues and address those who are involved, even the government.

5) Need to Encourage Vocations from the Minorities

As already stated, one of the major problems the American Church is having now is lack of vocations from the youths. According to Monsignor Frank Blood, this is a very big challenge to the Church in America.[451] It is a challenge because initially, as we saw in the above history of the Church, vocations from African Americans were not encouraged, and because of that most black youths who would have been interested in becoming Catholic priests lost their interest.

There are very few priests of color in many dioceses and in some, there are none at all. Many parishes have also been closed not only due to financial problems but due to lack of priests to manage such parishes. Encouraging youths of color to enter the seminaries and become priests will not only increase the number of priests to serve the people of God but also help the Catholics of color to feel welcomed. This will help in no small measure to correct past prejudices against the people of color in the Catholic Church.

6) Opening the Doors more to allow more Foreign Priests of Different Races

The American Catholic Church has been tolerant to allow foreign priests to work in the United States. There may be need to open the doors a bit wider to allow more foreign priests from Asia, South America, Africa, and Europe to work here, as some American missionaries are also working in the above areas. This is another way American dioceses could also improve race relations. Apart from race relations, this can also help to reflect more the universal character of the Catholic Church, and provide more priests to administer some parishes that would have been closed due to lack of priests.

7) Twinning of Parishes for Diversity and Mutual Understanding

Twinning of parishes refers to two parishes coming together occasionally to worship together and to carry out some activities together. This could involve an all-white parish and an all-black parish. This creates opportunity for the members of the two parishes to appreciate cultural diversity in worship. It also fosters mutual understanding. Most all-black parishes are poor, while many all-white parishes are rich. Twinning of parishes could also create an opportunity for financial help for the poor black parishes. Many white Catholics have never experienced worshipping with black Catholics or in all-black congregations. This will also give members opportunity to visit each other's parish and interact with them.

8) Appealing to the Government for a Dialogue

There is need to come together to discuss the racial problems of this country and how they are affecting lives every day, especially the problem of poverty. The segregation laws have been removed, but their effects are still very much felt, as many African Americans and other people of color who were deprived of certain rights that would have helped them economically are still languishing in poverty. An example is the Second World War and Korean War GI Bill of Rights which was not given to about two million African American GIs and women GIs of all races. Calling on the government to organize such a national dialogue to know how to handle such issues is very important. Catholic authorities really have to speak out in favor of this delayed but very important way of moving forward with finding lasting justice and peace in this country.

Jewish Religion

All the Jewish Rabbis and lay persons I interviewed testified that there is much discrimination existing in the Jewish synagogues and communities in the United States. The current discrimination in the synagogues and in the Jewish communities involves mostly white Jews against Jews of color and other people of color. ". . . White Jews in America have vehemently denied the existence of any legitimate African (Black/Colored/Afro, etc.) Jews, recognizing only Caucasian Euro-Jews from any place."[452] According to Kivel, "We need to challenge racism within the Jewish community, racism directed toward both Jewish and non Jewish people of color."[453] The following measures can be applied.

1. Awareness of Discrimination in Jewish Communities and Synagogues

American Jews of all colors need to be aware of what is happening in their synagogues and communities. The first step in the healing process is "admitting that the race problem exists. . . "[454] They also need to be aware that the problem is not mainly from outside but from inside, Jews discriminating against themselves, or to be more specific, white Jews against Jews of color.

The American white and middle class Jews also need to hear from their Rabbis, in the Orthodox, Conservative, and Reformed synagogues that financial security and whiteness or skin color does not define being Jewish and are no justifications for discriminating against others. Kivel asserts, "Jewish people . . . come in many shades and colors from nearly black Ethiopian Jews, to dark brown Jews from the Cochin coasts of India, to light brown Jews from Argentina and Morocco, to blond and light-skinned Jews in Denmark and England."[455] Diane Tobin, Gary A. Tobin, and Scott Rubin in their book, *In Every Tongue*, also point out that Jews come from diverse cultures and racial groups. However, understanding the multiple identities of being Jewish has been a source of confusion and conflict, as many Jews are not yet aware of the existence of Jewish diversity outside their own race.[456] So there is need to clear that confusion and to create awareness that is still lacking among some Jews, through enlightenment campaigns.

2. Joint Programs to encourage Cultural Diversity

Since Jews come from different shades and colors, it will be good to organize programs in synagogues that would gather Jews of different colors together to appreciate and to cherish their cultural diversity and what they share in common. I do observe the Central Reformed Congregation in St. Louis organizing musical concerts, joint worship, seminars, and workshops that involve both white and colored Jews. They invite speakers or Rabbis of different colors from different parts of the country to take part and to speak to their congregations about the things that Jews of all colors share in common. These unifying programs should also be held in Orthodox and Conservative synagogues, across the country, whether Ashkenazim or Sephardic by rite.

3. Bringing up Jewish Children to Avoid Snobbery and Cherish Diversity

Jewish children and youths need to hear from their teachers in Sabbath schools and from their parents that they also have brothers and sisters that may look different, and because they look different, does not mean that they are superior or inferior to them. They also need to be told about the dangers of discriminating against any human being, whether Jewish or not. They could be told stories about the historical consequences of anti-Semitism and racism both here in the United States and outside. Movies and pictures of the Nazi holocaust could be a good resource material to help them be conscious of the dangers of allowing hatred for whatever reason to continue.

Jewish parents also need to be careful about allowing difference in color to determine how they respond to their children. It was very shocking to hear the Jewish woman in the interview talk about how her parents rejected her because she was not white enough to be part of the family. To be ostracized from childhood by parents because of the accidental quality of color is horrible and could affect the person psychologically for the rest of the person's life.

4. Joint Condemnation of any Racist Behavior or Statement in the Society

Apart from discrimination in the Jewish Synagogues and communities, Jews also face discrimination in the wider American society. It is true that white Jews now assimilated to form part of the white majority in this country may not be facing a lot of discriminatory treatments, which people of color including Jews of color are still suffering. There was a time when white Jews were unequally treated, along with African Americans. Indeed, according to Rabbi Randy Fleisher, discrimination against white Jews by white supremacy groups in American is not yet completely over.[457] It will be helpful not to forget that period because Jews, whether whites or blacks, in the actual sense, are still part of the minority. White Jews need to join hands with other Americans to fight against injustice no matter who is the victim and who is the oppressor.

5. Appealing to the Government for a National Dialogue

As part of the effort to join hands with other minorities and other religious bodies, the American Jews also need to join in calling for a national discussion on the racial crisis of this country and its effects, especially poverty. In such a much needed dialogue, other problems bothering Jews in this country, whether connected to color or not, could be part of the dialogue for complete justice and peace.

CONCLUSION

Coming to America, I never ever planned to write a book on racism, because I had not experienced discrimination based on race or color before, and I did not know what it was all about, until I met the African American taxi driver. I did not want to believe all he told me about the role of religion in the racial crisis of this country, until I carried out this study to find out the truth. I started my search for true racial justice from the pastoral or religious perspective because of the taxi driver's dissatisfaction with the role religion played and continues to play. Another reason was because of the silence of religious officials and pro-life groups to the destructive statement made by an American statesman about the lives of black babies in the womb. I was desperate to know the reason for this silence and the truth about race relations in this country.

I discovered that despite freedom of speech and expression in America, there is also racism or racial injustice here. The color of a person's skin in some cases determines much how an individual is treated and the extent to which the person enjoys this freedom. Some citizens are truly more privileged than others. It started with human enslavement, moved to segregation laws, and from segregation laws to the present inequality and discrimination due to the color of skin. I also discovered that the different early religions played a major role in the racial crisis of this country as claimed by the taxi driver. John L. Kater agrees with the taxi driver. He observes, "American churches have been actively implicated throughout the encounter between race and religion. They have justified and prophesied, explained and criticized at every stage of the dialogue. Their publications are a historical reservoir of attitudes and rationales."[458]

Though there may have been other influences, I found out that the problem of racism in America started mainly as a result of the interpretation and application of the Protestant doctrine of divine election by the early Protestant immigrants who were escaping religious persecution in Europe.

They wanted to prove that having been denied freedom in Europe, they had been specially called by God to build a free Protestant empire in the new World. At the same time, the Catholic European immigrants also had genuine reasons to join their Protestant brothers and sisters if not for freedom of worship, then for greener pastures, while still loyal to Rome. The European Jews, having been expelled from different countries in Europe in the 1400s and 1500s, also had a good reason to migrate to a place in which they could be tolerated more.

The feeling of being specially called by God to build a Protestant empire in America initially gave rise to discrimination against Jews and Catholics. The early discrimination they received from the hands of the Protestant immigrants was not as bad as the horrible experiences of the African Americans and the Native American Indians who were enslaved and treated as sub humans, to keep the economy of this empire buoyant through forced labor. To keep the institution of slavery protected for centuries, religion had to team up with the state to propound racist theories and ideologies to calm the conscience. Theologians from both Protestant and Catholic Churches, in league with American social scientists did a fine job of making it look like God approved slavery, despite the fact that the slavery practiced in America, which was mixed with racism and total deprivation of the slave's human rights, was different from the one practiced in the Bible.

It is disturbing to find out that the Christian faith in particular "can function quite well on both sides of the issue of race. It can be a source of oppression and a source of liberation."[459] It was the same Christian religion, through the more radical Christian groups like the Mennonites and the Quakers that, out of sympathy for the victims of slavery, attacked the institution of slavery and branded it evil and inhuman. Many more Protestant groups in the North joined them to seek for the abolition of this human trafficking. As if it was not enough after about three to four centuries of enslavement, some Christian groups, especially in the South for economic reasons, still fought against abolitionism with theologies and pastoral letters, explaining why slavery is approved in the Bible and good for the children of *Canaan* who should serve the others. At the same time some religious leaders used the same Bible to prove that blacks and Indians are not inferior to whites and that the slavery in the Bible was different from slavery as practiced in America and so should be stopped.

Thus, the double game of religion continued and the doctrine of divine election continued to influence the order of things to the detriment of justice, love, and fairness.

The institution of slavery was so strong that a deadly Civil War had to be fought between Christians in the North who said no to slavery and Christians in the south who wanted to keep enslaving human beings. Materialism could be seen as the major reason why Christians could not give a united opposition to slavery because the nation's economy was a "slave based economy."[460] The Christians in the North and the state officials under Abraham Lincoln had to team up to make abolition of slavery prevail, leading to what looked like the liberation of the blacks. Abraham Lincoln's purpose for fighting the Civil War is still controversial. Some people argue that the war was fought mainly to keep the Union from collapsing, while some argue that without slavery, there wouldn't have been a Civil War. From all indications, both keeping the Union and stopping slavery were implied in the war, though Lincoln's letter to a personal friend indicates that keeping the Union seems to have been a first and major priority. Lincoln's inability to give freed slaves citizenship and voting rights complicates the issue and keeps the argument going on whether he was the Moses of blacks or not.

Since they had no voting rights and were not regarded as citizens, after a few years, under Jim Crow laws, they became very vulnerable and were subjected to another level of slavery, which deprived them of all rights and segregated them from all aspects of the society. How did religion respond to the laws? Why was it that those abolitionists did not defend the acclaimed freed slaves against Jim Crow laws? Religion welcomed the laws and applied them in church worship of different Christian denominations. This was a blessing for racism and segregation to continue for almost another century. The silence of the Church leaders of the different denominations gave government the power and the encouragement to formally and institutionally suppress and oppress the African Americans till the middle of the twentieth century.

At this time of segregation, priestly vocations from blacks were resisted; parishes were segregated including parochial or church schools of different denominations. Blacks were given a very inferior type of education in both church schools and government supported public schools. Misinterpreting social Darwinism, black children were taught even in church schools to believe that they were inferior to white children. Blacks were deprived of all economic benefits for many years and exposed to poverty. They were subjected to live in the ghettoes and slums. It is disturbing to find out that segregation already existed in most of the Churches long before the formal subjection of African Americans to Jim Crow Laws. Many of the Churches broke up into black and white congregations or denominations because of segregation or discrimination of white worshipers against black worshipers during the antebellum period long before the Civil War. Blacks, however, were not the only racial groups subjected to discrimination while the churches watched and co-operated. The subjection of Indians to reservations, the banning of Chinese, and all Asian immigrants, anti Semitism, and the expulsion of the Mexican labor force from the United Sates are evidences that it was not the blacks alone that suffered deprivations and discrimination.

Despite the long silence of religion, "many individual Christians and church leaders have been inspired by Christian teachings to work for social justice and for an end to racism and anti-Semitism."[461] The churches spoke in the 1950s and 1960s when the pressure and challenge came from the Civil Rights Movement led by Martin Luther King Junior, a black Baptist pastor. Rosa Park, a Christian woman of color prophetically resisted the evil laws, thus sparking off the Civil Rights Movement. Marin Luther King's leadership of nonviolence brought about the removal of the laws in 1964. The churches responded to the winds of change to save the Christian religion the embarrassment of continuous double standards.

The laws have been removed, Civil Rights offices have been established in many denominations, and many churches have officially condemned racism and rendered apologies to the people of color. Has racism stopped after the removal of the laws? Progress has been made, but still hearts and minds are not yet convinced of the equality of all human beings created in the image and likeness of God. After the assassination of Martin Luther King, Civil Rights seems to have died with him and the churches seem to be back to the usual silence, as if all is well. This is why at present, inequality, which is the modern phase of racism, is still being experienced in both church and society in the twenty first-century, as indicated in the interviews. It looks as if the country was deliberately planned and the different races are graded and placed at the different levels and sometimes things are done to make inequality look natural especially in the case of economy. I have observed careful management to reduce inequality more than I have observed careful management to totally eliminate inequality in America.

After verbal condemnation of racism by different churches, specific issues like poverty, caused by long history of deprivation is not yet effectively addressed. Social works are being organized in different churches to help the poor, but there isn't much being done to help them to be more self reliant by effectively addressing the historical roots of their poverty. White privileges continue as Kivel confesses, "Today, men and women and children of color still do the hardest, lowest paid, most dangerous work throughout the country. And we, white people, again depending on our relative economic circumstances, enjoy plentiful and inexpensive food, clothing and consumer goods because of that exploitation."[462] Unfortunately, some of the minorities seem to have accepted the economic and social conditions in which they have found themselves as if not much could be done to change the situation of things.

Racial stereotyping is being used by the media to blame only the victim for his or her poverty, thereby affecting and dampening even church pastoral empathy and response. Those who engage in racial stereotyping do not seem to know the history of this country well. I strongly recommend that all aspects of the history of this country be taught in all schools, if it is not yet being taught or if some aspects are being taught while some aspects are not. When people know the history well, they will feel more with the victims of racism and this could be one of the most effective ways of fighting against racism in both church and society. The present inequality is experienced every day in job hiring, education funding, and disparity in loans for business, police harassment, racial profiling, racial stereotyping, and discrimination from estate agents and so on. These forms of inequality are not adequately addressed by religion for the sake of justice and peace. One hardly hears about these problems in religious sermons, crusades, and revival ministries of various evangelical and religious institutions in this country. There seem to be little or no pastoral care plan for the *American Poor* by some of the rich Evangelical Movements who seem to be more supportive of the system or the administration than speaking for the poor. Some of their evangelists make very queer comments that could make one think that religion is a puppet of politics.

One surprising thing about the evolution of racism is that each ethnic group or religious group that is better treated turns to support and join in the oppression of the others that are still in the oppressed condition. Otis Turner observes the same problem in these words, "Oppressed ethnic groups often treat each other in ways that emulate the behavior of the oppressor. Instead of seeing a common cause in the struggle for racial justice across racial ethnic lines. . ."[463] American Judaism recently has also been implicated as a religion where white Jews in Synagogues and in Jewish communities discriminate against Jews of color and other people of color. It is like getting to the Promised Land and forgetting those who are still in the wilderness. At the same time, anti Semitic activities of certain white supremacy groups have not finally stopped. Many American feminists, fighting against discrimination and inequality in both church and state, are also implicated as racists, thereby making their struggle look hypocritical. Is discrimination an infectious disease?

In September, 2005, Hurricane Katrina in New Orleans exposed the worst effect of racism. The unfortunate event opened people's eyes to the amount of poverty that exists in the richest country of the world. Why are millions of people of color poor? Can their poverty still be dismissed as mere laziness? Or is their poverty due to a long period of economic exclusion? The history of the United States shows that the early Protestant immigrants influenced by the doctrine of divine election first saw it as a "Protestant empire." In the twenty first century, the continuation of inequality and special privileges, which some people are still enjoying, could make one ask if the doctrine of divine election is still influencing the order of things.

In my research in four hospitals with some African American psychiatric patients, who frequented the hospitals, I discovered that the poverty of millions of African American families has been largely due to some past government policies. For example, after the second World War and the Korean War, the federal government used the GI Bill, FHA and VA mortgages to disproportionately help 16 million white Euro-Americans including Jews to achieve economic progress up to middle class status. All the business loans, education loans, house loans, technical trainings, and job opportunities eluded about two million African American GIs and

Women GIs of all races. These deprived people whose names are possibly well documented in the war archives have not yet been compensated by the government.

The above unjust treatment (as many others), exposed millions of African American families to poverty and many young African American men and women to illiteracy, drug addiction, and imprisonment. Why couldn't the churches speak for these GIs and their descendants who suffered and staked their lives for this nation? Why was it only the white GIs and civilians that benefited from all these economic packages? Can the churches now speak for them, since the effect of the above injustice is still keeping millions of people of color in poverty and all the evils connected to it? This revelation is now a big pastoral challenge to American churches. What can the American churches still do to help these poor Americans besides the raising of money for charity?

I propose a dialogue which the American Churches as a team through the United States Conference of Religions for Peace have to advocate for and convince the government of why this should not be delayed any longer. The major reason for this dialogue is to discuss the problems of poverty in particular and racial inequality in general. If that is done, not only will poverty be drastically reduced, but crimes also. The most effective way of fighting crime is to fight poverty, especially poverty that was inflicted due to deprivations and unequal treatment. The dialogue could be seen as a step to what may be called *The Third Reconstruction*, as it will also involve discussions on other forms of racial inequality, with the intention of making a change in the racial history of this country.

Initially when I came here, I did not immediately experience racism and I felt that there was nothing like discrimination in this country, as the picture I had about United States was that of *the land of the free and equals*. Now, I am full of experiences and my testimonies in this book are based on careful daily observations. I have experienced racism here even as a pastor ministering to the sick. I now know how painful or hurt any one can feel when discriminated against based on color. Some of my white friends do not believe that there is racism in America because they are not victims. It is like a woman describing the pains of child bearing to a man. No matter how a woman explains her labor pains, the man will not fully understand her, especially when the man is made to believe that the pains of child bearing is the business of the woman and that there is nothing a man can do to help her, because that is the way God made it. However, I believe that men should feel with women and women should feel with men.

My concern to know the truth, my findings, and my call for dialogue for the sake of economic, social, and political justice is what I feel every pastor of any religion should do for humanity not minding the pastor's nationality and color. Sometimes, you need a visitor to say, "Yeah, this house is beautiful, but there are still lots of things that need to be put in order, to make every occupant of this house feel happy and protected." I strongly believe that the pastoral care ministry of those who really need our help or the oppressed should not be limited to the church offices, the hospital rooms, the prisons, and the schools. It should go beyond mere praying for them and wishing them God's blessing, to addressing the root causes of their problems at all levels.

This book is not written to deny the efforts the American churches are making to stop racial inequality, at the same time, it establishes the sober truth that there is no true racial justice here yet and that the religious institutions should not relax in their efforts to achieve complete justice and equality at all levels. This book, therefore, urges them to make more efforts and work closely with the American governments, especially to advocate for the reformation of the following institutions to accommodate equal treatment irrespective of race or color or sex. These include the security institutions, especially the police, the financial institutions, especially the banks, and the mass media. From some observations, these are currently the three major organs of suppression and marginalization of the minorities.

Though not much is said in this book to address the victim, that does not mean that the victim does not have his or her own homework to do, to help bring about a change in the race relations of this country or to put a stop to racial inequality. We need to accept that there is still problem with the system, at the same time the victim has something to do to help himself or herself. There will be time to address the victim too. However, from my findings, I feel that the image which I had about America as *the land of freedom and equality,* is yet a dream to come true in the twenty-first century. I agree with Otis Turner who believes that it is still a struggle that requires ". . . commitment, sacrifice, discernment, prayer, and worship-based action."[464] This dream of America as a *land of freedom and equality* can only come true when people are looked at and treated beyond the color of their skins. Racism continues to be an evil that can not be preached as normal and ordained by God in any serious religion. It requires equal pastoral attention like any other deadly social and moral problem. However, religion here continues to be a force that has not been fully or well utilized in the struggle against any form of inequality especially racial injustice in America.

NOTES

INTRODUCTION

[1] Paul Kivel, *Uprooting Racism: How White People can Work for Racial Justice* (Gabriola Island, BC: New Society Publishers, 1995), 95.

[2] Ibid.

CHAPTER ONE

[3] David A. Hogue, *Remembering the Future Imagining the Past* (Cleveland: The Pilgrim Press, 2003), 95.

[4] Ibid.., 105.

[5] Ibid.

[6] Ibid.

[7] Ibid.

[8] James L. Fredericks, *Faith among Faiths: Christian Theology and Non-Christian Religions* (Mahwah, New Jersey: Paulist Press, 1999), 2.

CHAPTER TWO

[9] James H. Smylie, "Racism, Religion, and the Continuing American Dilemma," *Church and Society* Vol. 91-92 (January/February 2001): 69.

[10] Joseph T. Leonard, "Racism," The *Catholic Encyclopedia for Schools and Homes*, 1979 ed.

[11] Thomas F. Gossett, *Race: The History of an Idea in America* (Dallas: Methodist University Press, 1963), 3.

[12] Virgil Elizondo, "The Church and Racism," *Concilium*, 1 (1982): 62.

[13] Ibid., 61.

[14] Thomas Powell, *The Persistence of Racism in America* (Maryland: Littlefield Adams Quality Paperbacks, 1992), 15-16.

[15] Frank G. Kirkpatrick, "Protestantism," in *Encyclopedia of the United States in the Nineteenth Century,* 2000 ed.

[16] Martin E. Marty, "Religion," in *Encyclopedia of the United States in the Nineteenth Century,* 2001 ed.

[17] O.C. Edwards, *A History of Preaching* (Nashville: Abingdon Press, 2004), 471.

[18] Peter M.J. Stravinskas, "Predestination," in *Our Sunday Visitor's Catholic Encyclopedia,* 1991 ed.

[19] Robert P. Lockwood, ed., *Anti Catholicism in American Culture* (New York: Our Sunday Visitor Publishing Division, 2000), 23.

[20] Smylie, "Racism, Religion, and the Continuing American Dilemma," 57.

[21] Elizondo, "The Church and Racism," 62.

[22] Winthrop Jordan, *White over Black: American Attitude toward the Negro, 1550-1812* (New York: W.W. Norton and Company, 1977), 95.

[23] Powell, *The Persistence of Racism,* 15.

[24] Ibid., 16.

[25] Karen Brodkin, *How Jews Became White Folks And What That Says About Race In America.* (New Jersey: Rutgers University Press, 2004), 30.

[26] Ibid.

[27] R. Knox, *Races of Men,* as quoted in Alan Davies "The ideology of Racism," *Concilium,* 1 (1982): 61.

[28] Marty Martin, *The Righteous Empire* as quoted in Elizondo, 62.

[29] Smylie, "Racism, Religion, and the Continuing American Dilemma," 57.

[30] Tim Alan Garrison, "Race and Racial Thinking," in *Encyclopedia of United States in the Nineteenth Century,* 2001 ed.

[31] Ibid.

[32] Ibid.

[33] Jospeh T. Leonard, "Racism," in *The Catholic Encyclopedia for Schools and Homes*: Racism, 1979 ed.

[34] Inderjit Bhopal, "The Ministry of Truth," *Christian Social Action,* Vol. 14, No. 1(March/April, 2001): 13.

[35] Ibid.

[36] Ibid.

[37] Anthony B. Pinn, *Religion and American Cultures: African American Religions,* Vol. 1 (Santa Barbara: ABC Clio, 2003), 4.

[38] Melvin Sylvester, *The African American: A Journey from Slavery to Freedom* http:// www.liu.edu/cwis/cwp/library/aaslavry.htm.

[39] Smylie, "Racism Religion, and the Continuing American Dilemma," 60.

[40] Smylie, 59.

[41] Frank G. Kirkpatrick, "Protestantism," in *Encyclopedia of the United States in the Nineteenth century,* 2001 ed.

[42] Smylie, 63.

[43] B. Davis Schwartz, http://www.liu.edu/cwis/library/aaslavry.htm.

[44] Paul Kivel, *Uprooting Racism: How White People can Work for Racial Justice* (Gabriola Island, BC: New Society Publishers, 1995), 121.

[45] Zinn Howard, *A People's History of the United States,* as Quoted in Kivel, 122.

[46] B.A. Meshack, *Is the Baptist Church Relevant to the Black Community* (San Francisco, California: R and E Research Associates, 1976), 15.

[47] Smylie, 63.

[48] B.A. Meshack, *Is the Baptist Church Relevant to the Black Community,* 15.

[49] Smylie, 63.

[50] Tim Alan Garrison, 49.

[51] Joel L. Alvis, *Religion and Race: Southern Presbyterians, 1946-1983* (Tuscalosa, Alabama: The University of Alabama Press, 1994), 7.

[52] William Sinclair, *The Aftermath of Slavery: A Study of the Condition and Environment of he American Negro* (Chicago: Afro-am Press, 1969), 85.

[53] Ibid.

[54] Jeremiah Asher, *African American Religious History: Protesting the "Negro Pew"* (Durham: Duke University, 1999), 224.

[55] Alvis, *Religion and Race,* 7.

[56] Smylie, 63.

[57] L.B. Brooks, "State of Country," New England Baptist Convention, 1922, as quoted in Leroy Fitts, *A History of Black Baptists* (Nashville, Tennessee: Broadman Press, 1985), 254.

[58] Ralph E. Luker, *The Social Gospel in Black and White: American Racial Reform 1885-1912* (North Carolina: University of North Carolina Press), 304.

[59] Ibid.

[60] Ibid.

[61] Brooks, as quoted in Fitts, 255.

[62] Leroy Fitts, *A History of Black Baptists* (Nashville, Tennessee: Broadman Press, 1985), 254.

[63] Stanley I. Kutler, ed., "Race Relations," in *Dictionary of American History*, 2003 ed.

[64] Elizondo, 62.

[65] Smylie, 67.

[66] Richard C. Dickinson, *Roses and Thorns: The Centennial Edition of Black Lutheran Mission and Ministry in the Lutheran Church—Missouri Synod* (St. Louis, Missouri: Concordia Publishing House, 1977), 19.

[67] Kevin Chappell, "The life and Legacy of the Mother of the Civil Rights Movement," *Ebony,* January 2006, 126.

[68] Alvis, *Religion and Race*, 9.

[69] Smylie, 68.

[70] Ibid.

[71] John L. Kater, "Experiment In Freedom: The Episcopal Church and the Black Power Movement," *Historical Magazine of the Protestant Episcopal Church*, Vol. XLVIII (March, 1979): 69.

[72] Smylie, 69.

[73] David L. Holmes, *A Brief History of the Episcopal Church* (Valley Forge, PA.: 1993), 20.

[74] Raymond W. Albright, *A History of the Protestant Episcopal Church* (New York: The Macmillan Company, 1964), 135.

[75] Martin E. Marty, "Protestantism," in *Encyclopedia of the United States in the Nineteenth Century,* 2001 ed.

[76] Harold Lewis, *Yet with A steady Beat: The African American struggle for recognition* (Valley Forge, Pennsylvania: Trinity International Press), 22.

[77] Edward L. Queen, Stephen R. Prothero, and Gardiner H. Shattuck, "African American Religion," in *Encyclopedia of American Religious History*, 2001 ed.

[78] Lewis, *Yet With A Steady Beat*, 22.

[79] Edward L. Queen, Stephen R. Prothero, and Gardiner H. Shattuck, "African American Religion," 2001 ed.

[80] R.E Hood, "The Historical Basis for Black Indifference Toward the Episcopal Church 1800-1860," *Historical Magazine of the Protestant Episcopal Church*, Vol. 51-52 (September, 1982):278.

[81] Albright, *A History of the Protestant Episcopal Church*, 32.

[82] Ibid.

[83] Holmes, *A Brief History of the Episcopal Church*, 80.

[84] Robert A. Bennett, "Black Episcoplians : A history from the Colonial Period to the Present." *Historical Magazine of the Protestant Episcopal Church*, September 1974, 239.

[85] Ibid.

[86] Ibid., 238.

[87] Ibid., 239.

[88] Ibid.

[89] W.E.B.DuBois, *The Negro Church* (Atlanta: Atlanta University Press, 1903), 39.

[90] Bennett, "Black Episcopalians: A history from the Colonial Period to the Present," 240.

[91] Lewis., 23.

[92] Ibid., 19.

[93] Ibid., 17.

[94] Ibid., 148.

[95] Ibid., 150.

[96] James H. Smylie, *A Brief History of the Presbyterians* (Louisville, Kentucky: Geneva Press, 1996), 39.

[97] Ibid.

[98] Ibid, 43.

[99] Joel L. Alvis, *Religion and Race: Southern Presbyterian, 1946-1983* (Tuscaloosa: The University of Alabama Press, 1994), 6-7.

[100] Edward L. Queen, Stephen R. Prothero, and Gardiner H. Shattuck, "African American Religion," in *Encyclopedia of American Religious History*, 2001 ed.

[101] Louis Weeks, "Presbyterians," in *Encyclopedia of the United States in the Nineteenth century: Presbyertrians*, 2001 ed.

[102] Smylie, *A Brief History of the Presbyterians*, 89.

[103] Ibid.

[104] Ibid.

[105] Joel L. Alvis, *Religion and Race,* 4.

[106] Smylie, *History of the Presbyterians*, 89.

[107] Alvis, *Religion and Race*, 1.

[108] Ibid., 6.

[109] Smylie, *History of the Presbyterians*, 129.

[110] Ibid.

[111] Ibid.

[112] John A. Hardon, *The Protestant Churches of America* (Westminster, Maryland: The Newman Press, 1957), 153.

[113] Charles Yrigoyen, "Methodists," in *Encyclopedia of the United States in the Nineteenth Century,* 2001 ed.

[114] Edward L. Queen, Stephen R. Prothero, and Gardiner H. Shattuck, "Methodism," in *Encyclopedia of American Religions,* 2001 ed.

[115] Edward L. Queen, Stephen R. Prothero, and Gardiner H. Shattuck, "African American Religion," in *Encyclopedia of American Religious History*, 2001 ed.

[116] Yrigoyen, "Methodists," in *Encyclopedia of the United States in the Nineteenth Century,* 2001 ed.

[117] Frederick A. Norwood, *The Story of American Methodism* (Nashville: Abingdon Press, 1974), 186.

[118] Chester Jones, "Coming to Terms With Our Methodist Roots," *Christian Social Action* Vol. 14 (March/April 2001): 4.

[119] Ibid., 5.

[120] William Warren Sweet, *Methodism in American History* (New York: Abingdon Press, 1961), 273.

[121] Ibid., 241.

[122] Edward L. Queen, Stephen R. Prothero, and Gardiner H. Shattuck, "Methodists," in *Encyclopedia of American Religious History*, 2001 ed.

[123] Ibid.

[124] Chester Jones, 7.

[125] Ibid.

[126] Hardon, *The Protestant Churches of America*, 21.

[127] Edward L. Queen, Stephen R. Prothero, and Gardiner H. Shattuck,

"African American Religion," in *Encyclopedia of American Religious History,* 2001 ed.

[128] Bill J. Leonard, *Baptist Ways A History* (Valley Forge, PA., Judson Press 2003), 263.

[129] Ibid.

[130] Ibid.

[131] O. K Armstrong and Majorie Armstrong, *The Baptists in America* (New York: A Doubleday Galilee Book, 1979), 236.

[132] Fitts, *A History of Black Baptists* 43.

[133] Nancy Good Sider and Cheryl Talley, *Ending Racism in America, One conversation at a time. http://www.edu./ctp/footpaths/vol2no3/page7.html.*

[134] Fitts, 24.

[135] Robert G. Torbet, *A History of the Baptists,* as quoted in Shelton Smith and Robert T. Handy, *American Christianity* 1820-1960, 169.

[136] Ibid., 30

[137] Stephen Gibson, *Was the "Revelation" Received in Response to Pressure? http://www.lightplanet.com/response/answer/pressure.htm.*

[138] Bill J. Leonard., "Protestantism," in *Encyclopedia of the United States in the Nineteenth century,* 2001 ed.

[139] Ibid.

[140] Edward L. Queen, Stephen R. Prothero, and Gardiner H. Shattuck, "Baptists," in *Encyclopedia of American Religious History,* 2001 ed.

[141] Stephen Gibson, *Was the "Revelation" Received in Response to Pressure? http://www.lightplanet.com/response/answer/pressure.htm.*

[142] Garner Taylor, *Baptist and the American Experience: Baptists and Human Rights* (Valley Forge, PA.: Judson Press, 1976), 68.

[143] Norman H. Maring, *American Baptists Whence and Whither* (Valley Forge: The Judson Press), 69.

[144] Ibid.

[145] Joel L. Alvis, *Religion and Race,* 9.

[146] Theodore G. Tappert, *Lutheran in North America: The Church's infancy* 1650-1790(Philadelphia: Fortress Press, 1975), 40.

[147] Hardon, *The Protestant Churches of America,* 127.

[148] Paul A. Baglyos, "Lutherans," in *Encyclopedia of the United States in the Nineteenth* Century, 2001 ed.

[149] Muhlenberg, *Selbstbiographie* as quoted in Theodore G. Tappert, *Lutherans in North America,* 74.

[150] Tappert, *The Lutherans in North America*, 74.

[151] Hallesche *Nachrichten,* as quoted in Tappert, 74.

[152] Douglas C. Stange, "Our Duty to Preach the Gospel to Negroes: Southern Lutherans and American Negroes" *Concordia Historical Institute Quarterly* Vol. 42-43 (November 1969): 173.

[153] Tappert, *The Lutherans in North America*, 74.

[154] George Anderson, *The Lutherans in North America: Early National Period* 1790-1840 (Philadelphia: Fortress Press, 1975), 141.

[155] Ibid., 142.

[156] Richard C. Dickinson, *Roses and Thorns: Black Lutheran Centennial* (St. Louis, Missouri: Concord Publishing House, 1977), 19.

[157] Ibid.

[158] Abel Ross Wentz, *The Lutheran Church in American History* (Philadelphia: The United Lutheran Publication House, 1933), 152.

[159] George Anderson, *The Lutherans in America*, 143.

[160] Ibid.

[161] Ibid.

[162] August R. Suelflow and E. Clifford Nelson, *The Lutherans in North America: Following the Frontier1840-1875* (Philadelphia: Fortress Press, 1975), 239.

[163] Ibid.

[164] Paul S. Baglyos, "Lutherans," in *Encyclopedia of The United States in the Nineteenth Century*, 2001 ed.

[165] Thomas Coates and Erwin L. Lueker, *Moving Frontiers: Four Decades of Expansion 1920—1960* (Saint Louis, Missouri: Concordia Publishing House, 1964), 405.

[166] Ibid.

[167] E. Clifford Nelson, *The Lutherans in North America: The New shape of Lutheranism* (Philadelphia: Fortress Press, 1975), 526.

[168] Ibid.

[169] Ibid., 527.

CHAPTER THREE

[170] http://news.aol.com/dailypulse/051806/_a/what-do-you-think-of-him/.

[171] Bennett, "Black Episcopalians: A History from the Colonial Period to the Present," *Historic Magazine of the Episcopal Church*, September, 1974, 243. Is 'Black Episcopalians:' part of the title?

[172] Ibid.

[173] Ibid., 244.

[174] Harold T. Lewis, *Yet With A Steady Beat*, 162.

[175] Ibid., 163.

[176] Ibid., 179.

[177] Ibid.

[178]Joel L. Alvis, *Religion and Race*: Southern *Presbyterians, 1946-1983* (Tuscaloosa, Alabama: The University of Alabama Press, 1994), 77.

[179] Ibid, 139.

[180] Betty J. Durrah, "Triple Jeopardy: The Impact of Race, Sex, and Class on Women of Color," *Church and Society* Vol. 81-82 (September/October 1991):49.

[181] Racial Ethnic Ministry Response, "Problems Caused by Racism," *Church and Society* Vol. 81-82 (September/October 1991): 71.

[182] Ibid., 70.

[183] Ibid.

[184] Jones, "Coming to Terms With Our Methodist Roots," 7.

[185] Yolanda Pupo-Ortiz, "Racism Lurks in the Corners" *Christian Social Action* Vol. 14 No. 1 (March/April 2001): 9.

[186] Ibid.

[187] Ibid.

[188] Dispatch, "Study Guide Aimed at Healing Wounds of Racial Divisions," *Christian Social Action* Vol. 14 No. 1 (March/ April 2001): 37.

[189] Ibid.

[190] Ibid.

[191] Yolanda Pupo-Ortiz, "Racism Lurks in the Corner," 8.

[192] Leroy Fitts, *A History of Black Baptists* (Nashville, Tennessee; Broadman Press, 1985), 301.

[193] Ibid., 302.

[194] Ibid.

[195] Ibid., 303.

[196] Ibid., 304.

[197] Ibid.

[198] Ibid.

[199] Was the "Revelation" Received in Response to Pressure? http://www.lightplanet.com/response/answers/Pressure.htm.

[200] Ibid.

[201] Fitts, *A History of Black Baptists*, 309.

[202] Richard C. Dickinson, *Roses and Thorns: The Centennial Edition of Black Lutheran Mission and Ministry in the Lutheran Church—Missouri Synod* (St. Louis: Concord Publishing House, 1977), 105.

[203] Ibid., 117.

CHAPTER FOUR

[204] Jay P. Dolan, "Catholicism," in *Dictionary of American History*, 2003 ed.

[205] Roberto S. Goizueta, *Religion and American Cultures: Catholicism in America*, Vol. 1 (Santa Barbara, California: ABC Clio, 2002), 75.

[206] Dolan, "Catholicism," 2003 ed.

[207] Roberto S. Goizueta, *Religion and American Cultures*, 75.

[208] Dolan, "Catholicism," 2003 ed.

[209] Goizueta, *Religion and American Cultures*, 76.

[210] Dolan, "Catholicism," 2003 ed.

[211] Edward L. Queen, Stephen R. Prothero, and Gardiner H. Shattuck, eds. "Roman Catholicism," in *Encyclopedia of American Religious History*, 2001 ed.

[212] Dolan, "Catholicism," 69.

[213] Kenneth J. Zanca, "Slavery and American Catholics," in *The Encyclopedia of American Catholic History*, 1997 ed.

[214] Ibid., 1320.

[215] Ibid.

[216] Cyprian Davis, *The History of Black Catholics in the United States* (New York: Crossroad, 1990), 37.

[217] Stafford Poole, and Douglas Slawson, *Church and Slave in Perry County, Missouri: 1818-1865*, as quoted in Davis, 38.

[218] Davis, *History of Black Catholics in the United States*, 38-39.

[219] Anna Blanche McGill, *The Sisters of Charity of Nazareth, Kentucky*, as quoted in Davis, 39.

[220] Camilius Maes, *The life of Rev. Charles Nerinckx*, as quoted in Davis, 39.

[221] Stephen J. Ochs, *Desegregating the Altar: The Josephites and Struggle for Black Priests, 1871-1960* (Louisiana: Louisiana State University Press), 18.

[222] John England, *Works*, as quoted in Davis, 39-40.

[223] Jay P. Dolan, *The American Catholic Experience* (New York: Double Day, 1985), 123.

[224] Poole, and Slawson, *Church and Slave in Perry County,* as quoted in Davis, 43.

[225] Zanca, "Slavery and American Catholics," in *The Encyclopedia of American Catholic History*, 1997 ed.

.

[226] Davis, *The History of Black Catholics in the United States*, 51.

[227] Ibid., 56.

[228] Ibid., 57.

[229] Ochs, *Desegregating the Altar*, 18.

[230] Jamie T. Phelps, *Many Rains Ago: Caught Between Thunder and Lightning A Historical Theological Critique of Episcopal Response to Slavery* (Washington D.C.: United States Catholic, 1990), 24.

[231] Ochs, *Desegregating the Altar*, 19.

[232] Davis *History of Black Catholics in the United States*, 47.

[233] Ochs, *Desegregating the Altar,* 20.

[234] Zanca, "Slavery and American Catholics," 1997 ed.

[235] Phelps, *Many Rains Ago,* 27.

[236] Ibid., 28

[237] Ibid.

[238] Davis, *History of Black Catholics*, 49

[239] Zanca, "Slavery and American Catholics," 1979 ed.

[240] Michael J. Curley, *Church and State in Spanish Floridas*, as quoted in Davis, 69.

[241] Davis, *The History of Black Catholics in the United States*, 70.

[242] John T. Pawlikowski, O.S.M. "Racism," in *The Modern Catholic Encyclopedia,* 1994 ed.

[243] Ibid.

[244] Edward J. Misch, The *American Bishops and the Negro from Civil War to the Third Plenary Council in Baltimore,* 1865-1884, as quoted in Ochs, 15.

[245] John T. Pawlikowski, O.S.M., "Racism," in *The Modern Catholic Encyclopedia,* 1994 ed.

[246] Phelps, Many *Rains Ago,* 23.

[247] Rice, as quoted in Phelps, *Many Rains Ago,* 26.

[248] Davis, *The History of Black Catholics, in the United States,* 53.

[249] Ibid., 62.

[250] Ibid., 65.

[251] E. Dupuy, Pastor at Iberville, to Blac, as quoted in Davis, 65.

[252] Ibid.

[253] J. Fairfax McLaughlin, "William Gatson: The First Student of Georgetown College," *Records of the American Historical Society,* as quoted in Davis, 65.

[254] Cyprian Davis and Jamie Phelps eds., *Stamped with the Image of God: African Americans as God's Image in Black* (New York: Orbis Books, 2003), 55.

[255] Phelps, *Many Rains Ago,* 27.

[256] Ibid., 28.

[257] Dolan, *Dictionary of American History,* 68.

[258] Ibid, 68.

[259] Morris J MacGregor, *The Emergence of a Black Catholic Community St. Augustine in Washington* (Washington D.C.: The Catholic University of America Press, 1999), 25.

[260] Edward D. Reynolds, *Jesuits for the Negroes* (New York: The University Press, 1949), 55.

[261] Davis, *The History of Black Catholics in the United States,* 159.

[262] Koren, *The Serpent and the Dove,* as quoted in Davis, 239.

[263] Ochs, *Desegregating the Altar,*

[264] Charles Hart, Interview by Author, Tape Recording, St. Louis, MO., 4 July 2005.

[265] John T. Gillard, *Colored Catholics in the United States.* (Baltimore: The Josephite Press, 1941), 196.

[266] Ibid., 198.

[267] Peter Clark, *A Free Church in a Free Society,* as quoted in Davis, 46.

[268] Mary A. Ward, A *Mission for Justice: A History of the First African American Catholic Church in Newark New Jersey* (Knoxville: The University of Tennessee Press, 2002), 17.

[269] Davis, *The History of Black Catholics in the United States*, 153.

[270] Josephs B. Connors, *The Journey Toward Fulfillment,* as quoted in Sharon M. Howell, *Many Rains Ago: The Consecrated Blizzard of the Northwest Archbishop John Ireland and His Relationship with the Black Catholic Community* (Washington D.C.: United States Catholic Conference, 1990), 41.

[271] Frank Blood, Interview by author, tape recording, St. Louis, MO., 10 June 2005.

[272] Powlikowski, 712.

[273] Ibid.

[274] Davis *The History of Black Catholics in the United States*, 154.

[275] Ibid, 156.

[276] Frank Blood, Interview by the author, Tape record, St. Louis MO, 10 June 2005.

[277] Ochs, *Desegregating the Altar*, 10.

[278] Ward, *Mission of Justice*, 22.

[279] Ibid.

[280] Sandra O Smithson, *To Be the Bridge: A commentary of Black/ White Catholicism In America* (Nashville, Tennessee: Winston Derek Publishers, 1984), 32.

[281] Ward, *Mission of Justice*, 23.

[282] Ochs, *Desegregating the Altar*, 10.

[283] Davis, *The History of Black Catholics In United States*, 252.

[284] MacGregor, *The Emergence of Black Catholic Community*, 255

[285] United States Conference of Archives, "Letters Proposed for the Hierarchy," as quoted in Davis, 252.

[286] L. B. Brooks, "State of County," New England Baptist Convention, as quoted in Fitts, 254.

[287] James H. Shyly, "Racism, Religion, And Continuing American Dilemma," *Church and Society* Vol. 91-92 (January/February 2001): 59.

[288]Davis, *The History of Black Catholics in the United States*, 253.

[289] Ibid.

[290] Ibid., 254.

[291] Davis, *The History of Black Catholics in the United States*, 255.

[292] MacGregor, *The Emergence of Black Catholic Community*, 340.

[293] Davis, 255.

[294] Diana L. Hayes and Cyprian Davis, eds., *Taking Down Our Harps: God of Our Weary Years* (New York: Orbis Books, 1998), 38.

[295] MacGregor, 340.

[296] Ibid., 340.

[297] Ibid., 341.

[298] Ibid.

[299] Davis, 256.

[300] Ibid.

[301] Ibid., 258.

CHAPTER FIVE

[302] Phelps, *Many Rains Ago,* 31.

[303] Gene Morris, Interview by Author, Tape recording, St. Louis MO, 7th June 2005.

[304] Phelps, 30-31.

CHAPTER SIX

[305] Robert M. Seltzer, ed., *Judaism A People and it History* (New York: Macmillan Publishing Company, 1989), 198.

[306] Edward L. Queen, Stephen R. Prothero, and Gardiner H. Shattuck, eds., "Judaism," in *Encyclopedia of American Religions*, 2001 ed.

[307] Ibid. 364.

[308] Seltzer, *Judaism A People and its History*, 199-200.

[309] Calvin Goldscheider and Jacob Neusner, eds., *Social Foundations of Judaism* (New Jersey: prince Hall, 1990), 115.

[310] Joyce Eisenberg & Ellen Scolnic, "Sephardim," in *The JPS Dictionary of Jewish Words*, 2001 ed.

[311] Geoffre Wigoder ed., "Sephardim," in *The Encyclopedia of Judaism*, 2002 ed.

[312] Eisenberg & Scolnic, "Sephardim," in *The JPS Dictionary of Jewish Words*, 2001 ed.

[313] Ibid.

[314] Geoffre Wigoder ed., "Sephardim," in *The Encyclopedia of Judaism*, 2002 ed.

[315] Ibid.

[316] Joyce Eisenberg & Ellen Scolnic "Sephardim," in *The JPS Dictionary of Jewish Words*, 2001 ed.

[317] Geoffre Wigoder, ed., "Sephardim," in *The Encyclopedia of Judaism*, 2002 ed.

[318] Ibid.,

[319] Ibid.

[320] Edward L. Queen, Stephen R. Prothero, and Gardiner H. Shattuck, "Black Jews," in *Encyclopedia of American Religious History*, 2001 ed.

[321] Ibid.

[322] Edward L. Queen, Stephen R. Prothero, and Gardiner H. Shattuck, "Judaism," in *Encyclopedia of American Religious History,* 2001 ed.

[323] Seltzer, *Jadaism A People and its History*, 199-200.

[324] Ibid., 201.

[325] Ibid.

[326] Ibid.

[327] Queen, Prothero, and Shattuck, "Judaism," in *Encyclopedia of American Religious History,* 2001 ed.

[328] Hubert G. Locke, *The Black Anti-Semitism Controversy: Protestant Views and Perspectives* (London and Toronto: Associated Press, 1994), 24.

[329] Queen, Prothero and Gardiner, "Anti Semitism," in *Encyclopedia of American Religious History,* 2001 ed.

[330] Calvin Goldscheider and Jacob Neusner, eds., *Social Foundations of Judaism*, 118-119.

[331] Charles Wagley and Marvin Harris, *Minorities in the New World* (New York: Columbia University Press, 1958), 227-228.

[332] Symlie, "Racism, Religion, and The Continuing American Dilemma," 63.

[333] Peter L. DeGroote, "White Supremacists Cloak Bigotry in Theology," *Christian Social Action,* (March/April 2001): 14.

[334] Myron I. Scholnick, *The New Deal and Anti Semitism in America* (New York: Garland Publshing, 1990).

[335] Hubert G. Locke, *The Black Anti Semitism Controversy*, 25.

[336] Myron I. Scholnick, *The New Deal and Anti Semitism in America*, 50.

[337] Dinnerstein, The Leo Frank Case, as quoted in Scholnick, 51.

[338] Charles Herbert Stember and Others, *Jews in the Mind of America* (New York: Basic Books, 1966), 302.

[339] Locke, *The Black Anti-Semitism Controversy*, 25.

[340] Edward L. Queen, Stephen R. Prothero, and Gardiner H. Shattuck,. "Judaism," in *Encyclopedia of American Religious History*, 2001 ed.

[341] Locke, *The Black Anti-Semitism*, 28-29.

[342] Ibid., 25.

[343] Karen Brodkin, *How Jews became White Folks & what that says about Race in America* (New Brunswick, New Jersey: Rutgers University Press, 2004), 50.

CHAPTER SEVEN

[344] L. Richard Bradley, "Lutheran Church and Slavery," *Concordia Historical Institute Quarterly* Vol. XLIV No. 1 (February 1971): 38-39.

[345] Alastair V. Campbell, "Pastoral Care Nature of," in *A Dictionary of Pastoral Care*, 1987 ed.

[346] Clifton E. Olmstead, *Religion In America Past and Present* (Englewood Cliffs, New Jersey: Prentice-Hall, 1961), 126.

[347] Emmanuel Y. Lartey, *In living Color: An Intercultural Approach to Pastoral Care and Counseling* (New York: Jessica Kingsley Publishers, 2003), 26.

[348] David A. Hogue, *Remembering the Future Imagining the Past: Stories, Ritual, and the Human Brian* (Cleveland Ohio: The Pilgrim Press, 2003), 81.

[349] Sharon G. Thornton *Broken yet Beloved: A pastoral Theology of the Cross* (New York: Chalice Press, 2002), 8.

[350] Ibid.

[351] Bill Bennett, "Radio show," 28th September 2005, Available @ http://mediamatters.org.

[352] Media Matters for America, http://mediamatters.org/issues topics/bill bennett and abortion.

[353] Ibid.

[354] Stuart E. Rosenberg, *Christianity Through Non-Christian Eyes: Christianity and the Holocaust* (Maryknoll, New York: Orbis Books, 1990), 41.

[355] Randy Fleisher, Interview by Author, Tape recording, St. Louis MO, 7th July 2005.

[356] Charles V. Gerkin, *An Introduction to Pastoral Care* (Nashville: Abingdon Press, 1997), 90.

[357] Ibid., 91.

[358] *Thornton, Broken Yet Beloved,* 34.

[359] G. Lee Ramsey, *Care—Full Preaching: From sermon To Caring Community* (St. Louis: Chalice Press, 2002), 88.

[360] Lartey, *In Living Color,* 29.

[361] Sharon G. Thornton, *Broken yet Beloved,* 6.

[362] Gerkin *An Introduction to Pastoral Care,* 125.

[363] mhtml:http://www.doc.missouri.gov/SVORI%20website.mht.

[364] Ibid.

[365] Missouri Department of Social Services Family Support Division: *Application for Food Stamp, available on line at http://dssweb/fsd/manual/fstamps/1105-015-10_1105-015-10-50.html.*

[366] Ibid., 88.

[367] Sharon G. Thornton. *Broken yet Beloved,* 29.

[368] Christine M. Smith, *Risking the Terror: Resurrection in this Life* (Cleveland, Ohio: The Pilgrim Press, 2001), 32.

[369] Karen Brodkin, How *Jews Became White Folks and what that has to say about Race in* America (New Jersey: Rutgers University Press, 2004), 26.

[370] Ibid., 51.

[371] Ibid., 50.

[372] Ibid., 38.

[373] Ibid.

[374] Ibid.

[375] Micheal J. Benneth, *When Dreams came True: The GI Bill and the making of Modern America,* as quoted in Katznelson, 113

[376] Ira Katznelson, *When Affirmative Action was White: An Untold History of Racial Inequality in Twentieth-Century America* (New York: W.W. Norton & Company, 2005), 114.

[377] F.J. Brown 1946; Hurd 1946; Mosch 1975; *"Post War Jobs for Veterans"* 1945; Willenz 1983 as quoted in Karen Brodkin, 38.

[378] Brodkin, *How Jews Became Whites,* 43-44.

[379] Ibid, 39.

[380] Katznelson, When *Affirmative Action was White*, 138.

[381] *Lubbock Avalanche*, June 6; 1945; *Los Angeles Tribune*, as quoted in Katznelson, 122.

[382] Brodkin, 39.

[383] J. Nash et al. as quoted in Karen Brodkin, 39.

[384] Brodkin, 45.

[385] Ibid., 51.

[386] Ibid.

[387] Ibid.

[388] MacGregor, 297.

[389] http// www.census.gov.

[390] Kivel, 30.

[391] Ibid.

[392] Ibid.

[393] H. Shelton Smith, Robert T. Handy and Lefferts A. Loetscher, *American Christianity: An Historical Interpretation with Representative Documents* (New York: Charles Scribner's Sons, 1963), 552.

[394] Ibid.

[395] Ira Katznelson, *When Affirmative Action was White*, 114.

[396] Truman K. Gibson, Jr. "Government Fails Negroes Vets: Systematic Denial of Rights under GI Bills Scored at Conference, New Technique Needed to Get Results Under Government Program," as quoted in Katznelson, 114.

[397] Jonathan Alter, "The Other America: Enduring the Shame," *Newsweek*, 19 September 2005, 43.

[398] Ibid., 45

[399] Ibid., 43.

[400] President Lyndon Johnson's commencement Address, "To Fulfill these Rights," June 4, 1965, as quoted in Katznelson, 173.

[401] Virgil Elizondo, "A Report on Racism: A Mexican American in the United States," 1 *Concilium*, (1982), 63.

[402] William Pannell, *The Coming Race War? A Cry for Reconciliation* (Grand Rapids, Michigan: Zondervan Publishing House, 1993), 61.

[403] Randall G. Sheldon, *Drug War Updates: Nothing Succeeds like Failure,* http://www.zmag.org/content/showarticle.cfm.

[404] Harrison Paige M. and Allen J. Beck, "Race, Prison and the Drug Laws," US Dept. of Justice, Bureau of Justice Statistics, also available @ http:// www.drugwarfacts.org/racepris.htm.

[405] Randall G. Sheldon, *Drug War Updates*.

[406] *Substance Abuse and Mental Health Services Administration, National Household Survey on Drug Abuse: Summary Report 1998*. (Rockville, MD: Substance Abuse and Mental Services Administration, 1999), P. 13; *Bureau of Justice Statistics, Sourcebook of Criminal Justice Statistics 1998* (Washington DC: US Department of Justice, August 1999) P. 343, Table 4.10, P. 435, Table 5.48, and P. 505, Table 6.52; Beck, Allen J., Ph. D. and Mumola, Christopher J., *Bureau of Justice Statistics, Prisoners in 1998* (Washington DC: US Department of Justice, August 1999), p. 10 Table 16; Beck J., PhD, and Paige M. Harrison, US Dept. of Justice, *Bureau of justice Statistics* (Washington DC: US Department of Justice, August 2001), p. 11, Table 16. Also available @ http://www.drugwarfacts.org/racepris.htm.

[407] Heather Ratcliffe, "After 5 years officials still disagree on racial profiling," *St. Louis Post Dispatch,* 6th April 2005.

[408] Harrison, Paige M., & Allen J. Beck, Race, *Prison and the Drug Laws, Bureau of Justice Statistics, Prison and Jail Inmates at Midyear 2004* (Washington, DC: US Dept. of Justice, April 2005), available @www. drugwarfacts.org/racepris.htm.

[409] *Drug, Minority Women and the US Prison Economy*, available @ http://www.saxakali.com/saxakali-magazine/saxmag3s.htm.

[410] Ibid.

[411] Lefferts A. Loetscher, *A Brief History of the Presbyterians* (Philadelphia: The Westminster Press, 1978), 93.

[412] Andrew Cherlin, as quoted by Jonathan Alter in "The Other America, Enduring the Shame," *Newsweek*, 43.

[413] Stanley I. Kutler, ed., *Dictionary of American History: Race Relations*, Vol. 7 (New York: Charles Scribner's Sons, 2003), 10.

[414] http://www.tulsalibrary.org/aarc/Riot/riot.htm.

[415] Michelle N. Jackson http://www.hartford-hwp.com/archives/ 45a/418.html.

[416] Ibid.

[417] Rick Montgomery, "Seventy-Eight Years later, Tulsa re-examines Deadly Race Riot," *Kansas City Star,* (September 7th, 1999).

[418] http://www.cnn.com/US/9908/03/tulsa.riots.probe/.

[419] Ibid.

[420] Olmstead, *Religion in America Past and Present*, 126.

[421] Ibid., 128.

[422] Sharon G. Thornton, *Broken Yet Beloved*, 27.

[423] Richard A. Kauffman, "U.S. leaders confess church failures," *The Christian Century*, March 21, 2006, 9.

[424] Ibid.

[425] "Diversity and Community: A Multi-Religious Statement on Social Responsibility in the Context of Ethnic, Cultural, Racial, and Religious Diversity in the United States by the Council of Presidents of the United States Conference of Religions for Peace November 3, 2000." *Church and Society*, (January/February 2001), 90.

[426] Ibid.

[427] Emma Vaughn and Patricia Ward Biederman, "Hurricane Katrina: Bush calls for end to Inequality," *Lost Angeles times* as Reported in *St Louis Post Dispatch*, (Saturday September 17, 2005): A5.

[428] Alter, "The Other America: Enduring the Shame", 43.

[429] Brodkin, *How Jews Became White Folks*, 50.

[430] Atler, "The Other America: Enduring the Shame," 44.

[431] Brodkin., 51.

[432] Hilary Herbold, "Never a level Playing Field: Blacks and the GI Bill," as quoted in Katznelson, 121.

[433] Sar A. Levitan and Karen A. Cleary, *Old Wars Remain Unfinished: The Veterans Benefits System* as quoted in Katznelson, 113.

[434] Turner, "Church and Society," 77.

CHAPTER EIGHT

[435] Spencer Perkins & Chris Rice, *More than Equals: Racial Healing for the Sake of the Gospel* (Downers Grove, Illinois: Intervarsity Press, 2000), 33.

[436] Ibid., 60.

[437] Bob Blauner, *Still the Big News Racial Oppression in America* Vol. 91-92 (Philadelphia: Temple University Press, 2001), viii.

[438] Otis Turner, "Addressing Racism An Agenda for Church Action," *Church and Society* (January/February 2001), 70.

[439] Otis Turner, "Addressing Racism An Agenda for Church Action," 75.

[440] Ibid., 72.

441 Chester Jones, "Coming to Terms with our Methodist Roots," *Christian Social Action* Vol. 14 No. 1(March/April, 2001), 4.

442 Otis Turner, 78.

443 Ibid.

444 Richard C. Dickinson,. Interview by author, tape recording, St Louis MO, August 15 2005.

445 Ibid.

446 Leodia Gooch, Interview by Author, Tape Recording, Monday 27 March, 2005.

447 *Catechism of the Catholic Church: The Mystery of the Church* (Vaticana: Liberia Editrice, 1997), 214.

448 Virgil Elizondo *A Report on Racism: A Mexican American in the United States*, 61.

449 Johannes Brosseder, *Program to Combat Racism*, 29.

450 Juanita Dick, Interview by Author, Tape Recording, (June 15th 2005).

451 Frank Blood. Interview by Author, Tape Recording, St. Louis, MO., 10th June, 2005.

452 Yosef A. A. Ben-Jochannan, *We the Black Jews* Vols. I & II (Baltimore, MD.: Black Classic Press, 1993).

453 Kivel, *Up Rooting Racism*, 154.

454 Spencer Perkins and Chris Rice, *More than Equals: Racial Healing for the sake of the Gospel* (Dovners Grove, Illinois: InterVarsity Press, 2000), 29.

455 Kivel *Uprooting Racism*, 150.

456 Daine Tobin, Gary A. Tobin, and Scott Rubin, *In Every Tongue: the Racial and Ethnic Diversity of the Jewish People* (San Francisco: Institute for Jewish and Community Research, 2005), 55.

457 Rabbi Randy Fleisher, Interview by author, Tape Recording, December 10th 2005.

CONCLUTION

458 John L. Kater, "Experiment In Freedom: The Episcopal Church and the Black Power Movment," *Historical Magazine* March, 1979, 67.

[459] Otis Turner, "Addressing Racism: An Agenda for Church Action," 74.

[460] Jay P. Dolan, *The American Catholic Experience* (New York: Double Day, 1985), 123.

[461] Kivel, *Uprooting Racism*, 198.

[462] Kivel, *Uprooting Racism*, 29.

[463] Otis Turner, 74.

[464] Turner, 74.

SELECTED BIBLIOGRAPY

Albright, Raymond W. *A History of the Protestant Episcopal Church.* New York: The Macmillan Company, 1964.

Alter, Jonathan. "The Other America: Enduring the Shame," *Newsweek,* September 19, 2005, 43-45.

Alvis, Joel. *Religion and Race: Southern Presbyterian, 1964-1983.* Tuscalosa, Alabama:The University of Alabama Press, 1994.

Anderson, George. *The Lutherans in North America: Early National Period 1790-1840.* Philadelphia: Fortress Press, 1975.

Armstrong , O. K and Majorie Armstrong. *The Baptists in America.* New York: A Doubleday Galilee Book, 1979.

Asher, Jeremial. *African American Religious History: Protesting the "Negro Pew."* Durban: Duke University, 1999.

Ben-Jochannan, Yosef A. *We the Black Jews* Vols. I & II. Baltimore, MD.: Black Classic Press, 1993.

Bennett, Robert A. "Black Episcoplians: A history from the Colonial Period to the Present." *Historical Magazine of the Protestant Episcopal Church*, September 1974, 240.

Bhopal, Inderjit. "The Ministry of Truth." *Christian Social Action* Vol. 14, No. 1 (March/April, 2001): 12-13.

Blauner, Bob. *Still the Big News Racial Oppression in America.* Philadelphia: Temple University Press, 2001.

Bradley, Richard L. "Lutheran Church and Slavery." *Concordia Historical Institute Quarterly* Vol. XLIV, No. 1 (February 1971): 32-41.

Brodkin, Karen. *How Jews Became Whites Folks And What That Says About Race In America.* New Jersey: Rutgers University Press, 2004.

Catechism of the Catholic Church: The Mystery of the Church. Vaticana: Liberia Editrice, 1997.

Chappell, Kevin."The life and Legacy of the Mother of the Civil Rights Movement." *Ebony.* January, 2006.

Coates, Thomas, and Erwin L. Lueker. *Moving Frontiers: Four Decades of Expansion 1920—1960.* Saint Louis, Missouri: Concordia Publishing House, 1964.

Davies, Alan. "The ideology of Racism." *Concilium* (1982.): 11-16.

Davis, Cyprian. *The History of Black Catholics in the United States.* New York: Crossroad, 1990.

- - -, and Jamie Phelps. eds., *Stamped with the Image of God: African Americans as God's Image in Black.* New York: Orbis Books, 2003.

DeGroote, Peter L. "White Supremacists Cloak Bigotry in Theology." *Christian Social Action* Vol. 14 No.1 (March/April 2001): 14-16.

Dickinson, Richard C. *Roses and Thorns: The Centennial Edition of Black Lutheran Mission and Ministry in the Lutheran Church— Missouri Synod.* St. Louis, Missouri: Concordia Publishing House, 1977.

Dispatch, "Study Guide Aimed at Healing Wounds of Racial Divisions." *Christian Social Action* Vol. 14, No. 1 (March/ April 2001): 37-38.

"Diversity and Community: A Multi-Religious Statement on Social Responsibility in the Context of Ethnic, Cultural, Racial, and Religious Diversity in the United States by the Council of Presidents of the United States Conference of Religions for Peace, November 3, 2000." *Church and Society* (January/ February 2001): 91-95.

Dolan, Jay P. *The American Catholic Experience.* New York: Doubleday, 1985.

DuBois, W.E.B. *The Negro Church.* Atlanta: Atlanta University Press, 1903.

Durrah, Betty J. "Triple Jeopardy: The Impact of Race, Sex, and Class on Women of Color." *Church and Society* Vol. 81-82 (September/ October 1991): 44-53.

Edwards, O.C. *A History of Preaching.* Nashville: Abingdon Press, 2004.

Elizondo, Virgil. "The Church and Racism." *Concilium* (1982): 61-64.

Fredericks, James L. *Faith among Faiths: Christian Theology and Non-Christian Religions.* Mahwah, New Jersey: Paulist Press, 1999.

Fitts, Leroy. *A History of Black Baptists.* Nashville, Tennessee: Broadman Press, 1985.

Gerkin, Charles V. *An Introduction to Pastoral Care.* Nashville: Abingdon Press, 1997.

Gillard, John T. *Colored Catholics in the United States.* Baltimore: The Josephite Press, 1941.

Goizueta, Roberto S. *Religion and American Cultures: Catholicism in America.* Vol. 1 Santa Barbara, California: ABC Clio, 2002.

Goldscheider, Calvin and Jacob Neusner. eds., *Social Foundations of Judaism.* New Jersey: Prince Hall, 1990.

Gossett, Thomas F. *Race: The History of an Idea in America.* Dallas: Methodist University Press, 1963.

Hardon, John A. *The Protestant Churches of America.* Westminster, Maryland: The Newman Press, 1957.

Hayes, Diana L. and Cyprian Davis, eds., *Taking Down Our Harps: God of Our Weary Years.* New York: Orbis Books, 1998.

Hogue, David A. *Remembering the Future: Imagining the Past.* Cleveland: The Pilgrim Press, 2003.

Holmes, David L. *A Brief History of the Episcopal Church.* Valley Forge, PA.: Judson Press 1993.

Hood R.E., "The Historical Basis for Black Indifference Toward the Episcopal Church 1800-1860." *Historical Magazine of the Protestant Episcopal Church,* September 1982, 278.

Howell, Sharon M. *Many Rains Ago: The Consecrated Blizzard of the Northwest Archbishop John Ireland and His Relationship with the Black Catholic Community.* Washington D.C.: United States Catholic Conference, 1990.

Jones, Chester. "Coming to Terms With Our Methodist Roots." *Christian Social Action* (March/April 2001): 4-7.

Jordan, Winthrop. *White over Black: American Attitude toward the Negro, 1550-1812.* New York: W.W. Norton and Company, 1977.

Kater, John L. "Experiment In Freedom: The Episcopal Church and the Black Power Movement." *Historical Magazine of the Protestant Episcopal Church,* March 1979, 69.

Katznelson, Ira. *When Affirmative Action was White: An Untold History of Racial Inequality in Twentieth-Century America.* New York: W.W. Norton & Company, 2005.

Kauffman, Richard A. "U.S. leaders Confess church failures." *The Christian Century.* 21 March 2006, 9.

Kivel, Paul. *Uprooting Racism: How White People can Work for Racial Justice.* Gabriola Island, BC: New Society Publishers, 1995.

Lartey, Emmanuel Y. *In living Color: An Intercultural Approach to Pastoral Care and Counseling.* New York: Jessica Kingsley Publishers, 2003.

Leonard, Bill J. *Baptist Ways A History.* Valley Forge, PA.: Judson Press 2003.

Lewis, Harold. *Yet with A steady Beat: The African American struggle for recognition.* Valley Forge, Pennsylvania: Trinity International Press, 1996.

Loetscher, Lefferts A. *A Brief History of the Presbyterians.* Philadelphia: The Westminster Press, 1978.

Locke, Hubert G. *The Black Anti-Semitism Controversy: Protestant Views and Perspectives.* London: Associated Press, 1994.

Lockwood, Robert P. ed., *Anti Catholicism in American Culture.* New York: Our Sunday Visitor Publishing Division, 2000.

Luker, Ralph E. *The Social Gospel in Black and White: American Racial Reform 1885-1912.* North Carolina: University of North Carolina Press, 1991.

MacGregor, Morris J. *The Emergence of a Black Catholic Community St. Augustine in Washington.* Washington D.C.: The Catholic University of America Press, 1999.

Maring, Norman H. *Baptist and American Experience: American Baptists Whence and whither.* Valley Forge: The Judson Press, 1976.

Meshack, B.A. *Is the Baptist Church Relevant to the Black Community.* San Francisco, California: R and E Research Associates, 1976.

Montgomery, Rick. "Seventy-Eight Years later, Tulsa re-examines Deadly Race Riot," *Kansas City Star,* September 7th, 1999.

Norwood, Frederick A. *The Story of American Methodism.* Nashville: Abingdon Press, 1974.

Nelson, Clifford E. *The Lutherans in North America: The New shape of Lutheranism.* Philadelphia: Fortress Press, 1975.

Ochs, Stephen J. *Desegregating the Altar: The Josephites and Struggle for Black Priests, 1871-1960.* Louisiana: Louisiana State University Press, 1949.

Olmstead, Clifton E. *Religion In America: Past and Present.* Englewood Cliffs, New `Jersey: Prentice-Hall, 1961.

Pannell, William. *The Coming Race War: A Cry for Reconciliation.* Grand Rapids, Michigan: Zondervan Publishing House, 1993.

Perkins, Spencer and Chris Rice. *More than Equals: Racial Healing for the Sake of the Gospel.* Downers Grove, Illinois: Intervarsity Press, 2000.

Phelps, Jamie T. *Many Rains Ago: Caught Between Thunder and Lightning: A Historical Theological Critique of Episcopal Response to Slavery.* Washington D.C.: United States Catholic, 1990.

Pinn, Anthony B. *Religion and American Cultures: African American Religion.* Vol. 1 Santa Barbara: ABC Clio, 2003.

Powell, Thomas. *The Persistence of Racism in America.* Maryland: Littlefield AdamsQuality Paperbacks, 1992.

Pupo-Ortiz, Yolanda. "Racism Lurks in the Corners." *Christian Social Action* Vol.14, No.1 (March/April 2001): 8-10.

Racial Ethnic Ministry Response. "Problems Caused by Racism." *Church and Society* Vol. 81-82 (September/October 1991): 66-73.

Ramsey, G. Lee. *Care—Full Preaching: From sermon To Caring Community.* St. Louis: Chalice Press, 2002.

Reynolds, Edward D. *Jesuits for the Negroes.* New York: The University Press, 1949.

Rosenberg, E. Stuart. *Christianity Through Non-Christian Eyes: Christianity and the Holocaust.* MaryKnoll, New York: Orbis Books, 1990.

Scholnick, Myron I. *The New Deal and Anti Semitism in America.* New York: Garland Publishing, 1990.

Seltzer, Robert M. ed., *Judaism A People and its History.* New York: Macmillan Publishing Company, 1989.

Sinclair, William A. *The Aftermath of Slavery: A Study of The Condition and Environment of the American Negro.* Chicago: Afro-am Press, 1969.

Smithson, Sandra O. *To Be the Bridge: A commentary of Black/ White Catholicism In America.* Nashville, Tennessee: Winston Derek Publishers, 1984.

Smith, Christine M. *Risking the Terror: Resurrection in this Life.* Cleveland, Ohio: The Pilgrim Press, 2001.

Smith, H. Shelton, Robert T. Handy, and Lefferts A. Loetscher. *American Christianity: An Historical Interpretation with Representative Documents.* New York: Charles Scribner's Sons, 1963.

Smylie James H., *A Brief History of the Presbyterians.* Louisville, Kentucky: Geneva Press, 1996.

- - -, "Racism, Religion, and the Continuing American Dilemma." *Church and Society* Vol. 91-92 (January/February 2001): 56-69.

Stange, Douglas C. "Our Duty to Preach the Gospel to Negroes: Southern Lutherans and American Negroes." *Concordia Historical Institute Quarterly* (November 1969): 171-182.

Stember, Charles Herbert et al. *Jews in the Mind of America*. New York: Basic Books, 1966.

Suelflow, August R. and E. Clifford Nelson, *The Lutherans in North America: Following*
the *Frontier1840-1875*. Philadelphia: Fortress Press,1975.

Sweet, William Warren. *Methodism in American History*. New York: Abingdon Press, 1961.

Tappert, Theodore G. *Lutheran in North America: The Church's infancy* 1650-1790. Philadelphia: Fortress Press, 1975.

Taylor, Garner. *Baptist and the American Experience: Baptists and Human Rights*. Valley Forge, PA.: Judson Press, 1976.

Tobin, Daine, Gary A. Tobin, and Scott Rubin. *In Every Tongue: the Racial and Ethnic Diversity of the Jewish People*. San Francisco: Institute for Jewish and Community Research, 2005.

Thornton, Sharon G. *Broken yet Beloved: A pastoral Theology of the Cross*. St. Louis: Chalice Press, 2002.

Turner, Otis. "Addressing Racism An Agenda for Church Action." *Church and Society* Vol. 91-92 (January/February 2001): 70-79.

Wentz, Abel Ross. *The Lutheran Church in American History*. Philadelphia: The United Lutheran Publication House, 1933.

Ward, Mary A. *A Mission for Justice: A History of the First African American Catholic Church in Newark New Jersey*. Knoxville: The University of Tennessee Press, 2002.

Wagley, Charles and Marvin Harris. *Minorities in the New World*. New York: Columbia University Press, 1958.

Vaughn, Emma and Patricia Ward Biederman. "Hurricane Katrina: Bush calls for end to Inequality," *Los Angeles Times* as Reported in *St Louis Post Dispatch*. Saturday September 17, 2005, A5.

204072

Made in the USA